The Sugar Bowl Feud

Gina N. Brown

novaheart
MEDIA

NovaHeart Media

ISBN Print: 978-1-9995741-4-7   Ebook: 978-1-9995741-5-4

I would like to acknowledge that this book was written in Mi'kma'ki, the ancestral territory of the Mi'kmaw people.

Book cover design by: Peggy & Co. Design and photo cover: Robert George Young Photography

NovaHeart Media website design: Crystal Picard Design & Marketing

Author photo: Nicola Davison, Snickerdoodle Photography

Dedicated to

My amazing stepchildren:
Rigel Crockett, Laurel Crockett and Joe Zsebenyi
You are caring, smart and fun!

And

My loving and supportive siblings:
Dale Brown, Reisa Muir and Tanya Brown

None of you inspired this story.

Also by Gina N. Brown

Author

Lucy McGee's Moment of Truth

Editor

Cross-eyed Optimist: How I Learned to See in 3-D and Straightened my Eyes with Vision Therapy. Written by Robert Bryan Crockett.

Definition: Family Tree

Noun: singular

Like the living plant for which it's named, a Family Tree has deep, tenacious roots and ever-growing branches—both supportive and non-supportive—which bear a wide variety of fruits and nuts.

Prologue

Courtney, the Executor

Where there's a *will* there's a way for someone in the family to behave like a jerk. That's my conclusion based on trying to settle my beloved mother's estate. Who knew it would take years, hundreds of documents and a lawyer on speed dial—and after all that rigamarole, my family would not be speaking to each other? Mostly the brawls were over the stupidest things. Honestly, it's embarrassing to think that we, as a family, couldn't work it out. But there you go.

Worse, it's hard to believe that my mother's once-reasonable estate came crashing down all because of her conniving fraudster of a friend and a wayward yellow sticky note. The mess picked up momentum like a turbo-charged bowling ball racing down an alley, then swerved into the gutter at the last second.

It wasn't even an authentic sticky note that would have done its job properly. Nope, this was a Mom special: a cheap, knock-off two-inch pad she bought from the Barely-a-Buck store across town. The brand should have been "Unsticky Notes."

The infamous "sticky note debacle" involved Doris, the alleged cleaner. My siblings and I called her that because there was no evidence that she ever lifted a finger to help Mom clean, despite charging thirty-five dollars an hour. They were childhood best friends, known as the "Doris and Babs daredevils," who remained friends through their endless escapades. Doris saw an opportunity when Mom became ill. She confused the phrase *seize the day* with *seize the assets*. It's funny how some people with no money can watch from a distance and become resentful when they see others who are better off than they are. And, how easily they can convince themselves they're entitled to somebody's hard-earned nest egg or an asset like a Maud Lewis painting. But whoa, I'm getting ahead of myself.

Sadly, the sticky note incident also marked the collapse of our shaky sibling foundation. While we built it from the ground up, one episode caused the whole to implode. The unwitting motto of the Martin family: divided we stand, united we fall.

When it comes to settling a loved one's estate, there's nothing like hindsight—that smug little blip on the timeline of life—to remind you what you did wrong, what you should have done instead and the mess you now have to mop up.

When Mom asked me to be her executor, I said yes, without giving it any thought. I was even flattered that she picked me. She had a will, and it was prepared by a lawyer, so she was already ahead of fifty percent of the population in Nova Scotia.

Despite her quirks, I loved her dearly. I admired her deeply for what she had overcome to look after us kids after she brought the twins home from the hospital. That's when my father offered to run to the corner store for baby food and never came back.

If my being the executor was her desire, I promised to do my utmost to honor her wishes. And I meant it. Mom and I discussed it at length, and out of the four kids, we both understood that it made the most sense for me to take on that role. First, I was the oldest and most responsible of the lot—her words (but honestly, she was right). Secondly, I had a lengthy career as an executive assistant, so I nearly had a PhD in organization, time management, budgets and schedules. At home, I even had an app for tracking how much time I spent on personal activities—driving the kids to soccer, movies or dance lessons. Nothing would get mixed up or lost on my watch, or so I believed.

It's not that my siblings were dishonest, it's just that they lacked... well, certain competencies and the character needed to do a decent job.

Next in line was the set of fraternal twins born less than two years after me (poor Mom!) They were a total yin and yang package deal, delivered twelve minutes apart. We nicknamed them the Brandies. The first-born, Brando, sounded like a typo. During introductions, everybody assumed we said Brandon, which then took five minutes to explain. Mom took to saying, "Bran*doh*," exaggerating the last syllable to make her point. In print, people added the letter n to the end of his name, as if he wouldn't know how to spell his name.

A born sales executive, Brando chose to see his name as a great talking point. "My name is Brando, not Brandon," he'd say to get the pitch rolling, retelling the same story with each new potential client. "My father named me after Marlon Brando in *The Wild One* but I'm not sure why, maybe he saw himself as a rebel." After a brief pause, he'd continue, "Mom chose Brandi for my twin sister. She was named for either a popular 1980s cocktail or a character in a soap opera—neither a good idea," he'd chuckle.

In daily life, the Brandies seemed like they didn't have to discuss certain responses; they simply glanced at each other, lifted an eyebrow or shrugged and the other understood. Like many pairs of twins who develop their own language and gestures, theirs was laughter. Somehow, they produced the exact number of ha-ha's as determined by how funny they found the subject. Sometimes there were four ha ha ha ha's in a row, other times ten—but they always started and stopped in sync. Maybe it was from the two of them watching too many sitcoms as kids. I guess when two fertilized eggs share the same space for nine months, they get to know each other quite well.

The twins remained close all their lives, living in the same subdivision. They hung out together, and their kids did too. Brando was brash, confident, and in love with money—more, more, more was his rallying cry. And Brandi went along with her brother's attitude because he was the alpha and asserted his opinion the most strongly. This meant that in the settling of the estate, they voted as a block (and they didn't have to discuss that either, for Pete's sake).

Then there's our half-sister Mona, born to my mother and her second husband, George Nichols. She arrived over a decade after me and the twins. Brando called her "Mona the moaner and complainer." Mean-spirited, yes, but she was all that. The twelve-year age difference was too much of a gulf for us to bond as a family. From her siblings' perspective, never was there a more entitled, failure-to-launch, peace-and-love gal who could get out of most forms of work. Plus, she despised capitalists and evil corporations, yet bought overpriced bohemian outfits, gadgets galore and lattés (on Mom's credit card, no doubt). She was very supportive of everybody else saving the planet.

When people would ask where Mona fit into the family, Brando would chime in, "she doesn't!" I cared about her as a human being and a half-sister, but it was hard to love her. It was even harder to watch Mom and George cater to her every whim when the rest of us had lived in deep poverty during our childhood when Mom was a single mother. We should have been happy for Mona to not want for a thing when we had grown up with hand-me-down clothes and the cheapest meals possible—lots of oatmeal with diced apples and brown sugar, vegetable soup and the occasional detestable serving of liver.

Technically, I'm called *executrix* because I'm female, but I refuse to use such an archaic Latin term from the 15th century. The first time I called a place to sell clothing and equipment to a second-hand store, I identified myself as the executrix. Buddy laughs then tells me they don't handle selling "those types of goods" and suggests I call the Adult X-rated play store in the next town over (which he seemed to know quite well). I was so furious; that's the first and last time I used that term. *Executor* it is.

All that aside, you know the worst thing about this whole estate thing and the will? It was the angst and jealousy that erupted over one little item: Mom's sugar bowl from our childhood. We all wanted it. I claimed it first, and then suddenly everybody else wanted it. Worse, we behaved like centurions prepared to fight to the death to have it. The more someone showed interest, the more the others believed they had to have it. It was petty and immature.

I'm embarrassed to say that the tug-of-war over the sugar bowl brought out the worst in us: at the first sign of things going sideways all civility flew out the window. Before you knew it, we were exchanging harsh words, and soon the in-laws and out-laws weighed in and all hell broke loose. Names were called and we realized we didn't really like some of our family.

Mom would have been mortified—but then again, she might have laughed about the mess. She did get a kick out of absurdities because she'd seen it all in her brief life. She was only sixty-three when we lost her. But she sure packed in a lot of fun, shenanigans and sorrow while she was around. She didn't deserve all the pain, but she never focused on that—"let's move on" and "better days ahead" is what she believed. I miss her so much. Honestly, there was no need of the sibling stupidity that unfolded over the sugar bowl, but that didn't stop us.

I now realize the persistence of grief is very real and sneaky, always lurking underneath the surface. A day can start perfectly well, yet when something goes wrong, a sense of sadness overwhelms you. Grief also does crazy things to people—it amplifies quirks and character flaws to jumbo proportions. The siblings who didn't visit their Mom enough or return her calls in a timely manner, behaved in weird ways as if they were trying to go back to make things right. Then the ones that live the farthest away make pronouncements about what should and shouldn't be done on behalf of their Mom.

The most annoying sentence from these people? "Mom would have wanted this or this, or not," when they hadn't been around enough to know.

What I've learned is that under pressure, a family member's neurosis morphs into psychosis. And before you know what's hit you, one of your siblings acts like Medusa springing out of a jack-in-the-box, scaring the bejesus out of you.

When it comes to family feuds one of my friends' grandpa used to say, "There's two sides to every story and then there's the truth." Not in our family. There were four sides to the sugar bowl story and four different truths. But the fair thing is to hear everybody's side of the story, so let's rewind to 2021 when Mom died and trouble started brewing. As airline pilots sometimes say, "Fasten your seatbelts, folks, we're in for a bumpy flight."

Chapter 1

Courtney

When my Mom's cancer spread quickly, she knew the end was in sight. Although it took months, I felt like it all happened in a blink of time. Mom was the bravest woman I knew. She never held a pity party in her life—she just dealt with every curveball that came her way. Unfortunately, none of us left behind realized just how much she was the glue that held our weird family together. We were all in pain and simply stumbling through the days leading up to the inevitable moment we couldn't face.

She had "the talk" with us each on our own, then with all of us together. She thought about all the things we'd need to deal with after she was gone. She made sure the others knew and accepted that I was the executor and she asked everyone to give me the respect that I deserved.

Mom forgot to tell the others that the executor is paid a fee of two to five percent of the estate for their time and trouble. Looking back, that amount didn't begin to cover my time and trouble, yet the sibs thought it was outrageous that I should be paid for my time—they didn't see the to-do lists that I dealt with for a couple of years. Also, they thought I took way too long to get things done. They also questioned my motives when I made decisions, which hurt me.

"Oh, Courtney Bea, not another family meeting!" Brando groaned. Bea was my middle name and he sometimes called me Queen Bea when he didn't like what I suggested. The sibs didn't want to meet for estate stuff, and when they did (begrudgingly) their attention spans could be measured in milliseconds. In the meetings they didn't care, until they did care later when the topic of money bubbled to the surface. By then they'd forgotten everything I'd told them and accused me of not informing them. I couldn't win for trying.

The Brandies only cared about the money they were getting from the estate, and they expected it right away. Brando wanted to buy a new truck and Brandi and her husband Milo set their hearts on a kitchen reno—even though I warned everybody to not spend money until they got it in their hands. That's because an executor has no idea about the final value of the estate until probate is closed. Nobody likes to believe there will be debt, but it can spring out of nowhere. Meanwhile, Mona was such a walking financial disaster she wasn't even dreaming of spending on big projects—she had rent to pay, and groceries and premium cocktails to juggle on a maxed-out credit card. I feared my siblings were busy spending money based on hunches about Mom's net worth.

At our first meeting at Mom's house, I arrived early and walked around the house which was packed floor to rafters with stuff. So was the garage where Mom traded in antiques and second-hand goods. She scoured charity shops and bought estate lots and boxes of things at auctions, which meant that she constantly had goods coming and going. Certain items yielded high returns, other items languished in boxes for years and even decades. She loved the never-ending parade of buyers and sellers hanging out in her garage where all the action took place. Her prices were fair, and she was even known to help young people and newcomers who couldn't afford much. If an old set of dishes hadn't moved in a couple of years, she'd give it to somebody in need. Her inventory system was all tucked away in her head.

She had a modest three-bedroom house which still had a mortgage on it. She and George lived there with Mona when she was growing up. It was a far cry from the trailer park the Brandies and I grew up in, over at the Eastern Wind trailer park. We called it the Breaking Wind trailer park because of its lingering stench, which seemed impossible in an outdoor setting, but was all too real.

When our scummy father had jumped ship back in the 1980s Mom worked frantically to get a roof over our heads at a price she could afford. Fortunately for her, she had cared for an elderly gentleman who had to go into long-term care, with no family nearby. She treated him like a father and helped him buy things for his home. They got along well—she even coaxed laughs out of him, even though nothing in either of their lives was funny. He must have felt sorry for Babs being a single Mom with a daughter and a pair of twins under three, trying to live on welfare (as it was called then) and any money she could earn under the table. Mr. Vincente rented the trailer to her for only a hundred bucks a month. He saved us kids from God knows what fate—possibly being put up for adoption. When he passed away, I overheard her crying as she discussed our situation with her friend.

"What's going to happen to us?" she wailed, not realizing I was seated by the window.

When Mr. Vincente's will was read, we discovered that he had left the trailer and the land it sat on to Mom. She cried for days out of relief. Our home wasn't worth much, but hey... it did the trick. The modest piece of land had enough room for the trailer, driveway and a small yard—and it was tucked away close to a wooded area that led to a lake. Even with no trailer payment, we barely got by. There were only two bedrooms, and Mom had to sleep on the couch every night. She never complained and we didn't notice her discomfort—we were just kids. She also made sure we had food in our tummies every day, though sometimes meals were... uninspired. There was the "vegetarian soup" as she called it because she couldn't always afford meat.

We often had oatmeal for breakfast with one apple cooked into it because oats were cheap, and she got apples for free from an apple tree nearby. As Brando got older, his complaints about food grew but Mom always said without apology, "You've got two choices for the meal: take it or leave it." After Brando went to school angry and hungry a few times, he begrudgingly ate the oatmeal. I always liked oatmeal for breakfast because it was one of the few times that Mom let us eat brown sugar. I recall digging the tiny spoon into the soft mound of crumbly sugar in the eight-sided bowl and sprinkling it on my oatmeal. It made me feel loved by my mother that she would treat us to this special breakfast topping that had no nutritional value, but that clearly made us happy.

Brando developed incredible charm to score all kinds of treats, earn a bit of money in the better-off area of town and improve his lot in life. It's no wonder he became a sales rep; at a young age, he learned the importance of customer service, charging well for your worth and closing the deal. Years later when I asked him about his career choice, he said he decided very early on he would never get caught in a mess like Mom's. I think all of us understood the importance of having a different outcome than she had.

For me, I set my sights on being the best executive assistant, because I would always be able to get a job. It wasn't fancy and the pay was nothing exciting, but it had worked out. Brando, though, wanted more, a lot more. Sales had served him extremely well. There was more risk and harder work involved as well as traveling, yet the rewards were high. Working on commissions would have stressed me entirely, but he thrived on it.

And Brandi? She entered the hotel management business which provided a steady career and decent pay. She also met and married Milo Pach, a rising star in the art world, to give her even greater financial stability. She doted on Milo and his daughter, Olivia. She made sure he was always happy, and in exchange, he understood her happiness was dependent on a big house filled with expensive furniture, the best appliances and exquisite decor. Nothing could be second-hand or antique—it all had to be new. I think with each purchase of an expensive item, she felt a momentary jolt of satisfaction go right through her. No more depriving herself of the things she wanted. I guess we each had our beliefs and motivations about money.

For the first few weeks after Mom was gone, I couldn't get started on anything—I just didn't know what to do. I felt like I was stumbling through life, and barely present for my kids and husband. They were all patient, but when you're used to running the show and keeping things going on the home front, you can only fumble around in a fog for so long. I took time off work but wasn't getting anything done at home.

One day, I jumped in the car and drove to Mom's place. It was so weird going inside. I was used to Mom having the radio on and her energy lighting up the place. Everything felt so sad and quiet now. It was like her life just stopped, with books and notepads lying around on the coffee table. I'm not sure what I was expecting: did I believe she'd do a big clear-out before entering the hospital? Of course not.

I wandered over to the beat-up desk where my mother did her paperwork. I shuddered about the work facing us. Even though I was the executor, it felt weird rifling through Mom's things. I couldn't figure out how to get started handling her affairs. Yes, I knew there were bank accounts, but she also had a lifetime of hustles and side hustles, with plenty of transactions to organize. I picked things up, set them down and sometimes moved them around which did nothing to settle the estate. I wanted all of this to unfold properly with the family and make sure everything was transparent. I folded up and replaced Mom's things as if I were expecting someone to note what I'd been up to. I returned home without a single task completed on this trip. I felt like I had let myself, my Mom and the estate down.

Finally, I met with Mom's lawyer, Megan Blume. She reviewed the spreadsheet that I'd created with all the assets I could think of, including the debts and account numbers. After reviewing it, she looked at me and said, "This is one of the best prepared family documents I've seen."

"Thanks," I said, reviewing my carefully written notes. At least I was on the right path. Her comment was a great motivator for me.

She then helped me to map out the steps and process-es that needed to be followed. "You know this could take years, right?"

"I guess so," I said nodding slowly. I was shocked.

"It depends on the complexity of the estate. I suggest you meet with the other beneficiaries to go over every-thing, as soon as possible." Megan said it was important for them to find out how long it takes. "Most people have no clue," she added.

"I'm on it," I said, full of business. I sent an email and requested a family meeting, to share what I had discovered.

I bought bankers' boxes at the stationery store and headed to Mom's place to start organizing. I stared at the desk, trying to figure out her system. Everybody has a system—even if it's simply piling things on top of a desk. The most recent papers were at the top of the desk and went backward in time as you moved down the drawers. At the bottom, I pulled out a long drawer and my eye caught a blue Hilroy notebook that I remembered seeing on her desk when I was a kid. In Mom's handwriting, it was labeled Dirk the Jerk. Knowing that was my mother's nickname for our father, I flopped into an armchair, dangling a knee over the arm. I flipped it open, shocked by what I read.

Chapter 2

Mona

The blinding morning sun filtered through tie-dyed curtains that didn't quite cover the windows in her bedroom. Mona blinked a couple of times to wake herself up. She raised herself on her right arm and scanned the room, then flopped her limp body back on the mattress. Then she remembered: her mother was gone. Her sniffles shifted to wailing, until her dog Shiva, galloped in from the living room and cuddled up to her, as if trying to take away her pain. Mona threw her arms around the dog who waited patiently for the sobbing to ease.

"There's a good girl," said Mona, petting her in long strokes. Shiva leaned into Mona's shoulder, with an expression of pure compassion. "You're my savior," Mona said, burying her face in Shiva's long hair. "And I know the retriever in you will never turn down a petting session." In the soft morning light, dog hair filled the air like a storm in a Snow Globe. She lifted clumps of ginger dog hair off the duvet, packed it with her hands and tossed it to the side of the bed for the vacuum to pick up. She hadn't vacuumed in weeks. Today was not the day.

She normally loved bright summery days, but now she couldn't summon up energy. She revisited her life in a nutshell: her Dad had died six years ago, and now her Mom was gone too. At the age of thirty, she was officially an orphan cast adrift in a world already thrown upside down by the Covid pandemic. Yes, she had three half-siblings who were technically family, but she didn't think of them that way. They were older and showed little interest in her. It was clear they only gathered as a family to please their mother for a birthday, Thanksgiving or Christmas. Her Mom used to talk up every gathering as if it would be a rollicking good time, but it never delivered.

Mona didn't have kids and had nothing in common with the others (other than sharing the same mother), so when they got together it felt like a tortuous affair. It was just the three half-siblings, their spouses and kids who never asked her anything and only replied to questions in short syllables and spent the rest of the time staring at their cellphones. Courtney was the alpha oldest child who would walk into Mom's house and shout, "Okay, what can I do to help?" That was code for her taking over the kitchen, right down to wearing the apron.

"What's this, Mom?" Courtney would ask, holding up a glass jar full of white liquid.

"Uh, thickening for the gravy," Mom would say, darting around the kitchen, opening cupboard doors, searching for items.

"Flour or corn starch?"

Suddenly, Mona recalled their Mom looking unsure of herself, almost trying to predict what Courtney's preference would be so that she wouldn't have to defend her choice.

"Flour."

Wrong. As soon as Courtney heard that, she'd start questioning her food and cooking decisions. Soon the two of them would be snapping at each other. As the years rolled by, everybody realized it was just easier to let Courtney run the show.

Then there was Brando—according to Mom, a new and improved version of his father, but to Mona, still an overbearing oaf. He behaved more responsibly than his father had in not abandoning his family, but other than that, Mona didn't care for his in-your-face attitude. At the table, he sat at the end and did most of the talking—as if everyone should be fascinated by his every word. He was mouthy, opinionated and self-centered with a voice that grew in volume and intensity after a drink or five. Based on his behavior, it was obvious he believed men should be the strong masculine type, without showing a speck of emotion. Mona's friends included men, women and others, and it was just assumed they'd all share their feelings. While Brandi, his twin, was sweet, she was eclipsed by her big bro, which meant she didn't talk much and nodded in agreement with his statements.

As soon as everybody gathered at their Mom's place, the siblings would slip into their childhood roles. Even their faces took on childish expressions. The few times Mona tried to say something to get them off their petty topics, Brando shut her down or made fun of her. Their mother would try to rein in Brando or at least have them include Mona, but he was another one with whom it was easier to just let him do what he needed to do. Eventually, Mona realized they had only one thing in common: they shared the most amazing mother.

Mona's half-sibs shared the same father. And by all accounts, their father Dirk was a horse's arse of epic proportions. While the three kids may have bonded negatively over the drama of an absent father, they still bonded in their own way.

Mona was like a second-generation, only child. Her parents loved her to bits and showed it in so many ways. While her Mom acted like a tough-love mama, Mona knew she was as gooey as a toasted marshmallow on the inside. Early in life, Mona figured out that her mother couldn't say no to any of her requests. Mona sometimes wondered how she got so lucky but didn't dare ask in case her mother suddenly realized she should say no occasionally. The other kids knew their mother enjoyed giving Mona things she couldn't give them when they were small and Mona welcomed being showered with love.

Then there was her father, whom she called Georgie or Daddy while he called her Goldie for her flaxen hair. Thanks to his steady job and decent pay in the insurance business, he didn't need any persuading that she should have anything she desired. The more she squealed when opening extravagant gifts, the bigger the gifts grew.

Mona had heard endless comments at her birthday gatherings, which the siblings were guilted into attending by their mother. While Mona tore a giant bow off a designer girly bike in metallic pink, Courtney remarked bitterly that she only ever got socks and toques for her birthday.

Then Brando piled on. "That's some birthday bike there, Mona," he'd sneer. "We had to share a rusty, hand-me-down bike when we were kids."

It sounded like a recycled script, and Mona wished she didn't have to listen to their annual complaining while she opened her gifts. Yes, the gifts were special, a notch or two above those of kids in the area. Yet was it her fault that their Mom had met a man who loved making their daughter happy? The girls in the neighborhood gathered around to see the bike, gasping at it and envying Mona for having a wonderful father. Mona was anointed queen of neighborhood bikes.

As a teen, she had full access to her parents' car—they'd even joke and ask her to borrow the car. Mona was so grateful that she was their only child because that meant she didn't have to share or negotiate with anyone. While some people felt sorry for her having no siblings her age, Mona celebrated it. She could choose her "family," and enjoyed endless friend groups. First, there were school friends, and while that group dwindled after graduation with many now raising families and buying homes, some stayed in touch. She formed deep bonds with friends she did incredibly stupid things with as teenagers. Mona also had her yoga sisters, who met weekly at the Good Vibes Studio, and they'd socialize before and after a session. She created a crafters' group called Knit One, Purl Two. They'd gather in a friend's coffee shop, where they'd knit, crochet—and share their feelings.

After her Mom died, she joined a grief circle where she admired everybody for their love and vulnerability. Mona had held the spotlight recently, due to her

Mom's passing. Mona loved this group deeply. She invited Courtney and the Brandies, but they didn't show any interest. Mona could see why: Courtney was the executor and in charge of the estate. She had never shown any weakness or vulnerability in her life, and she wasn't about to change. Yet under that big front of stoicism, Mona saw a woman in her forties, as frightened as a child.

As for the Brandies, Brando looked horrified as she described sitting in a circle and sharing grief. When she invited them, Brando blurted out, "There's no time to grieve, Mona." She tried to point out that he was grieving whether he knew it or not, and further, the grieving process would take as long as it took. But he just shut her down and busied himself trying to forget his pain. She thought Brandi might have been interested in the healing circle, but with the other two siblings saying no, Mona knew she'd do the same.

Mona's favorite craft and sustainability group was called the RBs, short for the Recyclin' Babes. It all started when Mona had worked alongside her Mom in her second-hand enterprise and learned the business. Instead of trading in second-hand goods, she learned how to sew and got into new and vintage fabrics, big time. She launched a small business online, calling it the Recyclin' Babes, creating one-of-a-kind pieces of clothing and home décor items.

At a yard sale, she discovered a bolt of fabric from the 1950s. "OMG!" she shouted to her friends, who raced to see what was so exciting. "The pattern is dancing martinis, and the colors are turquoise and pink!" For a five-dollar bolt, she made thirty lounge cushions that sold for over a hundred dollars apiece. Her signature pieces were revamped denim jean jackets with new knitted sleeves and collars or added lace bought at yard sales. Soon, she met a tribe of women nearby doing the same thing. To get enough supplies, they created the Recyclin' Babes co-op where they met once a month to exchange items scoured from charity shops, church sales and estate sales. When they met up, everything was dumped on a table. No money was exchanged. Everybody took what they needed, and they all agreed to donate a small percentage of the money they earned to local charities. Mona insisted on that. They'd start the exchange with a drink and break into a chorus of "I'll Grow up Tomorrow," by The Beaches. They called it their millennial anthem because it was about twenty-somethings who just couldn't get the concept of adulting and defaulted to partying, overspending and stumbling through life.

While she loved her endless groups of friends, it was now hitting her she had nobody to share the happy memories of her parents while growing up. She never dreamed she'd lose her folks at such an early age. She felt alone and a sensation that she was merely floating—she'd lost her anchors. She'd start a journal entry but couldn't focus. She tossed the pen aside.

At Shiva's urging, Mona stumbled out of bed and walked to the fridge. When she opened it, there was a group of empty condiment bottles with crusty tops, and an egg carton with one egg inside, a month past its sell-by date. Her eyes teared up: normally she would have walked over to her Mom's three streets away. Mona loved weekends because her Mom always had coffee on and breakfast awaiting her late morning arrival. Whether it was homemade yogurt with granola or toast, her mother loved rustling something up for her. Mona wished she had known those were perfect times, times she took for granted. It wasn't the trips to spas, New York, or expensive birthday gifts from her parents that she was missing; it was the shared weekend coffee and chats that made her weep. In hindsight, she wished somebody could have pointed out, "Enjoy these moments; these are the good old days."

She glanced at Shiva while staring at the empty fridge. Mona hadn't bought dog food lately and mainly fed her with scraps from her meals. She figured the dog didn't mind, but Shiva deserved a square meal.

"Okay, my darling pooch," she said to Shiva, as she grabbed her bank card and phone. Worried her credit card was maxed, she pulled out a caddy with dozens of gift cards from birthdays, Christmas and the like. That was the other advantage of being mostly an only child—she got endless gift cards from relatives who didn't have a clue what to buy. The cards never ran out. What she really wished for was a gift card to pay her back rent. Without her Mom's support, she'd lost her financial cushion. She needed to sell stuff online but had no energy. Mona flipped through the caddy, grabbing a coffee and a grocery card.

"Let's go to the bank machine," she said, putting the leash on Shiva. The dog's ears perked up and she danced lightly, ready to bolt out the door. Mona wondered if Shiva expected to go to her Mom's place. She hugged Shiva who was now officially her best friend.

Then she remembered Raj, her boyfriend. He meant well, but the relationship was lopsided. He loved her more than she loved him, even though he was a catch and was loaded with money. One of the problems was his controlling parents in India who wanted him to marry a nice Indian girl. She saw it as reverse racism; this time the white girl was not wanted. She found it interesting to be in a situation with the tables turned, yet she wasn't afraid to challenge inequality. "What is your opinion on arranged marriages?" she once asked them at dinner when they visited Nova Scotia. When they skirted the issue, she continued, "And how about this caste system—isn't it time to let that go?" Their hasty departure and Raj's subsequent gloomy mood for days said it all.

Mona strolled to the bank, Shiva's tail waving in a full circle. Shiva sat down by the ATM and waited patiently; there was no need to chain her to a parking meter. Mona pushed the card in and entered her PIN. The screen pop-up said the transaction couldn't go through.

"Come on," she muttered to the screen, then looked at Shiva's tilted head. "Sorry, not you, pup." She tried again. After the third round, she went inside the bank; to her dismay, she saw Heather at the teller's counter. The downside of living in a small town. Heather was a wannabe Recyclin' Babe and begged to join the group, but she lacked the talent. Rather than insult her about her missing skills, Mona told her they were at their max.

"You let Melanie join last week," argued Heather.

Busted, Mona thought. "Right, and now we're full, Heather," she added, refusing to discuss it further.

Once it was clear Heather wasn't getting into the group, she expressed strong opinions about the group's work. That was the other reason nobody wanted her around—too much negativity. But today, Mona needed her help.

"Hey, Heather. How's it going?" she said, inserting her card.

"Good. I saw your jean jacket for sale online."

"Did you," she replied as a statement rather than a question, showing as little interest as possible while she keyed in her PIN.

"That was a weird take on your usual jean jacket, using purple yarn. Was it acrylic? Maybe that's why it hasn't sold."

Who cares? Mona wanted to shout at her. "Uh...not sure. I made it a while ago," Mona said, trying to sound vague.

"I'm impressed you feel confident enough to put three hundred dollars on it," Heather added in her passive-aggressive tone.

Mona knew that Heather was insulting her, she didn't get that the jacket was a work of art, and Mona didn't care what Heather thought. "I will sell it. It just takes time," said Mona, re-entering the PIN. It beeped a loser tone. "This is so annoying. Same thing at the ATM. My card is not working."

"Okay, let me have a look here," said Heather, typing furiously. She tilted her head sideways. It was never a good sign when a person tilted their head while studying something—it meant there was a problem.

"I'm sure there's a good chunk of change in there," Mona said, smiling, as if that would solve the issue.

"Hmmm, Mo. I see what the problem is," Heather said slowly, still typing incessantly.

Mona cringed. Her full name was Ramona, but most people called her Mona. She reserved Mo for her besties only, and she figured Heather heard that nickname while eavesdropping at the pub. Mona didn't correct her because she needed money.

"Hmm."

Mona tapped the card, which made her appear impatient. "Geez, I just wanted fifty bucks for a latté and something to eat."

"Sorry, it was your mother's account, Mona," she said, sounding serious.

"I know. Mom gave me a card."

"Yes, that's true. But when someone passes away, the bank automatically freezes the account."

"What the hell?" Mona blurted before she could stop herself.

"It's to protect the estate. Otherwise, somebody could clear out an account that belongs to all the beneficiaries."

"Well, you know I'm not going to do that."

"I know. Still, I can't give you anything today."

Mona's voice quivered. "So how do I unfreeze the account?"

"The executor has to do it."

"C'mon, Heather," Mona groaned. "You know that Mom gave me a card on her account. There's no fraud here."

"This isn't a joint account. It was in Babs' name only, so I can't unlock it. Do you know who the executor is?"

Oh no. "Courtney," she stated simply. No last names needed; they both knew that Courtney was her half-sister and the designated adult of the family.

"You'll have to talk to her, Mona. But keep in mind: settling an estate moves very slowly."

"We'll see about that," Mona said, yanking out her card. She shot Heather the stink eye and strode toward the door. It wasn't one bit fair being blocked from withdrawing money. She could use gift cards in the short term, but she knew a bigger financial problem was brewing. Mona was fired up and ready to fight for her share of the money. Fuming, she texted Courtney: *On my way over. Bank issue.*

After she sent it, Mona thought about how Courtney might interpret the message. That's when she remembered a problem: Courtney had no idea about her mother giving money to Mona. It was perfectly legal, except her mother hadn't told the siblings. They both knew the first three kids were squirrelly about money.

And now Miss-By-the-Book executor, Courtney, could make decisions that would impact her livelihood. Mona needed her mother's financial support—at least for now—because she was too bummed out to earn a living. She didn't want to get a job in town. She never liked bosses lording their pathetic little power over her just because they owned a business, especially ordering her to start work at 8:00 a.m. That wasn't civilized.

The closer Mona got to Courtney's place, the more she dreaded the conversation. She knew she couldn't do this today—she was too emotional. Courtney had set a family meeting for the estate for next week. Mona had no idea what it was about, but she was willing to hear her out—if it didn't affect her livelihood. Before Courtney had a chance to reply to the first text, she sent another: *Sorry, something's come up. Can't come after all. Talk later.*

That gave Mona a week to figure out how to make a case for maintaining her mother's financial arrangement a case nobody was going to like.

Chapter 3

"The Brandies" — Brando and Brandi

It was annoying when our big sister Courtney Bea called a family meeting about the estate. Queen Bea said we had to decide as a family what to do with all of Mom's stuff. It wasn't just a typical house packed to the ceiling with trinkets; it also included an overflowing garage full of items that was headquarters for Mom's second-hand store, What Goes Around.

We knew Mom meant well with her second-hand household and furniture business, but we had had enough of that as kids. We had worked hard to become financially stable, so we felt no need to revisit the past that was all about second-hand stuff. And those customers of hers? OMG. Every one of them had a hard luck story. Mom, the saint, listened to all their painful details. You'd swear she was part psychologist. When she listened to their boring tales of woe and poverty, she was known to discount items or even give stuff away. That was Mom's choice, even if we reminded her it wasn't a great business model. The stockpile of junk in her garage was constantly replenished to keep the business going, and when she passed away, the building was mostly full. So, clearing it out wasn't something we wanted to tackle. We knew the store would yield very little, so why should we take time out of our busy lives to peddle low-budget goods?

We both lived in the suburbs with brand-new spacious homes, and late model trucks and SUVs—and proud of it. We fought our way out of terrible childhood poverty by pursuing two solid careers: an award-winning salesman and a hotel administrator. We knew the real value in Mom's estate was the Maud Lewis painting and Mom's home, although it was modest. Not to our taste, but Mom never lived a high life, even after she married George Nichols, who was a much nicer second husband than our deadbeat father who still owed Mom a ton of alimony. But that was another sordid tale. Mom and George lived in the house that Mom bought originally and then George helped to improve. It was old and rickety, so it always needed repairs. But the real money pit in that house was our half-sister, Mona, who was spoiled beyond belief. She believed working for someone else was beneath her. We couldn't figure out how she stumbled through life with her pathetic little clothing business.

We tried to help her once, with advice about how to run her business. She didn't want our help. She had learned at an early age that she didn't like to earn money, but she sure loved to spend it. They say some were born with a silver spoon in their mouths. Mona was born with an overpriced latté in one hand, and an ice-berg-sourced bottle of water in the other. She never held a part-time job as a teen, and even in her twenties, she rarely looked for work. On the rare occasion when she got a job, she was usually fired because she criticized every aspect of the job and the company. Her firing then helped to prove her warped theory that all businesses were owned by evil capitalists—which, she seemed to believe, put her on the moral high ground. Getting fired regularly enabled Mona to label herself as a victim in her "career path." What a joke. We think Mom and George propped her up financially, but Mom wouldn't talk about it. We suffered so much as kids, with barely enough food on the table and clothes on our backs. Meanwhile, Mona never once worried about financial responsibilities because there was an endless flow of money pouring into her hands all her life.

Anyway, we didn't want a big fuss, but honestly, we didn't want to participate in Courtney's big estate inventory game at the house and the garage. We just wanted the money. There was no need to drag the executor thing out like she did, but we knew she couldn't help herself because Courtney had gone into official mode. Queen Bea wanted to show off how good she was at organizing everything. In no time, she had spreadsheets, file folders and everything was color-coded. Good for her, but our golden rule was to keep it simple. She ignored that rule.

Problems crept up when we both started renovations on our houses, based on what we thought we'd be getting from Mom's estate. Queen Bea said, "Don't spend a cent until we have a better handle on Mom's assets and debts." She would say that just to lord over us and exert her control. We said she could kiss our assets: we'd spend if we wanted to. Except our lines of credit crept upward. We didn't tell Courtney we needed an influx of cash to avoid renovation disasters because she would have launched into a round of "I told you so." Sadly, that meant we had to attend family meetings and participate in some of her assigned duties. But we did what we needed to do to move things along. Otherwise, Courtney would have dragged everything out, mostly to feel important.

We knew why Mom picked Courtney as the executor because she was the oldest, most obsessed with details and liked being Miss Perfect. We needed to light a fire under her. At first, she amused us with her talk about the estate being settled as a democracy where we'd vote on everything. Yawn. Within a very short amount of time, old family rivalries surfaced, and her little plan started to erode. That's because the two Brandies see eye-to-eye on everything, so we were one half of the so-called Martin family democracy.

We also knew that uptight Courtney and the much younger Mona put on a brave face, but they were hardly a team to take on the two of us. Mona thought Courtney was controlling and bound by rules. And Courtney thought Mona had no discipline and was spoiled beyond comprehension. All true, which made it harder for them to battle us. When it came to voting, it got a little messy. With their shaky alliance, we believed the Brandies would decide the vote, every freakin' time. But sometimes life doesn't work out that way, and yes, things happen. We didn't know what would unfold. So, we agreed to attend Courtney's precious meetings. And that triggered the chain of events that broke up the family.

Chapter 4

Courtney

Between work, the estate and home, I felt overwhelmed and took a week off work to get on top of the estate tasks. I'd been reading about estates and being an executor, and it hit me how much there is to do. I learned that one of the biggest mistakes is that executors don't communicate enough with beneficiaries, which can put pressure on families already weighed down by grief. Noted. I vowed to keep everybody up to date, but what I didn't realize was that not all siblings wanted updates—until they did. The second misunderstanding was that people don't realize how long it takes to settle an estate. It can take two to five years—sometimes more—and that information usually upsets beneficiaries.

When I first started working on the estate, I told the Brandies and Mona about this timeline. They nodded, but I could tell it didn't sink in. Based on their comments, they acted like it should have taken weeks to settle, not years. That's crazy. Also, I said they wouldn't get any money until all of Mom's debts and taxes were paid off.

There was still a mortgage on the house, and I knew there'd be other things as well. Yet my siblings thought I could wave a wand and make it all happen.

Of course, there were priorities. First, we had to organize a memorial service for Mom and work around Covid restrictions. Even though we were no longer in lockdown, there were limitations. What a pain. That meant we had to restrict the number of people who could attend the service so that they could sit several seats apart. It all felt so impersonal. This wasn't how I wanted to honor my mother.

At home, my husband Jamie was supportive of my new executor role and tried to do more around the house to help, but he had no idea what was coming. Our daughter Ava was fifteen and semi-independent, except for all the taxiing to and from her endless activities. She was active and busy, and that made me happy. Our Jacob was eleven and satisfied if he was fed and clothed. I loved him to bits because he was so easy to look after and still let me hug him. Ava was already showing signs of asserting independence, requesting drop-offs further away from the school, instead of our usual out front. Sigh. But I was like that in my teens. As a parent, I had my standards: I insisted we all eat dinner together, with no cellphones at the table, so I knew we'd have at least one group conversation most days.

Mom's cat Fluffy, sashayed sideways towards me, food clearly on her mind. I had taken her in after Mom passed away; she was a lovely cat and Mom adored her. A rescue, of course. Mom couldn't bear to see anybody in pain, human or animal. I loved Fluffy too, except Jacob was allergic to cats, especially long-haired ones.

He didn't complain, but I had to put her in the basement at night, otherwise Jacob's eyes would puff up. Worse, since her arrival, our house had turned into a tumbleweed factory with tufts of cat hair falling off Fluffy's back, forming a ball and somersaulting all over the house. I used to vacuum every week or two, but suddenly I had to do it twice a week, or Jacob would be wheezing. Somehow in this household, I was the only one who vacuumed. How did that happen?

Fluffy was not happy to be a boarder here and seemed to sense that I was in the process of finding her a new home. She knew something was up. Mom begged me to keep her in the family and I was doing my best, but it wasn't easy. Mona had a dog, and the two pets didn't get along. Besides, from what I observed, Mona could barely look after herself and Shiva, never mind adding a cat. Brandi and Milo loved cats; their daughter, Olivia, not so much. But she didn't like anything at her age. However, they had just purchased a very high-end Sphynx cat. If Brandi told me one more time what they paid for it, I would scream. I wanted to say, "You paid five grand for a cat, and it doesn't even come with fur?" It was one of those creepy cats with a soft hide of leathery skin instead of fur. To each their own, I guess, but give me Mom's fluffball any day. That left Brando, who was fine with cats, but with anything asked of him, he was automatically non-committal. Both he and his daughter DeeDee (from his first marriage to Twyla) liked cats, as did his new girlfriend, Roxy. He could have easily taken Fluffy and eased our family burden, but he dithered when I repeatedly asked him about it. Depending on the day and mood he was in, he'd agree to take her but then didn't follow through.

I worked on the estate to-do list. It had edged up over one hundred items long. I had started all the work of registering Mom's death with umpteen government departments—and then had to redo forms because of their mistakes. I logged onto Mom's bank account; right away, I felt uncomfortable going through her affairs, but it was what I was supposed to do. There were a couple of accounts with the usual monthly transactions—except for one weird thing: every month, her Canadian Pension Plan payment of seven hundred and thirty-two dollars was deposited electronically and was withdrawn in cash the next day. I found it odd; it was too much of a pattern to ignore. What was she doing? If George had still been alive and she was better off, I wouldn't have wondered, but she needed it all. I traced back to the first time she received her pension, at the age of sixty, and it was the same thing every month. It didn't mean there was anything wrong, but if a mistake were made, or she had a monthly commitment, I needed to know. Besides, it bugged me. I mean, what the hell? I gathered the bank papers, the will and the death certificate. I decided to get to the bottom of it at the bank.

Chapter 5

Doris

Doris wriggled, trying to propel herself up from the cozy armchair. Her arthritic knees hurt, which told her it was going to rain. With her car not running, she'd have to walk to her cleaning job, and she wasn't looking forward to it. Outside her window, she noticed Booter, the long-time postie in the neighborhood.

He stopped outside her door and rustled around his mailbag, then launched into his usual whistling of an old song, "I'm Gonna Knock on Your Door," followed by rapid knocking on her door which meant there was postal business. Over forty years, she watched his looks morph from those of a long-haired hippy with a dark, unruly ponytail to an older man with a balding head and a cluster of gray wiry bristles that looked like the steel wool she used for cleaning pots and pans.

"Hey Booter," she said, easing the door open.

"Morning. Got a registered letter for you," he said extending it outward with both hands.

"Okay," said Doris, cocking her head to see who it was from. As she looked up, she spotted her cousin, Carl, walking by and waving madly. He was a motor-mouth and very nosy, so she was careful what she shared with him. She sighed when he turned down the walkway toward them. Carl didn't miss an opportunity to catch up on family news.

"What's up, Doris?" said Carl, moving in for a close-up of the envelope. "Hey, it's from the big law firm in town."

"That so," said Doris. Her heart pounded. In her world, a registered letter was never a good thing and her mind fired up with little paranoid thoughts about what could be the problem. Her friends had told her for years she should get insurance for her small business in case somebody was to take her to court, but she always replied that cleaning people's homes wasn't exactly a business. Besides, she couldn't afford the insurance. Puzzled, she stared at the letter, front and back, as if it might reveal something.

She took the envelope and said, "Where do I sign Booter?"

Booter handed her a pen and a mini clipboard, pointing to the blank line. "Right here." She scribbled her signature and passed it back to him. "Thanks, Doris. See you, Carl," he said.

Doris could tell Booter was scrambling to get away before Carl took a deep breath and started a story.

"You going to open it?" asked Carl.

"Not now, Nosy Parker," she said, slipping the envelope into the back pocket of her jeans. "Listen, Carl. I have to take off for my cleaning gig," she said, closing the door as he tried to keep the conversation going. Good thing he wasn't offended by her curt responses.

She figured he'd just move on to annoy the next person he saw.

She stared at the envelope. It was lightweight, but she figured there was enough paperwork inside that it would cost her something. It wasn't fair; she felt like she was always getting blindsided by things in life. She threw the letter on the table and walked over to the plastic tray of lemon cookies she picked up at the Barely-a-Buck store. The cookies weren't great, but for the price, they did the job. She munched on two in a row without registering that she'd eaten them.

All morning, as she cleaned, she wondered what was in the envelope and if it was going to spring something bad on her. She wondered if she should have signed for it, but it was too late now. Whatever it was, it was going to cost her, and she couldn't afford it.

She picked up Babs' house key, tossing it back and forth in her hands, trying to decide if it would be okay to enter her late friend's home. She needed money soon. Doris knew selling the knick-knacks that Babs had promised her and marked with a signed sticky note would bring in a few bucks. She could pick them up today and start selling. Yet she had to be careful because Drill Sargent Courtney was now running the show. "Am I even allowed to enter the house?" she wondered aloud, or would she have to wait for an invitation from Courtney?

She still couldn't believe her best friend was gone. Babs was tough, and Doris figured her friend would be the last to go from their childhood gang. In many ways, they were the same, but also different.

Doris had more health issues than Babs, yet she noted to herself, she was still kicking. Doris decided early on that she didn't want to work herself to death like Babs did, hustling for every job to support her three kids at the age of twenty-one, while Doris had two kids in five years and a couple of husbands. Babs and Doris had both grown up in poverty and joked about coming from the wrong side of the tracks and on the wrong side of town. Babs was determined to get out of there and make something of herself. She eventually got her wish and moved to a nicer part of Danbyville. Doris didn't exactly aim high and felt good because she mostly got by in life. Except she now found herself living in a basement apartment at the age of sixty-four, which Babs nicknamed "The Hobbit Hovel." Babs called it that in response to the landlord packing the exterior cement walls with moss to insulate the house in the winter.

Her thoughts returned to her immediate problem: cleaning. It was her only skill, and she didn't think she could keep doing it with her arthritis getting worse. She had to keep a steady flow of new customers to keep things going, and it took endless energy to cobble together a decent income. Her cousin Pam said she could get Doris a job at the company where she worked, Home Sweet Home, helping senior citizens in their homes. All she'd have to do is light housework, help them move around their homes and keep them company. She'd have to take a two-week unpaid training course, which sucked but was doable. The bigger problem: Doris detested all the stupid paperwork. You signed in when you arrived, and at every turn, a supervisor would be breathing down her neck. Last resort, she decided.

Babs was her favorite customer (or "client" as they now called them at the Unemployment Office, now called the Employment Office. *Whatever*). It helped that she and Babs were best friends from way back. Doris was proud that she called Babs as soon as she heard about the cancer and jumped right in to help her friend. She offered to clean her house for free, but Babs insisted on paying her. Thanks to Babs' shared life with her second husband George, she had built up some savings and finally had enough to live on. She was super frugal when she was young and broke, yet always generous when she had money. *Bless her*, Doris thought. Her friend sure deserved more comfort after having three kids with her first husband Dirk, or "Dirk Bag" as the gang called him. They knew him when he was a teenage train wreck. She wondered what Babs ever saw in him, but then remembered that she had dated him briefly in high school, so she was no better. He charmed Doris long enough to get her into bed, then dumped her right afterward. "Lucky me, getting dumped right away" she used to joke with Babs.

It was three years ago that Babs started feeling off, and it took time for the doctors to diagnose the cancer. Doris knew how hard Babs worked to keep her house clean over the years, so she figured it was the one place where Doris could make a difference. However, Doris felt any of Babs' four adult kids could have pitched in on the work. Courtney did help, but she focused on the errands and groceries. Brando and Brandi were too busy running their massive suburban homes in the ritzy part of town. They hired people to clean their own homes (not Doris, she noted), so she knew they sure as hell wouldn't stoop to clean their Mom's house. And Mona, well, Doris knew that girl was a pickle, who never lifted a finger to clean. One time, Babs got all excited and paid Doris to "spring clean" Mona's apartment.

"How did it go?" Babs asked Doris.

"Well, let's just say Mona forgot spring cleaning for the last five seasons, so there was a serious buildup of grime," said Doris, refusing to gloss over the negative stuff. "It was clear she didn't like me being there."

"Don't take it personally, Doris," said Babs. "She never liked me cleaning her room as a teenager. She said she'd look after it, which she never did. I thought she might appreciate some help."

Doris recalled when she wrapped up the job, Mona muttered something about not cleaning properly. *Well, look who's calling the kettle black*, she wanted to toss back to Mona but didn't want to hurt Babs' feelings. Within a couple of weeks, Mona's apartment returned to its state of natural disaster, so Doris figured it was obvious who was prone to sloppiness.

Cleaning Babs' place was a totally different experience—it was a laugh-a-minute and her best job. Doris dropped by three times a week to help cook and clean. She'd put the kettle on for tea when she first arrived. If there were no cookies around, she'd bake some and Babs always insisted that she take the rest home. They'd talk, laugh and catch up on all the news. Then Doris would haul out cleaning stuff and get started before lunch.

"Don't get too bogged down in cleaning, Doris," Babs would say, sipping a beer like they did in old times, and biting into one of Doris's barbequed burgers one summer's day.

"Why not?"

"Maybe I was too focused on cleaning for most of my life and passed that on to Courtney."

"Yup. Life's short." Doris nodded to her friend. She wished Babs could point that out to Courtney. Doris tensed up whenever Courtney dropped by unexpectedly. It usually happened when she was resting her knees. Courtney would cast her hawk eye around the room with that snooty look of hers as if challenging her cleaning. Babs would tell her to relax, but Courtney didn't relax. Brando and Brandi were worse. They only stopped by a couple of times, and both times she'd been sitting with Babs. What were the odds? Brando didn't mince words—he barked at her to get back to work. Babs tried to calm him down, but we both knew he was saddled with his father's short fuse. Brandi never said a word. When they left, Babs waved her hand dismissively, and said, "Don't worry about it."

Mona was there a fair bit when Doris would arrive, giving her mother a big hug and kiss on the cheek—as sweet as one of her double caramel lattés. Doris knew she was only there to hit her mother up for some dough. Lord, that kid was a moocher of the first order—always scarfing down her mother's food, doing laundry at her house, or bumming money. She should have just moved back to keep her mother company after George died, but no sir, she needed her own "safe space" as she called it, which was code for having sex with one of her boyfriends.

Doris figured Babs was a little lonely in the last year. Yes, the kids visited, but not often and they didn't stay long. She went way beyond the call of duty for her friend Babs. She cleaned, but she did much more—she was her friend.

"How about just sitting and visiting?" Babs would say sometimes.

Doris visited often. And she'd make meals to make sure Babs ate something. She only charged for cleaning, never for visiting, because Doris knew where to draw the line. Yet she appreciated Babs' generosity because she needed payment for the hours she worked each week. The job kept her hovering slightly above the poverty line. With that income stream now gone, she was at a loss. Plus, her car, which she and Babs named "El Crappo," was now on the fritz and she didn't have the money to fix it. And it wasn't like there was a bus in this one-horse town. With her arthritis, life was getting tougher. She so wanted to quit the cleaning business, but she needed the money. Bad.

That was the other thing, Babs saved her butt multiple times when she couldn't pay her oil bill or buy groceries. Doris would start explaining a problem when Babs would pony up a bunch of twenties without her even asking.

"Don't forget, Doris, there's also cash in the old tobacco tin at the top of the cupboard that's full of rolled bills if you ever need them."

"You sure?"

"Yes, of course. Keep in mind it's there for Mona, too."

At first, Doris turned down her kind offers, until she realized Babs' income had been rising over the years and hers wasn't. She figured, "Why not?" That's what she and the gang did: they helped each other in times of need. Babs found ways to help Doris without making her feel like she was a mooch. She didn't want to be like Mona.

One day when Doris was dusting Babs' china cabinet, she happened to admire her collection of painted ceramic figurines. Doris had just seen an article in a magazine about how valuable certain items were. Babs had many of them from all her wheeling and dealing.

"Which ones do you like?" said Babs, standing beside her at the cabinet.

"Oh geez, I don't know," said Doris, randomly pointing to the clown on a bench with balloons, a high-class lady in purple with a matching parasol, and a mother with her child.

"You're good," Babs laughed. "Those are the most valuable ones of the lot."

"No way. That must be from my refined upbringing," she joked.

They both howled at the absurdity of it. Babs scribbled on three sticky notes and said, "I'm putting your name on these three. You can have them when I'm gone. Keep them or sell them if you need money. I don't care."

Doris tried not to look too eager. "Don't you want these to go to your kids?"

"C'mon, Doris. The kids won't want any of those; they're too old-fashioned. Besides, I know you'd like them to resell. And I'm okay with that."

"Got me," she laughed, as Babs placed the stickies on the bottom. It was true, she didn't care one iota for them, but she sure liked the idea of swapping them for cash. She knew she'd have to be careful about what she

admired because as Babs got closer to the end, she'd
kept saying she could have items and hand her a yellow
square. Doris didn't want to appear greedy, so she didn't
always respond. She figured once Babs was gone, her
money-grubbing children would be ready to sell anything.

"So, tell me about this Maud Lewis painting," Doris
asked one day, pointing to the small canvas showing a
sleigh ride in the countryside. "I don't know much about
her." She had heard the story before but loved to see
Babs light up when she recalled the event.

"I used to attend all-day estate sales. The place would
be packed all morning, and the bidding was frenzied.
But by mid-afternoon, people fizzled out," Babs said,
walking over to the painting and smiling at it. "Of course,
prices were creeping upward, but this was before prices
went through the roof."

"Uh huh, then what happened?"

"There weren't a lot of people there, so I got it for a
thousand bucks," she beamed.

"That's quite a story, Babs. You were so ahead of your
time with Maud Lewis paintings," said Doris." In hindsight, Doris recalled Babs hinting about giving it to her
that day but then went off on another topic. Doris didn't
come right out and ask for an official sticky note from
her at the time. "That must be worth a fortune, now."

"Yes, it's crazy. They are going for thirty to fifty thousand at auction these days."

Doris nearly choked on her tea. "You serious?"

"Yes ma'am. I lost money on lots of crap that I bought
over the years, but this one is my pride and joy. In
addition to enjoying it for years, it's an incredible nest

egg. It gave me so much comfort during the years that if things ever got bad, I could sell it," said Babs.

Doris strained her memory. Hadn't Babs once said, "maybe you'd like it?" She couldn't quite recall. She knew it wasn't a reward for her cleaning in the past years; maybe it was about their deep friendship from childhood. They were just getting to the nitty gritty of her generous gift when Courtney burst through the door and said they were late for her mother's doctor's appointment. Courtney glanced at her standing by the painting with Babs, her eyebrows squished into interrogation mode. "What's going on?"

"We were just dusting Maud Lewis and Babs is supervising," Doris joked, pulling out a rag from her apron.

"For God's sake, Doris, don't wipe that painting with a dirty rag," Courtney barked. "It's extremely valuable and has to be cleaned by a professional."

"Sorry." Doris tucked the rag back in her pocket.

Babs eased out of her chair and did a slow-motion hustle to get ready. Doris kicked herself for not getting Babs to write out a sticky note for Courtney to witness that day. Babs thought better of it with Courtney standing there. The next time Doris admired it, Babs didn't say anything.

Doris never relied on anybody in her life, so she wasn't going to make a fuss. And she refused to grovel. Babs' kids all had enough money to live on (well, maybe not Mona because she spent money like water), yet all they could think about was how to spruce up their homes, show off a new SUV or head to a sunny destination. And here she was stuck in her life with nothing—after all the years she had been such a good friend to dear Babs. It wasn't fair.

She fumed as she turned on the TV, but she couldn't focus on anything. She needed cash soon, or she'd be in deep trouble. As a stopgap, she wondered if she could get Courtney to pay her for her last week of work with Babs. That made her feel better for a minute.

She walked back to the table and opened the envelope from the law office; she might as well find out what the damage was. Sticking her thumb in at the end, she tore into it, her heart pumping. It was an official copy of Babs' will. She skimmed through all the legal mumbo jumbo until she found her name. Her eyes popped. It wasn't a lawsuit or a bill; Babs had left her a gift of two thousand dollars. She gasped. Aside from being desperate for money, she was moved by Babs' generosity. Suddenly, she perked up. She grabbed another cookie and put the kettle on. Her brain was on fire, wondering how fast she could get the money. That meant a conversation with Courtney, which she dreaded. Would Courtney try to get out of paying her? Plus, she wanted her last week of pay. She needed to get herself organized so that she could talk to the Drill Sargent, or "Queen Bea" as Brando called her, which always made Doris laugh.

Chapter 6

Courtney

"You ready for this?" said Jamie. "Your family can be a handful."

"I'm good thanks, hon," I said, kissing his cheek and handing him a coffee as he checked his phone at the breakfast counter. "You're right, though; they can all act like wild cards. I'm glad Mom's lawyer will be running the meeting."

Instead of sleeping, I spent the night worrying about reviewing the will this morning. Even though I had prepared for hours for this family meeting with the lawyer, Megan Blume, I still felt like I was standing on a tiny mat which could be pulled out from under me at any second. I trusted her completely, but in one of our earlier meetings, I warned her about my siblings. She thanked me and said not to worry, explaining that it was important to hear from everybody and let them ask their questions. I was happy because if one of the siblings asked a curveball question, it would be best for the lawyer to answer. Knowing the Brandies and Mona, they could argue about legal matters like they were in a courtroom when in fact, they were merely spouting their opinion. I told my siblings I'd take notes and distribute them afterward so that we had everything documented. I know that sounded official, and it wasn't my siblings' style, but they'd appreciate it later. I grabbed an apple and shouted "bye" to my husband and kids heading out for school.

I turned into the law office parking lot and spotted the Brandies pulling up beside my car. I knew they'd traveled together so they could strategize. Plus, Brando wanted to vape cannabis before the meeting because his girlfriend Roxy wouldn't let him do it in the house. He was so simple to figure out.

"Hi, Brando and Brandi, how's it going?" I asked, hoping to get things off to a friendly start. "Hey there," they nodded and smiled.

"Mona here?" asked Brando, looking around.

"I'm expecting her any minute," I said, checking my watch. I don't know why I bothered to put a positive spin on Mona's arrival time. We all knew she'd be late. We exchanged small talk as we waited for Mona, each of us scanning cars driving by, in case it was her.

"Courtney, I hope this doesn't become a habit," said Brando.

"What?"

"Spending money on a lawyer," said Brando. "It's crazy to pay hundreds of bucks an hour to someone—you'll drain the estate."

Here we go. I knew he'd complain. "Look, settling an estate is complex. There are legal issues that I don't know anything about," I said.

"You're the executor; you should inform yourself."

"I'll pretend I didn't hear that jerky comment. Lawyers spend their careers 'informing themselves,'" I said with air quotes. "If we do this ourselves and get something wrong, you'll be the first one to complain," I said, looking at my watch and ignoring his smug face. "Well, our meeting starts in five minutes. There's no sign of her and I refuse to be late," I said.

"Agreed," chimed the Brandies. We walked inside to the reception. Brando announced our arrival in his booming sales rep voice. Within seconds, we were hustled into a meeting room. I explained that Mona was running late but would be joining us. Megan looked to be our age, in her mid-forties, which I thought would work well for us. Her thick wavy hair and smart blazer and skirt gave her confident lawyer cred, but she'd added a small-town twist: an expensive T-shirt sporting ample cleavage. Brando started joking and flirting to get her attention; God, he was obvious.

"You must be Brando Martin," she said smiling. "And by process of elimination, you're his twin, Brandi Martin-Pach." She shook everybody's hand in quick succession as if she were working the room at a networking event.

"Please, grab yourself a coffee while we wait for Mona so that we don't waste time," she said, pointing to a food and drink station in the corner.

"Thanks, Megan," I said. I liked her already. That's what you want from a lawyer when you pay by the hour. I texted Mona. She replied she was almost here, which meant she was just leaving. Fortunately, it was a small town, and she wasn't far away. Mona liked attention. And whether she knew it or not, she usually arrived late to make an entrance or cause disruption.

Megan glanced at her watch. "While we are waiting, let me note your pronouns for correspondence. Brando, are you *he/him*?"

"Yup."

"Courtney and Brandi, are you both *she/her*?"

"Yes," I said, and Brandi nodded.

Megan scribbled in her notebook. "Thanks. And do you know Mona's preferred pronouns?"

"Me, myself and I," joked Brando.

In a millisecond, I saw the Brandies exchange their catty glance that I called the "virtual high five." I had seen that during childhood when one of them one-upped somebody. While there was truth to Brando's remark about Mona, I didn't want our family to show our true colors in the first meeting.

"Sorry, I think it's *she/her*. I should know that." I spent half my day at work carefully noting that information about my colleagues, yet I'd never asked my siblings.

"Don't worry, I'll verify later," Megan said, picking up the will and taking a breath to speak.

Right on cue, we heard a commotion out in the reception area including a dog barking. Mona breezed in with Shiva. Now, I love Shiva, and she was a friendly retriever which meant that she loved everybody and wanted them to pet her. She also shed continuously, her full swishy red tail dusting any person or object in her path. But why, oh why, did Mona have to bring Shiva to the meeting?

"Hi, I'm Megan. You're late. You must be Mona Nichols. Please have a seat here," Megan said, pointing to a chair at the table. Her tone was neutral, not angry—yet in a couple of sentences she had gained control of the meeting. Looking startled, Mona eased into the chair without debating the request, a first for her. She had her bucket-sized latté with her, so at least we didn't have to wait for her to fetch a coffee.

When Megan saw Shiva, she stopped. "And who's your fur baby?" she said, looking at the dog.

"Shiva," Mona announced meekly. "Sorry, I couldn't get her to stay home."

"No problem," Megan said, looking around. "Anybody here allergic to peanut butter?"

We glanced at each other, a little surprised by the question, and shook our heads. Megan then pressed a phone button and said, "Aaliyah, could you please bring a pet cushion and a doggy treat ball." While she was waiting, she handed a copy of the will to everybody. In seconds, Megan's assistant arrived, placing everything in the corner. She showed Shiva the light plastic ball with deep dents in it, like a golf ball on steroids. Each cavity was filled with peanut butter, a treat that would keep a dog busy for ages. Shiva trotted to the corner and settled in on the cushion.

"Wow, that's a great idea. How'd you think of that?" I said to Megan, glancing at the now-settled dog and then at the Brandies and Mona.

"Well, pets sometimes attend meetings and we're ready for them," said Megan looking at Shiva. "They are usually the best-behaved attendees at the meeting."

I laughed nervously. I think she was joking but wouldn't have bet my first-born on it. I felt relieved that a canine wasn't going to hijack the meeting, even if the room reeked of peanut butter and we had to listen to Shiva slurping the ball like a ravenous anteater after a long winter. Mona appeared confused because the dog issue was addressed in two minutes flat. I could see Brando's knee tapping up and down under the table, which meant he was either bored, stressed or in a hurry. Knowing him, all three.

"Okay, shall we start?" Megan asked, without waiting for an answer. Everybody nodded as if it were the first day of school and they'd been assigned the strictest teacher in the school.

I was glad Mom picked her; this woman was serious. Mom was smart enough to hire Megan to draw up the will, so barring unforeseen circumstances, this should be straightforward. I'd already read it, so I knew what was coming. The Brandies and Mona hadn't—although Mom had given them a high-level outline.

Megan looked at everybody as she read. "First, just to reconfirm, Courtney Bea Martin-Wilkie is the executrix. It is her responsibility to ensure your mother's wishes are carried out as directed in the will." She confirmed that the estate was divided equally among the four siblings, and we all knew that included Mom's house and the contents, her car, second-hand goods business and bank accounts. "Is that clear to everyone?"

"Yes," I said, and the others nodded.

"And there is a specific bequest here," said Megan reading. "'I hereby give, devise and bequeath a specific gift to my long-time friend Doris Lynn Wheatly, of Danbyville, the sum of two thousand dollars. And there are three knick-knacks that I've promised to her in my home, signed by me on yellow sticky notes.'"

"How'd Doris talk her into that?" said Brando. The Brandies shot a sideways glance at each other.

Megan looked at Brando. "I was with your mother when she wrote this will, so it's valid."

"I think it's sweet," said Mona, suddenly awake. "They'd been besties since their younger years, and she knew Doris was hard up for money."

"I agree," I said. "Mom probably didn't need convincing." I could see Mona was moved by our mother's display of kindness. In the bigger scheme of things, I knew the money would benefit Doris more than the rest of us. Although I had my issues with Doris—she was neither a competent nor motivated cleaner—she was still Mom's dear friend. Plus, she was in her sixties with multiple health problems. Her life wasn't easy.

"Whatever," snapped Brando, scribbling on the side of the will. His face showed he didn't like it one bit. "Anything else?"

"Yes, there's one other request from your mother," says Megan. "Here's what she said: 'When the time comes, I would like Fluffy, my adorable cat, to be cremated and buried with my ashes.'"

"Whaaaattt?" said the Brandies.

"This might be a stupid question," said Brandi, her face flushing, "but is that allowed?"

"While it's not common, it happens," said Megan. "Pets are an integral part of many families now."

"Well, for the record, I'm part of the family and I don't want that to happen to me," said Brando.

"Noted." Megan flashed him a condescending smile.

I wrote a note in the file. We'd have to make sure there was enough money in the estate to feed and care for the cat, as well as pet cremation later, once I found out how long cats lived. I put a star in the margin so that I could get an estimate and then add in an inflation factor. Since Fluffy was only three years old, we'd have to inform whoever was taking care of her about our mother's final wishes.

"Still, seems kind of mean to me," said Brando shrugging. His heel was tapping as fast as a disco beat at a 1970s wedding.

"Cats are very intuitive, you know," said Mona, gulping her coffee. "I suspect Mom and Fluffy had an understanding about the cremation plans when she passed, so I think it's okay."

"Well... they can debate that in their next life," said Brando.

Brando was unemotional about everything—why did he suddenly sound like a caring guy? And why did Mona think she could weigh in on Mom and her cat whispering conversations? I looked to Megan for help with S.O.S. written all over my face.

"Yes, well, none of us can answer that, so we won't waste time debating it," said Megan, shuffling her files. "So, before we go any further, are there any questions?"

"How long will this estate stuff take?" Brando asked, doodling bubbles on his legal pad.

"Hmm..." said Megan. "It's a bit like asking me 'How long is a piece of string?'"

"I didn't mean to go all philosophical on you," Brando joked, then turned serious. "You must have some idea. Are we talking weeks? Months?"

"Much longer, Brando," said Megan, looking directly at him. "Minimum one tax year, maybe two or more. It depends on what we find. It will take as long as it takes."

"Wow, I had no idea," said Brandi.

I looked at Mona, Brando and Brandi as a shockwave rippled across their faces. I don't know if they thought I was going to cut a check for each of them at this meeting and wrap it up, but clearly, they didn't have a clue about the process. To be fair, I didn't either until I read a bunch of books and blogs. I was glad this came up at the meeting so that Megan could break the news to everyone.

"Could you help me to understand what you mean by 'depending on what we find?'" asked Mona. I sensed unease brewing in her question.

Megan tapped a pen on her pad. "Here's how it works. We'll put the estate through probate. That means we have to identify all her assets and debts. We can liquidate all the assets like selling the house, the car and the business inventory. We pay the probate and income taxes, gifts and debts, then we distribute whatever is leftover."

"So, as you can see, this is going to take a good chunk of time," I said, supporting Megan's point.

"No, I don't see, Queen Bea," said Brando. "Anyone with competency should be able to push this through in a few months."

I stiffened. Our first official meeting, and already, Brando was being... Brando.

"Brando," said Megan, her tone firm. "First of all, we'll put a notice in the *Royal Gazette* for six months, which is a government newspaper that announces your mother's passing and invites anybody who claims to have a debt with her to contact us."

"Mom didn't have any debts, so we can skip that step," said Brando. "That will shave six months off."

"We are legally required to do it. It's not up for discussion."

"How often does it happen that someone has an unknown debt?" asked Mona.

I looked at Mona. Knowing that girl, it wouldn't surprise me to find out Mom had co-signed a loan for Mona at some point. Mona had so many carefree spending habits like buying clothes and cars, attending college, and starting businesses... who knew what she'd been hiding?

Megan leaned toward Mona and said, "You'd be surprised. Sometimes people forget. Last month, we had two men arrive from Prince Edward Island. They saw the obituary of an old friend and said their late friend owed them a hefty sum from a poker game thirty years ago."

"Well, Mom didn't gamble," said Brando. "Forget that."

Megan raised one eyebrow. "We still have to go through the legal process. The good news is that they have six months to step up. And if they don't within that time frame, well, too bad for them. Any other questions?"

"What are the next steps?" I asked, even though I knew the answer. Since we were paying Megan the big bucks, I wanted her to break the news to everybody.

"Well, I know you are organizing a service for your mother. After that, you can provide me with a list of all the assets and debts—that you know of—and then start liquidating or dividing the estate. You as a family should get together and discuss how to do that."

"Another meeting," groaned Brando.

Brando believed I lived for meetings. I didn't, but we had responsibilities. My siblings just wanted the estate money, yet there was so much we had to do before we got there. I knew he'd be a fly in the ointment and try to amuse himself while doing it. He didn't want to be the executor because that would be too much detailed work for him, but he did want to run the show. And Mona would be right behind, waiting to join him. She might sound friendlier, but she had the same urge to run the show without doing a lick of work. And her opinions would be the opposite of everyone else's. I left the meeting with a growing knot in my stomach, knowing it was my job to get everybody on board to do the work. It was only day one, and already I wondered, *Are we there yet?*

Chapter 7

Mona

Mona walked into her apartment and tossed her bulging bag on the chair. She felt unsettled about the reading of the will earlier that day. While it was good to reconfirm that she'd get one-quarter of the estate, the timeline wasn't in her favor. She needed money before her rent arrears turned into a crisis. Well, it was already a crisis and could become an even bigger one without cash flow.

She logged into her online retail account to see if any of her designs had sold. Just one cushion at a hundred bucks. *Big deal*, she thought. She switched to her social media accounts and saw comments from her customers encouraging her to add new items. She knew she should add new inventory, but she just didn't have the "oomph," as her Mom used to say. To take the pressure off, she posted about her mother passing away. Grief-stricken emojis popped up like mushrooms. She could hardly keep up with the love that flowed. Normally, she'd welcome so much traffic, but it was not helping now. She didn't know those people—they were just names and weird nicknames "out there" somewhere in a virtual world. Each post made her feel lonelier. She needed a friend in person.

Just then a text swooped in from her friend Stella, begging her to go to the bar for drinks. She replied: *Of course!* She hoped Stella was buying. But first, she needed to eat. She texted Raj and invited him over for dinner (which meant he would pay for it).

Mona: *Hey-o, Raj. Coming over to dinner?*

Raj: *Curried chickpeas, or Tarka dhal?*

Mona: *Surprise me, but I am hungry. LOL. Don't forget rice, naan and chutney.*

I can't believe I found a found a guy so kind and accommodating, she mused. She wished she loved him more. Early on, she was smitten with him and even named her dog Shiva in honor of the Hindi God—he laughed and said a retriever wasn't exactly a "destroyer" kind of dog.

She laid down on the sofa and patted a spot for Shiva to join her. Shiva tried to fit into a tiny space beside her on the sofa. They wiggled and moved until they both fit and curled up together like a pretzel. Within minutes, she'd nodded off into a late-afternoon nap. When a knock at the door pulled her out of a deep sleep, she exchanged glances with Shiva. She had no idea how much time had passed and vaguely remembered Raj was picking up food.

"Come in," she shouted at the door, not ready to sit up yet. Silence. There was another knock, and she sighed, wondering why Raj didn't use his key. She nudged Shiva off the sofa and stood up, walking to the door.

"Coming, Raj!" When she opened the door, she jumped. It was her landlord Bruce who lived at the front of the house. She was annoyed with herself for not checking first because she wanted to duck him. He wasn't a bad guy, but his wife Cilla or Sylvia (or whatever she was called) was a miserable person with a scowl tattooed on her forehead. A murky brown aura surrounded his wife and Mona preferred to give her a wide berth.

"Hey, Mona," he said, glancing back toward the deck where his wife lurked. Mona figured she was coaching her husband with messages that she was too chicken to say. This annoyed Mona, so she did her best to make them state exactly what they wanted to say. She once invited them in for tea so they could have a rational conversation, but Bruce's wife made up a lame excuse to avoid a face-to-face conversation.

Mona raised her hands to her shoulder and tossed back her golden hair, illuminated by the golden afternoon sun. Mona knew Bruce found her attractive, but he was respectful and nerdy and responded by acting nervous around her. He never said a word or behaved inappropriately around her, so she felt hair-tossing was a harmless tactic. Besides, with a large negative energy field simmering on the deck, Mona was not worried something untoward would happen.

"Hi, Bruce. Look, I know why you're here," she said. She didn't want to make it more awkward for him. "I'm a month or two behind in rent, but don't worry," she said, flashing her mega-watt smile and waiting for him to dissolve.

The deck let out a creak and a sigh. "Six," he slipped in, staring at his worn-out running shoes, followed by a glance at the deck.

She briefly lost her focus. "Six what?" Mona said.

"Months. You're behind six months in rent."

It couldn't be. "Oh, my goodness no, Bruce," she said. "You must be mistaken." She knew she sounded patronizing, as if he was either a child incapable of tracking such things or he was losing his mind, and she was trying to be gentle with the news. She was delaying the conversation because she couldn't recall the last time she did an eTransfer to him. This wasn't good.

"Last December. The fifteenth."

"Let me check," she said bringing up her bank account on her phone. She scrolled full of purpose, chattering away as if it were a casual item to be searched. The account was an endless list of debits at her friend's coffee shop, the sewing and notions store and service charges. She flinched when she saw that she had paid seventy dollars in service charges for one month. *How did that happen? Why didn't she notice?* She finally spotted the amount for her rent transfer and checked the date.

"Oh, dear. Yes, about five months ago. I'm so sorry, Bruce. How did that happen?" she asked.

"Six," creaked a voice from the deck.

"Yes, six, I'm afraid," said Bruce.

"What, is there a ventriloquist on the deck or something?" Mona joked, but she remembered her father urged her to be careful with sarcasm.

Bruce pulled in a deep breath. "But that's not why I'm here."

"Oh?" Mona said, kicking herself for raising the topic of rent arrears when she didn't need to.

"It's the lease ending... you know, the letter we sent six months ago," he said. "You haven't let us know about leaving, and we need the apartment back."

Mona felt like someone was spinning her head like a top. She had no idea about a letter, and all that sunk in was that he wanted her apartment back. "Why do you need it?" She knew she sounded a bit accusing, but it snuck out before she could filter it.

"For my mother. She can't stay in her home. We need to make the apartment accessible for her."

"What? You're renovicting me?" she gasped.

Bruce blushed. "That's not how I'd describe it, Mona."

Mona scrambled to figure something out quickly. Rentals in Danbyville were in short supply and overpriced. While this one wasn't perfect, she had spent time making it pretty—all for nothing. "And what about this supposed letter, Bruce?"

There was a thump on the deck, and Bruce fumbled with a file folder. "Uh...we gave you notice six months ago. I have the letter here."

"Well, I didn't get any letter," she snapped. "Let's just deal with one thing at a time, shall we?" She didn't know what she meant by that, but it sounded good.

He flipped through the folder and pulled out a piece of paper. "Here you go. It's a receipt that shows you signed for it."

Mona's mind raced. Did she really receive a letter? And worse, did she sign for it? She couldn't remember. The last year was a haze for her.

She leaned toward him and whispered, "You know my Mom died, right?" She did that on purpose to rile up his wife who was just out of earshot.

Bruce nodded. "Yes, everybody knows. And I'm so sorry Mona."

"Okay, but I need notice. I can't believe this, after all I've done for you and your wife."

"Bugger all," whispered the voice on the deck. Bruce stared downward.

Her mind raced to blurt out things to prove what a good tenant she was. There was a time last winter when Bruce fractured his wrist and couldn't shovel. She had started to shovel the driveway to great fanfare. For half an hour, she cleared enough to get her car out, but then realized Bruce couldn't drive anyway so she stopped. She reminded herself she always paid her rent, even if it took time, well, except for this latest round. So that wasn't the best example.

She decided to ignore the puppeteer's comments on the deck. "So, Bruce, what can you do for me?"

Bruce ran his hands through his hair. "I suppose I could make a few calls to people who have rentals."

Mona fumed. She didn't need this hassle on top of everything else. Yet she was hardly in a position of strength. "I suppose. But how about two months' notice?"

"My mother has to leave her old place now. I don't have any choice," he said pausing. A stomp came from the deck. "Sorry, Mona, but you are already past the deadline."

She realized she'd lost the battle. It wouldn't look good for a thirty-year-old to get into a tussle to block an octogenarian from moving in. "Well, the least you can do is give me thirty days' grace," said Mona, looking directly at Bruce. "I mean, that's only fair, isn't it, Bruce? You don't want to push a young woman onto the streets, do you?"

"Yes, we do," croaked the shadow above.

"Bruce?" Mona said softly, ignoring the deck. She half closed one eye in the afternoon sun—it could be interpreted as a squint or a wink. She'd let him decide.

"Well, I guess that wouldn't be too neighborly," Bruce replied.

"Thank you, Bruce. I appreciate your kind and warm heart. I will get this sorted out within thirty days. And let me know what you find with your rental friends," she added.

Bruce nodded and turned toward the deck; his face twisted lightly with fear. Mona felt sorry for him because she knew he was in for a good shellacking with his wife. But annoying her was a bonus. "Oh, and say hi to Sylvia for me," she added as he left.

"Cecilia."

Whatever. Mona smiled and closed the door. Curious, she started searching for the letter. Once Bruce was gone, she walked back to the door and stuck her hand in the mailbox. It was chock full; she hadn't checked it in months. Most of it was junk, and she couldn't stand the waste of paper that went in there weekly, so she just ignored it. She grabbed it all and tossed everything on the table, recycling as she sorted. There was no letter in there, but she realized if she signed for it, it wouldn't have been there anyway.

In little bursts, she wandered around the apartment lifting things in piles and looking for places where she stowed mail and documents. There was no central hub. She found lots of useless bits of mail, but no letter. She walked to the living room and plunked herself on the sofa. Spying a stack of books on the lower shelf of the coffee table, she noted white envelopes and letters collecting dust. She pulled one out and blew the dust and dog hair away. She found the letter, and yes, she had signed for it. *How could she have forgotten that?* The date was six months earlier and for the life of her, she couldn't remember it—except a vague conversation with her mother. She choked up thinking about how much she missed her mother at a time like this. Her Mom would have simply made all this go away. She didn't know what she'd do without her. However, she reminded herself she was her mother's daughter and could be very resourceful when she needed to solve dire situations. This was big and it needed an extreme plan.

Chapter 8

Doris

Doris glanced at the sign "Welcome to Ocean Breeze community" which made her chuckle because it didn't look welcoming, and it was nowhere near the ocean. This was Courtney's subdivision and Doris dreaded both the visit to Courtney and the extra walk on streets that were designed to meander—except people mostly drove. Yes, there were shuffling seniors, taking a ten-minute walk, but not a lot of neighborly strolls like in the brochures.

Early summer was finally arriving in Nova Scotia. While she loved it, the last few years had been too hot for her. Sweat trickled down the sides of her head, neck and back as she walked toward Courtney's home.

Doris had dithered about whether to call and ask to come over or just land on her doorstep. She was worried if she called, Courtney would put her off. While Courtney was pushy and annoying, she also had certain manners—so Doris believed her best bet was to arrive unannounced. After a fifteen-minute walk, she winced at how many steps there were to the front door, especially with her knee starting to swell. She stopped at the landing to catch her breath, hoping Courtney wouldn't spot her. Finally, she reached the top and breathed deeply before ringing the doorbell. She had barely pushed the button when the door flew open. Courtney was surrounded by luggage and looked like she was in a hurry—but she was always in a hurry, according to Babs.

"Hi, Doris. This is a surprise. What are you doing here?" said Courtney, more focused on spinning a weekender bag in the right direction.

"I'm sorry to bother you, Courtney," she said, gathering her thoughts. Courtney wore an expensive suit, the latest handbag and delicate strappy shoes with high heels and little support. Doris called them "sitting shoes" because you could only wear them to sit in. The lady was headed somewhere.

Courtney cut in right away. "That's okay, Doris. What can I do for you?"

"I got a copy of the will and saw the gift your Mom left to me. Bless her soul, I just cried to think about how kind Babs was to remember me." Doris choked up just trying to spit out what she wanted to say.

Courtney shifted slightly. "Yes, Mom was a good person, and I know you two go way back."

"Thick as thieves," joked Doris. She had already launched into a lengthy anecdote when she heard a couple of pings.

Courtney checked her fitness watch. "Apologies, Doris. I'm off to a conference. Is there a quick question?"

Doris jolted. She wasn't used to operating at Courtney's warp speed. "Oh, sorry, dear. I just wondered if I could pick up my check for two thousand dollars," she blurted. Courtney's eyes widened.

"OMG, Doris. You just got the letter yesterday, right?"

Doris nodded. She wondered what that question was for, but it was clear Courtney was about to explain it.

"There are so many steps and hoops to jump through before we can start distributing money. It will be months, possibly a year before we can do that."

Doris froze. "But... I need it now."

Courtney pushed and pulled her suitcases, corralling them to the door. "Sorry, but that's not going to happen. Two days ago, you didn't even know about it. Look, when I get back, I would be happy to sit down with you and go over the legal process. Is that okay?"

Doris knew that she didn't have any choice, but her financial woes egged her on. "Well then, could I get paid for my last week?" she blurted out, thinking she might as well aim for something. In the distance, she spied Fluffy the cat clawing at the French doors to the dining room, mewing and trying to escape. Doris felt sorry for the cat. She would try to escape too if she lived with Courtney.

Courtney sighed deeply. "I thought Mom paid you cash the minute you finished your cleaning."

"Well, as you know the last few weeks were different. Your Mom wasn't herself," she said. Courtney's look of agitation grew with Fluffy's cries of despair.

"Look, I'd need an invoice. Now that it's an estate, I need to account for every single transaction."

"You can't do it today?" Doris didn't even know how to do an invoice, but she figured Courtney would tell her what to write.

Courtney checked her watch. "No, Doris, I am now running late," she said with a tone saved for hosing down unruly people and indicating there was no negotiating. "Like I said, I'm back in three days. We can talk then. Is that okay?"

"Guess so," said Doris. She looked at the luggage stash. "Do you want a hand with that bag?"

"Thanks, Doris," she said sliding the bag toward her, as if Doris were just standing by like hired help, waiting to do hard labor.

Doris lifted the bag and struggled down the steps. Courtney, with the heavier bag, brushed past her and wobbled to the car on her heels. When Doris made it to the bottom, Courtney grabbed the bag and muttered a quick thanks. She backed out of the driveway as fast as possible, not even offering Doris a lift out of the long and winding road in the Ocean Breeze community.

Doris sat at the bottom of the steps to catch her breath. She was unimportant in Courtney's eyes—just a pest with a request to put off until later. Doris knew that Babs would be mortified to see her friend treated like she didn't matter. Also, she would have wanted her daughter to drive her arthritic friend out of the suburb—especially in hot weather. After five minutes, Doris walked over to the garden hose at the side of the house and gulped a deep drink of lukewarm water that tasted like plastic. Although she felt humiliation coursing through her body, she pushed everything back. From an early age, her mother drilled it into her to never feel ashamed about where she came from, and even if she did, never let it show. As teens, she and Babs perfected the art of acting tough and never appearing weak.

The sun beat down on her, and she wished she had brought a hat because her hair was thinning at the top. She picked up the unread newspaper on the steps and made a hat, pirate style, the way they did as kids. She knew she'd get stares from passersby, but she didn't care as she began the long trudge home.

***

Twenty minutes later, she emerged from the pristine suburb into central Danbyville. She was thirsty again, her knees hurt, and she had to pee, but she still had a way to go. Then she stopped. One street over was Babs' house. Rattling around her purse, she checked that Babs' key ring was still there. A full set of keys to everything—the house, basement and garage—that's how much Babs had trusted her friend. Doris decided a pit stop at her best friend's place was the perfect solution. Knowing that Drill Sargent Courtney was headed out of town, Doris could slip in there unnoticed. The Brandies never ventured to this part of town, and Mona wasn't likely to stop by now that her mother's pot of gold was gone. Even if others saw her going in there, it would just look like she was still cleaning.

She let herself inside. It felt cool and damp. Babs' favorite glass sat on the counter. Doris filled it from the tap and guzzled it in one shot. She washed it by hand as she always did and felt a deep sense of loss. When Babs was around, they'd be laughing the minute Doris arrived, and the laughter wouldn't stop until she left. Even when she was quite ill, Babs still had a sense of humor.

Doris had an urge to clean; it was now such a pattern for her in Babs' place, but she figured Courtney would be angry if she did anything. Doris looked up to the top of the shelf. The tobacco can with the cash stash was still there. It was always stocked up with rolled twenties, tens and fives. She remembered Babs telling her if she ever needed money, take it. She bet Courtney wouldn't even know about it. Still, things were different now with Courtney in charge. She decided to have a look to see how much money was there. She pulled the kitchen ladder from the pantry and started up the steps. She felt a shooting pain in her knee and wobbled a bit, but she took a little break at each step. Finally, at the top, she reached for the can. It was empty. She figured Mona got her grubby little mitts on that right away. Disappointed, she stepped down.

She wandered into the living room and gazed at the ceramic figurines that would soon be hers. They were so hokey, she couldn't imagine people paying hundreds of dollars for them, but she sure hoped they would. She never thought Babs was a huge fan, but it was probably a point of pride to say she could now afford them. She had to get those items to liquidate them as soon as possible.

The Maud Lewis painting caught her eye. She wandered over and stared at it. Everybody in Nova Scotia knew about Maud Lewis. A poor woman with multiple physical disabilities who lived in a one-room house in rural Nova Scotia and who still managed to see the good in life. Back in the sixties and seventies, she painted everything in the house: the walls, doors, stairs and every surface she could find. And when she ran out of places to paint, she painted on cardboard, wood, or whatever was at hand. She'd put the paintings outside for sale for five dollars. Passersby saw the heart and soul that she poured into her work, each painting lighting up somebody's life for a couple of dollars. Doris heard about Everett, Maud's husband, who didn't care about her paintings until he saw they could sell. Even then, he was stingy about buying Maud paints and supplies, but he sure liked the growing interest in her work. He even tried to paint like her after she died to keep things rolling.

Over the next four decades, her artwork grew in popularity, but she didn't live to see the frantic bidding for her paintings at prestigious auction houses. From five bucks for a painting to thirty or forty thousand dollars today, Maud's work became the darling of the folk-art world.

She studied the painting with a winter scene and a sleigh—the setting would have come from Maud's childhood in the Digby area. The colors were so bright and cheerful, and it seemed to her that Maud was trying to paint herself into a happier life. Doris hadn't spent any time looking at Maud's work because it was well above her snack bracket, although she enjoyed a trip that she and Babs had once taken to the exhibition at the Art Gallery of Nova Scotia in Halifax that even included Maud's tiny house that had been moved and installed inside the Gallery.

Doris wondered if Babs had wanted her to have this painting. Even though her memory was a little foggy, she felt like her friend was looking for a way for Doris to enjoy a retirement that was more secure than what she'd ever imagined. She thought about the kids and their situation: Courtney and her family in the expensive part of town, the Brandies and their insistence on showing off how far they'd come with their big homes, brand-new vehicles and sun vacations in the winter. Then there was Mona who was used to living high on the hog, but only thanks to her mother's and father's hard work.

Doris seethed as she thought about her situation: why did they all have so much while she had so little? What would they do with that Maud Lewis painting? Sell it for sure and then divide up the proceeds, so they could buy more expensive things for their homes.

She wandered over to the china cabinet and looked at the three figurines that Babs called "knick-knacks" in the will. She looked at the sticky notes on the bottom with Babs' handwriting. A brilliant idea flashed through her head, but it was so nervy she wondered if she'd lost her mind. She thought about when she and Babs were teenagers; they were a wild and crazy twosome who loved to break rules. Babs would dream up dares and Doris would do the deeds. They were a perfect team. They pulled off numerous antics that people never heard about because they kept them secret. After they'd finish a dare, they'd get a bottle of lemon gin from a bootlegger who didn't care that they were underage—and go to the wooded area near their house. They'd drink, smoke, recount the event and laugh their heads off. Doris would always start by saying, "I can't believe you did that!" Doris always felt a shiver of excitement for pulling it off without getting caught. And their successes would fire them up to do more.

Even though Babs was no longer with her, she started feeling the itch to pull off one last caper in honor of her departed friend.

Suddenly, the phone rang. Doris froze. Most people would know Babs had passed away, so who on earth was calling? Could Courtney have somehow figured out she'd stop there, or was Mona up to something? There was no call display, so she stood still like an idiot in the middle of the floor. After five rings it stopped. Probably a telemarketer. Doris took a breath and let herself out the side door.

Chapter 9

Brando

Brando groaned when he saw Courtney turn into the driveway. Mornings were busy enough without having someone stop by. She had texted to say she had a special delivery, and he knew right away it was Fluffy. Under different circumstances, he'd have put her off, but he knew his nephew was suffering from allergies that were getting worse, and it was the third time she had asked him, so he finally said yes.

She jumped out of the car and opened the back door, pulling out Fluffy in a cage. Of course, Fluffy was scratching and meowing to get out. She marched to the house and walked in the side door shouting a quick "hi ya" and setting the cage down. Then she beetled back to the car, got out a box full of cat accessories and brought them in.

Brando sighed; he felt like he was getting stiffed with this Fluffy burden. "Geez, got enough stuff, do you?"

"Just one more item," she said, not stopping to take a breath. This time she hauled out a massive bag and wrestled it to the door. Then she lifted it one step at a time until it was on the back porch.

"What the hell is that?" he asked. It didn't occur to him to help Courtney; instead, he was hoping she'd change her mind. Not a chance.

"I told you; it's a year's supply of cat food."

"Big deal," he snapped. "A lot of good that will do." Now he'd have to find a place to store that stuff or give it away.

Puffing lightly from her big exertion, she smiled and said, "Thanks, Bud. I know you're busy getting ready for school and work, and so am I. Gotta run."

"Smell ya later," he said, as he had since childhood. He picked up Fluffy's carrier and brought it to the kitchen. He couldn't very well leave her caged all day, so he opened the door. She bolted out and raced to a hiding place under the sofa. He didn't have time to cajole her. "Here we go," he muttered to himself. He pulled out a dish for water and one for food and filled them up.

Roxy flew by him in the hallway with an outfit draped over her arms. "Coming through!" she shouted to Brando as she headed for the basement.

"Can I help you with anything, Babe?" he said to Roxy, who looked more like a blur.

"If you are in the mood for ironing," she replied.

"Well, maybe not that. But anything else."

"I was just messing with you," she laughed. You are the worst ironer ever."

Relieved to get out of that chore, he checked his watch. "DeeDee?" Brando shouted from the bottom of the stairs. "You coming for breakfast or what?" He used his urgent voice with his daughter because he would soon be late if she didn't get a move on. He couldn't understand why she needed so much time getting ready for school, but based on the clothes tornado in her room, he realized she must change at least ten times a morning.

He wanted to challenge her on that, but growing up in an all-female household, he learned to not challenge things that seemed illogical to him. He prided himself on being a simple guy: he kept a few good outfits in his closet, and he'd grab the first pair of pants and shirt he saw in the morning then add his running shoes. No muss, no fuss, he'd be done. As a teenager, he once suggested his brilliant dressing solution to his sisters, and they looked at him like he was an alien. Well, he was, kind of. At home, he had a mother, and two sisters close to his age, followed by Mona many years later. He was grateful he didn't have to interact with her because she was ten times worse than Courtney and Brandi. His stepfather George was very careful not to take sides with Babs' children, so Brando had no father role model or brothers to commiserate with—it was just him amongst a bunch of females. He felt like he was always on guard.

When he graduated from high school and entered the sales arena for his career, it was all guys. They trained to-gether, attending sporting events and conferences. He'd met his tribe. Finally, his gross jokes, burping on demand and roughhousing were appreciated—it was like they'd been hidden away for years and could finally be brought out for entertainment purposes. Then he got married to Twyla, and their daughter DeeDee was born, and he was right back to square one with a female household. He loved his daughter more than anything, but it surprised him how he'd never had more male presence in his world.

"DeeDee. *NOW*," he shouted up the stairwell, then walked back to the breakfast nook and sat on the edge of the stool, checking his email. He knew if he were running super late, his girlfriend Roxy would drop his daughter off at school, but DeeDee was his responsibility. After what he experienced with his absent father, Brando wanted to be a good father—even if his daughter referred to him as "old school Dad." He spoke bluntly which wasn't always politic these days. Fortunately, Roxy was a bit tomboyish and fun—she even laughed at his fart jokes. She also liked that he was "manly," as she described him. He was so much happier with Roxy than he had been when he was married to Twyla, who wore a permanent look of disgust on her face about everything he said.

DeeDee descended the stairs still sizing up her outfit. She checked herself in the hall mirror and just as she turned back toward the stairwell, Brando said, "Don't even think about it, Deeds. We're leaving in ten minutes." He saw her scowl as she came into the kitchen.

"What can I get you for breakfast?" he said.

"Uhm, what is there?"

Brando bit his tongue. It was the same question every day, and yet she never remembered. "We've got juice, yogurt, cereal, or toast. What'll you have?"

DeeDee lifted her nose like a sniffy cat. "Pass."

Brando thought about his childhood and the anger he sometimes felt with his mother for serving oatmeal too often. Some days the meals were okay, others terrible. And yes, he complained, but he ate them. Back then, he just didn't understand his mother didn't have other options. He looked at his daughter and felt frustrated that she was turning down healthy food. He would have given anything to have had that selection as a kid.

"You have to eat something," he said, looking into her eyes. "You are not attending school on an empty stomach." *Oh shit,* he thought, watch out for the waterworks. He was in a rush but had to calm her down, or there'd be a teen crisis. He decided to try another angle: "I'll make whatever you want, DeeDee, but you need to pick something. What about a smoothie?" He held his breath in case that insulted her.

"Okay."

"Smoothie for my girl," he said smiling, relieved that he hit the jackpot in the breakfast lottery. He raced around tossing healthy things into the blender, adding protein powder and a tablespoon of maple syrup—but not a drop more because of her latest diet. But at least she was eating. He poured the smoothie into a drink container and handed it to her, along with a packed lunch.

She took it and picked up her backpack. "Okay, let's go," she barked as if Brando was the one holding things up. "And I need forty bucks for our class trip."

Chauffeur and ATM, that's what he was for his daughter. She had no idea how tough he had it growing up. If he wanted money, he had to earn it by mowing lawns or charming an elderly lady with household repairs that he barely knew how to do. The few times he'd tried to tell DeeDee about his childhood poverty, she'd rolled her eyes with boredom. All she had to do was hold out her hand or utter a syllable and either he or Twyla would pony up. DeeDee was just like Twyla—a sense of entitlement that didn't quit. He sighed. But then he realized he allowed it, so that's what he got.

When she came up from the basement, Brando kissed Roxy and promised to watch her play softball that evening. It was dull to watch, but he'd made friends with the husbands in the stands, so there was at least something to keep him occupied.

On the way to school, Brando tried to pry information out of DeeDee about school, sports, or anything. She answered in monosyllables while she sipped her smoothie. Then she turned to him and said, "Dad, what's going to happen to Gram's house?"

"Well, it's likely that we'll sell it, hon. Why?"

"I dunno. I guess it's just weird with her gone. I miss her. We didn't go there much, but she was real fun to be around," said DeeDee, staring out the window. "There were always so many things to look at. But there's also a ton of junk in her house and garage to be cleaned out..."

"Hey," he said, his eyes narrowing. "Don't talk about your grandmother like that."

She turned her head and looked at him. "That's exactly what you said months ago."

Brando sniffed. Kids could be very annoying when it came to remembering all the stupid things their parents said. "Yeah, well, I shoot from the hip when I talk. Besides, that was when she was alive. I know, that's no excuse—so I apologize, it wasn't the nicest thing to say."

He turned into the school drop-off and pulled up at the curb. DeeDee was practically bursting out of the car before he could even stop.

"Love you, Deedsy," he said, as she released the seatbelt and pushed open the door.

"Uh huh," she replied, distracted by her group of friends waving to her.

"Don't forget your smoothie," he shouted, lifting it out of the holder as she slammed the door.

He held the smoothie in his hand—it was three-quarters full. He worried she could be heading for an eating disorder. He'd have to talk to Twyla to see if she noticed anything. His ex had a long history of eating issues, even though she looked slim and fit.

A text pinged letting him know his meeting was canceled. Great, all that rushing and now he had forty minutes to kill before his next meeting. He checked his messages—nothing urgent. He could make sales calls, but he felt a little bummed out thinking about his Mom.

He pulled out of the school and drove over to her house a few minutes away. He stared at the modest house that she was so proud to own. The paint was starting to peel, and the greenery out front was sprouting in all directions. They'd need to do repairs and tidy up before it went up for sale. He wasn't looking forward to that.

Despite its shabby appearance, it was a decent starter home. As a kid, it had seemed like a big move up from when they were living in a trailer. Back then, Brando had never invited any kids over to play and vowed when he grew up, he was never, ever going to live in a trailer. He would make sure that he made plenty of money, and if he married, he'd never want his wife or children to feel shame about their home.

When his mother finally saved up enough money to make a down payment and get a mortgage on the house, they celebrated like they were moving into a mansion. Brando finally got a bedroom that, while modest, was bigger than the trailer, where he could touch both walls with his arms outstretched. Courtney and Brandi had to share a room, which led to endless arguing, but they worked it out. And finally, his Mom got a bedroom, so she no longer had to sleep on the couch. He hadn't thought about it at the time, but he realized she must have made up that bed every night and morning because there were never any sheets showing when the family plonked themselves on the sofa to watch TV at night. Yet he never heard her complain about it. She just got on with things. The woman was a saint.

However, as time went on and he went to high school, he started feeling shame about the house. Courtney was more practical and helped with housework while their Mom worked. He and Brandi hung out with friends at their homes but never invited them over. He may have even complained about the place being a dump, but his mother would just let the comments roll off her back and tell him he was lucky to have a roof over his head and food on the table. She was doing her best, and he wished he hadn't been such a jerk about it. Besides, the house wasn't that bad. True, it wasn't like his three thousand square foot home and two-acre yard that he was so proud of, but his Mom was right, it did the trick. And besides, back in the eighties that's how many people in town lived. Why was he so high and mighty? Just like his daughter today.

And now, here he was, wondering why his daughter was being so mean about everything. Had he raised her that way? And what was DeeDee talking about when she said they didn't visit his mother very often? That hurt. He thought they had—at least on holidays and birthdays, which he never enjoyed with everybody pretending to be on their best behavior. The more drinks he had, the more irritating he found people like Mona. She was such a hypocrite: save the planet was her rallying cry when it suited her. Make nasty comments about business own-ers and harp on about the importance of low-income housing and equality for all while over-charging people for her little crafts.

One of Brando's colleagues at work had dated Mona—once. The next day Brando asked him how it went. He described her as a "Champagne Socialist," de-crying the evils of capitalism, while wearing fashionable clothes and tossing back glasses of expensive Prosecco that somebody else bought.

He thought about DeeDee's comment that they hadn't visited his mother very much in the past year. It was true, even though he had convinced himself he was visiting of-ten enough. He wanted to see his mother, he truly did. It nearly crushed him the way she'd light up when he came to visit. He didn't deserve her unconditional love—and yet she gave it with no expectation of anything in return. With Brando, she set her expectations low and even then, he failed to meet them. Courtney and Brandi used to complain that they were there every week and Mom didn't light up like that when they arrived. It made him feel even worse that she was excited to see him at all, given his poor visiting attendance and her late stage of cancer. He would have preferred for her to tell him to get lost, but she didn't. Worse, even with all his guilt, it didn't move the needle on his behavior. Not one iota. The girls begged, and still, he didn't go enough.

On one miserable rainy night when they met in the local pub to talk about helping their mother, they asked him why he didn't visit. He was in no mood to be ambushed. He barked at them and told them to back off loudly enough for everybody in the pub to pause briefly to see what the ruckus was. The truth was that he didn't even know why back then. It wasn't until after her passing that he realized the truth: he couldn't bear to watch his mother's slow miserable death.

He leaned his head back and stared upward out the sunroof. He hated this whole mess—his mother was gone and now he'd have to spend a whack of time dealing with the estate. Worse, Queen Bea would be running the show and telling everybody what to do. That meant numerous trips to his mother's house, reminding him how little he did to help her out at the end. He couldn't deal with it. His sisters liked to sit and go over things endlessly, sniffling and letting all their sadness hang out. Especially Mona. He could see she'd chosen to be a victim and would squeeze every opportunity for people to feel sorry for her and help her out in some way. He couldn't stand her underlying assumption that *her* problem was everybody else's until it was resolved to her satisfaction.

His head rested until his phone pinged with a fifteen-minute reminder of his next meeting. He pressed the ignition, plugged in his phone and cranked the vol-

ume on a Nickelback song to drown out how he felt as
he drove to his meeting.

Chapter 10

Courtney

I pulled into the driveway at Mom's house, ready to tackle the next phase of activities with the Brandies and Mona. We had key decisions to make, and I wanted to be ready for any questions. I could tell Brando was dragging his heels with Mom's estate and business affairs, but there was no time to lallygag. At least they all agreed to meet on this Saturday morning when we wouldn't have to rush things.

I shoved my estate notebook into my handbag and pulled out a fat key ring that contained the keys to my mother's place, the office and fobs for three cars. I felt like a janitor.

After three tries, I found the key to Mom's garage that hadn't had a car parked inside for years. I pushed the door and switched on the light, gasping at the task which now lay before me. Every square inch of the place was choked with goods for sale—there were toys, tools, long tables of china, glassware, household items and stacks of books. Piled-up items looked like they'd been aging there for a long time like a vintage wine just waiting for the right buyer. And there were obsolete items like VHS tapes, cassettes and CDs that could hardly be given away, never mind sold. Plush toys hung from the rafters, matted and balding, like runaways from the county fair in the nineteen fifties.

Some items had prices, but many didn't. That's because Mom loved striking up conversations with people when they asked the price. I recalled at one point when Mom tried to draft Mona into a partnership. The enterprise fizzled when Mona realized she'd have to source vintage items from other yard sales and auctions, which mostly took place on the weekends. After Mona had let Mom down on several occasions, Mom realized it was a lost cause. Mom loved that scene; she always claimed it didn't feel like work to her to be constantly replenishing her inventory. She loved it when George showed interest. They spent weekends scouring yard sales and church sales, looking for hidden gems. She was also known to stop at old farmhouses with empty barns and outbuildings, asking the owners if they had anything to sell. That led to fascinating conversations with strangers and even lifelong friendships.

My head hurt as I thought about the work ahead of us. I knew a lot would fall on my shoulders, but one thing I knew, it was all the siblings' responsibility. Megan, the lawyer, told to me remember that, because she'd seen many families sit idle, expecting the executor to do all the work. And she reminded me that the executor was entitled to take a percentage commission of the estate—because it took so much time and energy to complete the work. Early on, I figured I wouldn't take an executor's fee because we'd be able to divide up the estate without much of a problem. Now that seemed like an incredibly naïve thought, but I believed it at the time.

I walked up the steps to the house and jiggled the key in the crappy lock that would only keep out honest people. In the kitchen, there was more of the same: stuff everywhere. The house was like a hybrid of my mother's personal goods and a warehouse with other items for sale. If someone needed an old-style colander for making jams or a fluted Pyrex pie plate, she'd tell them to wait and she'd come back from the kitchen with five of them to choose from. Then she'd only charge a dollar because it made her happy to see them get something they wanted.

I realized my mother's business wasn't about making money, it was more of a social enterprise—but not in the traditional way. She had been careful about her sales and sticking to a fair price in her younger days when she had three kids under five. But as time rolled on and her finances improved, she saw it as her way of helping buyers who couldn't afford new things at the store. There were many single mothers, newcomers and seniors who adored her for her "elastic" pricing. I could hardly fault my mother; it was quite noble what she was doing. I just wished she weren't quite so noble.

I pulled out my notebook and made notes about items that might be valuable and what could go at fire sale prices. Now all I needed was my siblings to show up. Let the games begin.

Chapter 11

Mona

A crash in the kitchen jolted Mona out of a deep dream in which her mother was dressed like a museum guide, wearing a smart navy uniform with cream-colored piping. She was providing a guided tour of her house and garage, pointing out the most valuable antiques, along with estimated prices. Mona was part of a crowd hanging on her every word; most of the visitors were strangers, except for Courtney and the Brandies. They didn't look anything like her half-siblings, but she knew it was them—and they all showed great interest in their mother's tour.

She sat up in bed, then stood up quickly trying to get her bearings. Her head was full of specific information from her Mom, and she needed to jot everything down before she forgot it. It felt like more than a dream. She couldn't say exactly, but it seemed like her mother was right there in front of her. As she discussed specific items in her collection, words like *Ming Dynasty*, *Wedgwood* and *Derby* floated through Mona's head, but they were wispy phrases wrapped in a fog. She then recalled her mother specifically saying, "There are a few rare pieces hidden in plain sight" in the house. She raised her hand in the group and asked her mother why she had never sold them if they were so valuable. Her mother, sporting a half-smile like Mona Lisa, said, "Remember what I told you?" Mona blushed and said, "I've forgotten, Mom, could you tell me again?" Just as her mother leaned to whisper in her ear, there was a crash in the kitchen. The dream had ended and the spell was broken.

She sighed and walked to the kitchen in case there was an intruder (not likely), or Shiva was up to something (most likely). She glanced at the clock; it was six-thirty in the morning. She rarely surfaced before nine, so the early hours felt disorienting to her. Moving past the two-seater dining table pushed against the wall with the pass-through to the kitchen, she spotted Shiva, who was grazing on the spillage from an aluminum bowl she'd flipped over. Mona remembered that she had poured a sprinkle of dry food into the dog's dish last night but left it on the counter. Shiva was normally well-behaved, but she was not afraid to get food off the counter when she was hungry.

"Hey, pooch," she whispered to Shiva. "Sorry—you should have had that last night." The dog looked up briefly with the guilty expression retrievers wear on their faces. When she understood she wasn't in trouble, she returned to her meal. Satisfied that there was no disaster in the kitchen, Mona walked to the living room and picked up her journal and pen. She opened the journal to the page with the purple velvet bookmark that her Mom had given her when she was ten. Mona treasured it. It felt soothing to run her hand over it.

She jotted the date and time on the page, then waited for details to flow from her pen. The dream seemed so real, that she wondered if it was a dream, or if her Mom was trying to communicate vital information to her. She wrote the names given to her by her Mom and sat there quietly hoping and praying that the rest of the dream would replay. Nothing. After fifteen minutes, she finally accepted defeat. Not a thing. She was annoyed because her mother had told her similar information several years ago when she was trying to convince Mona to take over the business. Her mother had rambled on and on about Ming this, and Derby that—but Mona found the tour so boring, she lost her focus. Did her mother say the word *Ming* or was it something else? It couldn't have been Ming, or she'd have been sitting on a fortune. And surely, she would have sold an item like that. Perhaps she said the item resembled Ming pottery, but it was still valuable. That would make more sense. Why hadn't she paid closer attention at the time?

Now she needed money, and it would have been so much easier if she could have coincidentally requested one of those items as a keepsake of her Mom. Courtney had mentioned something about each one of them picking an item as part of their meeting at their mother's house. For the life of her, she couldn't remember any of the valuable pieces—and sadly, they could be covered in dust, sitting alongside a crappy cup and saucer worth two bucks. She wondered if she should point this out to Courtney and the Brandies or figure it out herself first.

Her brain felt like mush. She walked over to the cupboard and found a jar of instant coffee left behind by the last house guest. It looked like freeze-dried desperation, instead of her usual standard of freshly-ground espresso beans. Resigned to her fate, she poured boiling water over the light brown granules and watched a cup of coffee materialize. She sipped it and decided the only people who should drink this stuff were those who had cooking limitations: astronauts and campers.

She opened the cupboard and grabbed the honey jar that was sealed with stickiness—it hadn't been opened in months. For five minutes she tried to wrench the thing open, but it wouldn't budge. Lately, she cried when things like this flared up because it reminded her that she missed her Mom. She didn't know the exact connection, but it was the comforts that were no longer in her life. Her mother would have had quality coffee to begin with, so she wouldn't have to drink the crap now in her mug. And if she wanted honey, the lid would have come off in one try because her mother always wiped the lid with a damp tissue before putting it away. And there would have been fresh milk or cream in her fridge with no concerns about sell-by dates. That's what she missed, the love and care of her mother. Everything her parents did reminded Mona that they loved her.

She needed to pull herself together for today and not get bogged down. Still, she longed for cream in her coffee. Returning to the cupboard, she found a jar of powdered coffee whitener, which some joker had labeled "White Death." She'd already sunk low, so she slopped a heaping teaspoon in her mug, half of which landed on the counter. She added another, then watched the lump turn into a sludgy drink that tasted nothing like coffee. Whatever, it had caffeine, and it would do until she made it to a coffee shop. Plus, it would make for a funny story at her grief group.

Now a little calmer, she thought about the details she couldn't retrieve from the dream. Perhaps its message was to draw attention to possibilities at her mother's place.

She knew that the Brandies and Courtney were super keen on money—they were the "it's- never-enough" types with big lifestyles to maintain. She could just picture the visit to their mother's place: the Brandies would behave like metal detectors, entering the garage and scanning for the most valuable items in a sea of mostly worthless junk. That wasn't how she and her friends rolled. Yes, they liked money to have what they needed, but after that none of them cared—they didn't feel the need to have everything new and expensive to show off to others. They got more excited about finding a cool pair of linen pants for five bucks at a second-hand clothing store.

Suddenly another thread of her dream came back. Her mother presented her with a gift wrapped in vintage paper with a pink bow. When she tore it open, it was an old book with a decrepit cover. She looked closer and saw that it wasn't just any old book. It was the pottery marks identification guide that served her mother for decades. Her Mom filled that book with little notes on dog-eared pages. Mona shivered: was the information about the treasures noted in the book? She tried to remember where her mother kept the book at the house but drew a blank. She'd find it. This could solve all her problems. She had to be out of her apartment in thirty days and would need an infusion of cash to get set up in a new place. Some property owners wanted first and last month's rent, or a damage deposit. The thought of that had been overwhelming, so she stopped thinking about it. Now, if she could get a leg up through her Mom's estate, she could picture possibilities for the next phase of her life.

She checked the clock; the meeting was in just over an hour. If she showered quickly and rushed there on her bike, she could arrive ahead of everybody else and do a little "reconnaissance mission," as her mother used to call it. She needed to find that book and stow it in her knapsack before anybody arrived. Was that a sign from her Mom? It felt like the dream was telling her something. The siblings didn't know the book existed; it would only be known and useful to those buying and selling antiques—which Mona almost did. So, if she kept her backpack zipped and her mouth shut, everything would be fine.

Her brain was on fire, and she couldn't wait to sleuth around the house in search of the "antiques' bible," as her mother called it. "Now we're cooking with gas," she said, rubbing Shiva's ears as she made her way to the shower.

Chapter 12

Brandi

"Milo, Olivia, I'm heading out soon," said Brandi as she gathered her keys and jacket. What did a person need for a family meeting about an estate? Courtney would know and would be fully prepared, so she'd let her figure it out.

"Remind me: what are you doing at your mother's house?" asked Milo as he walked inside from the studio attached to the house. He wrapped his arms around her and kissed her neck as she tossed her hair into place.

"We're going to talk about the service for Mom, as well as her estate," she said. Then added, "I think." She figured that's what they were doing but wasn't sure if she had mixed it up. The number of emails from Courtney was growing weekly. Brandi scanned them, yet nothing sunk in. Still, she was ahead of Brando, who often deleted them unread, depending on his mood.

"You think?" said Milo, raising his eyebrows. "Why do you always add that to the end of a sentence?"

"I don't know, dear," she replied absentmindedly. She had no clue why she did that and didn't care. She wasn't in the mood to have her sentences checked by her husband, but she knew she could wrap up the conversation more quickly by simply agreeing. He had to be right in most conversations, but fortunately, she didn't feel the same way. Brando was like that too: he had to be right and worse, he wouldn't ever give in. As a teenager, the Tom Petty song, "I Won't Back Down," was his favorite and he bellowed it from the top of his lungs. Brando's and Milo's shared dominant attitude had resulted in heated exchanges between them over the years, but they always worked it out.

"Well, it just undermines the last thing you said, is all."

"Got it, Milo... Now, if I could just find my water bottle."

"Be careful with your family today," said Milo.

"What do you mean?" She hoped he wasn't going to launch into a lecture. He had his issues with her family; she did too, but it was *her* family.

"Your family can be a little... volatile," he said, choosing his words carefully. "Grief does weird things to people, so they can behave oddly. Trivial things can trigger them, and they may respond in ways that are emotionally immature, stubborn, or half-crazy. Your brother believes that it's wrong to show feelings—he pushes all his emotions down deep, so he doesn't have to deal with him. He keeps everything on simmer and it's not good."

"And how do you deal with emotional issues?" she asked, trying to sound curious, not defensive. Milo had the answer to everything.

"Simple. I paint," he said sweeping up the cat into his arms. "And I pet Bastet. She's a beautiful breed. Look at her body—it's like soft leather." He rested his head on her head.

Brandi walked over and petted the cat, who perched herself like a queen in Milo's arms. She was indeed soft, and Brandi was surprised she enjoyed having a furless cat, mostly because it didn't shed and leave furballs everywhere. Their last long-haired cat wore out the vacuum cleaner.

Although she bristled when Milo had described her family as volatile, and even crazy at times, he was right. She thought back to her childhood when she was always the peacekeeper of the family and one of the few people who could calm Brando down when he was riled up. Her Mom was the best at it and sometimes they'd work together to great effect. But Brandi couldn't stand confrontation and went to great lengths to avoid it with both Brando and Courtney.

Yes, she and Brando had minor skirmishes as kids, fighting over shared bikes, games and worn-out Lego pieces, but she didn't care about the outcome, so she'd let Brando win. He knew he'd win with Brandi, so he'd save his energy for Courtney. Sometimes, when Brandi and her Mom were folding clothes in the kitchen, they'd hear Courtney and Brando battling in the living room. Her Mom would give her a big hug and praise her, telling her she was the family diplomat who was too smart to get into feuds with her siblings. This always made her feel special because there weren't many instances where Brandi was the star. It motivated her even more to not rock the boat or cause a fuss. But now, forty years on, and with their Mom's passing, she was starting to feel the old rivalries bubble to the surface. She missed her dear mom terribly. They were a quiet team working together to keep things calm and restore order.

Now Brandi felt like she was on her own to provide the calming effect, not only for Brando and Courtney, but Mona too. Mostly she had gotten along with Mona over the years because there wasn't much at stake at family events or Christmas dinners. But the estate changed everything, and tensions rose in the family. While Mona wasn't hotheaded like Brando and Courtney, she had a will of iron that nobody could bend. She might not holler and stomp her feet, but she could sure dig her heels in. Somebody had to keep cool and not add to the chaos. *I'm still the peacekeeper, Mom, but I sure wish you were here to help me.*

A car horn blasted outside in the driveway. Brandi knew by the sound of irritation in the horn that it was Brando. She kissed Milo and walked to the staircase. "Leaving, Olivia. I love you!" she shouted up the stairs. She heard a grumble but had no idea what she said. Milo stood with her jacket open to help her into it quickly. "Thank you, kind sir," she said, loving him for his manners. He was that old-style European male who always made her feel special with these simple gestures. Not one guy in Danbyville would ever have thought of that. She grabbed her keys and bent over to wiggle her feet into her shoes. Brando laid on the horn again—he always counted to thirty and then honked again.

"Coming!" she shouted to him as she rushed down the steps.

Chapter 13

Mona

Mona cycled onto her mother's lawn with Shiva running alongside her and dropped her bike by the door. She spotted Courtney's car in the driveway and then saw her half-sister at the kitchen window, her sharp eyes patrolling the front lawn like a half-starved eagle watching for prey. Mona's plan of arriving early to search for the book was scuppered.

"Hi," said Courtney as she opened the front door and stuck her head out. "There must be some mistake. You're early," she said, with an LOL grin on her face.

"Ha ha, funny Courtney," Mona said, moving her bike to the side of the house and clapping her hands for Shiva to join her. She wished that she weren't always labeled the late sibling. It was tiresome. Those three siblings had rigid roles like hardened metal in a mold, and they all acted like they weren't allowed to change. The same tensions ruled every gathering: Courtney would assert her authority, Brando would argue about everything she said, even if he agreed with her, and then he'd misbehave to get attention. Brandi would watch the same scenario play out every time, never participating—she always looked like an expressionless doll who never said a word.

"What's up?" Courtney said with a slight edge to her voice before Mona and Shiva could squeeze through the door.

"Well, I know the Brandies aren't the least bit interested in Mom's stuff, so I thought we could take a quick tour of the place before they got here—to get the lay of the land," said Mona. She thought that sounded impressive for a spontaneous answer. Plus, it would allow her to keep her eyes open for the antique identification book that she believed was the Holy Grail of her mother's collection.

"Okay. Let me grab my notebook," said Courtney, digging into a leather bag so vast, that it could carry Shiva and a week's worth of clothes in it. Courtney unearthed a navy book, with an elastic around it and a pen holder on the side. Mona admired Courtney's commitment to her responsibilities, which meant that she was never caught without her organizing tools. Such a level of organization was beyond the realm of possibility for Mona.

Excited to be back in the house, Shiva bolted to the kitchen and rooted around in search of her usual treats. There was even a Milk Bone cupboard that their Mom kept stocked for Shiva's visits. Treats helped to distract the dog from chasing Fluffy until they were both settled.

"Geez, Mona. Can you keep an eye on Shiva? I know she likes to run, but we're indoors and she's a little haphazard with her bushy tail. There's a lot of stuff to knock over."

"Come, Shiva," she called. "No problem, Courtney. But remember, she's been coming here since she was a pup. She may look like she's all over the map, but she's quite skilled at moving through the spaces and has never knocked over an item."

"Okay, but now we have an estate and it's important to keep everything under control. That's why I didn't bring Fluffy over, even though I know she misses this house."

"Understood," said Mona. She'd learned to let Courtney have the last word, or Brando, depending on who was dominating the conversation. She used to fight it, and one day, she realized it drained her energy. She knew that Shiva was an obedient dog (well, she did like to chase Fluffy which both she and her mother enjoyed watching) but she understood not everyone had the same patience for canines.

They walked around the house and discussed assorted items, with Courtney writing furiously. Mona was surprised she remembered as much as she did about pieces and pricing, but she had also forgotten even more, which she would never reveal to Courtney because it gave her the upper hand to sound so informed. They had been there half an hour, talking animatedly and Mona was almost enjoying the moment, except she hadn't spotted the spiral book anywhere. But she didn't fret; it could be in so many places.

Then they heard Shiva woof lightly and race to the top of the sofa where she could watch the activities on the street. She was on "driveway patrol" as their mother described it.

"Down, Shiva," clipped Courtney. Shiva turned her head briefly but ignored her and returned to her duties, barking playfully at the incoming siblings.

"Looks like the Brandies are here," said Mona as she petted Shiva whining at the window. Shiva shook with excitement when she spotted Brando. He was good with her, and Mona appreciated his love of throwing frisbees and balls for her dog.

"Yup," said Courtney. "And they travel together so they can plan their strategy on the way over."

"Are you nervous?" asked Mona. She sensed Courtney was preparing for battle.

"No, not at all," she shrugged. "Just get ready for some curveballs."

***

Out front, the heavy stomp of Brando's footsteps and Brandi's featherweight steps triggered another bark fest from Shiva. Mona glanced at Courtney; she knew she'd be complaining soon about bringing Shiva to meetings, but she didn't like to leave Shiva at home, alone.

Besides, it was early days, and everybody was hoping the estate work would be self-policing. At an earlier meeting, Courtney had talked about families getting into petty spats over the stupidest things, and she didn't want the family to go there. Mona knew everybody had varying points of view, so she hoped everybody would work together. It's what their Mom would have wanted.

"Hey, Brando and Brandi, come on into the kitchen," Courtney said, waving them in. "I brought iced tea, fizzy water and snacks. Help yourself." Mona could see Courtney wanting to run the show.

Mona scanned Brando's face to detect his mood. His face pulsed slightly red, which sometimes meant he was impatient, but on this day, it was warm outside. Sweat beads rolling down his temple confirmed it. With everybody seated at the table and refreshments served, Mona settled in for Courtney's tightly-run meeting agenda. If Brando got antsy, it could get ugly.

"Thanks for coming today," Courtney said. "I've been working hard on the estate for the last couple of weeks and I know it's important to keep you updated. So, there are two main things I wanted to talk about: Mom's memorial service and dealing with the estate. I know this is hard..." Brando sighed, and Courtney continued. "Even though I'm the executor, I'd like us to make decisions as a group. The outcome will be better."

"How does that work?" said Brando. "I mean like, there's four of us, so what happens if two say yes to something, and the other two say no?"

"Good question," Courtney nodded with a forced smile.

Mona knew exactly what he was getting at. If there was a vote, it would automatically be the Brandies voting together. Mona didn't like all the jockeying and political voting—she voted for something because that's how she felt. She didn't care what the others thought. But the three of them could be well and truly out there at times.

"Well, for major decisions," said Courtney, choosing her words carefully. We each get to state our opinion, and it's my hope we can reach an agreement—"

"If not?" Brando said, cutting in.

"Yes, as I was going to add, if we can't reach an agreement, we'll vote and majority rules."

"Good luck with that," Brando said with his patented smirk.

"Um, Courtney?" said Mona, raising a hand, then scrunching her hair into a ponytail, flipping it up, then releasing it. "Before we get started, I'm wondering if we should write a values statement." She saw Courtney stiffen.

Brando rolled his eyes. "Oh boy. Mona's going to take a dip in the touchy-feeling pond." He looked at Courtney. "Queen Bea, is that allowed?"

Mona saw Courtney's *oh-my-God-no* expression. *Too bad*, Mona thought. She had her standards. To make it look like it was okay to continue with the plan, she unrolled a lengthy piece of paper and dug out markers from a plaid pencil case. Mona knew that Courtney was used to this kind of activity at work, so she figured it would be no problem. She knew it would be a tough sell to Brando, whose values were inspired by *Lord of the Flies*, his favorite book from grade school.

"What exactly is a values statement, Moan?" Brando said, grinning.

Mona intensely disliked the nickname but realized the best way to deal with Brando's insults was to ignore him. Sometimes she regretted being named Mona, it was so old-school. Her Mom told her she was named for her great-grandmother, Ramona MacNeill, who was an amazing woman. Aside from the many domestic skills required of a farmer's wife back then, she created exquisite wedding dresses for families and neighbors. Mona treasured the one dress she inherited, with tulle and lace everywhere and delicate white pearls sewed on by hand. Besides, Brando would find something else to make fun of her, if not her name.

"We are about to embark on a journey," Mona began, a little too earnestly, watching Brando's eyes glaze over. "Sometimes we'll have to make tough decisions and it could get tense. If we start by stating our values—and by values, I mean beliefs that we hold as a group—it will guide our decisions."

"Okay, thanks for sharing, Mona," Courtney said, which Mona knew was the standard response at work meetings when somebody offered their opinion and nobody cared.

"You're welcome," said Mona. "I think it's important that we allow each person to contribute in ways that are comfortable for them. So is a values statement okay for everyone?" Courtney nodded.

"Whatever," Brando shrugged.

"Sure, Mona. But I'm not sure what to say," said Brandi. "Could you start?"

"Sure thing," Mona said, grinning at the group. She picked up a purple marker. She taped the sheet of paper to the wall and marked *Values* at the top. She studied the paper with a marker poised in her hand, ready for action—and then underlined the word Values. She waited a bit longer until the right word landed, then turned to the group. "How about *honesty*?" Yes, she liked that choice very much. They were off to a good start.

"Okay, but keep in mind, I like to tell it like it is," said Brando. "If you can handle the truth, I'm in. But don't bite back if I speak honestly in a situation."

She looked around and everyone was nodding. Mona was relieved Brando bought into the first one. "*Honesty* it is," she noted.

"Good one, Mona," Courtney said to keep things rolling. "My suggestion is *transparency*—"

"Meaning?" said Brando.

"As the executor, for example, I know it's going to be important to share the details so that you are all informed about the progress of the estate."

"Kind of stating the obvious," said Brando. "But if that's important to you, go for it."

"Obvious, maybe, Brando, but I think Courtney's value has—" said Mona, pausing.

"Value?" Brando joked.

Mona twitched lightly, but she wasn't going to let it slow her down. "Right, so let's go with it," Mona nodded. "And how about you two?"

"*Respect*," said Brandi. Her cheeks washed to a deep crimson when everybody focused on her. "What I mean, like, is accepting that people have different views. And we may not agree with them, but they still count."

"I like that, Brandi," said Mona. She wrote R-E-S-P-E-C-T in block capitals and underlined it, humming the Aretha Franklin tune. She looked at Brando as if to say, "Got that?"

"One more. Brando, thoughts?"

He paused and raised his feet onto the chair. Mona leaned toward the paper like a studious high schooler, ready to record something profound for a student council meeting. "*Hurry*," he said.

Mona paused, her marker capped and tapping her chin. "*Hurry*...mmm," she said gazing out the window, giving it careful thought. "Is that a value?" Mona asked looking at Courtney, hoping she might say out loud what was clearly expressed on her face: *Hell no*, hurry *isn't a value. It's an impatient command by a man who has spent his entire life going against the grain, simply to get a rise out of people.*

"Look, there's merit in what he's saying," Courtney said. "This is a stressful time, and we all want to get this work done as soon as possible. So, yes, *hurry* works for me."

Mona was surprised that Courtney was so compliant. She felt the word *expediency* would have been better, but she knew that Brando wouldn't like swapping a two-syllable word for a five-syllable. Worse, Courtney was sending her a look, *Now can we please move on to more important things?* Mona paused until they all squirmed, then nodded. "Okay, I think we've got our values," Mona said. She took a photo of the values, which she then texted to everybody.

"That is such a relief, to get a confirmation of our values, Moan," chirped Brando. "Well, that's about enough for today," he said, gathering his papers and phone.

"Hang on, Brando," Courtney said, pulling out her files. "Now we can talk about the memorial service for Mom."

Chapter 14

Courtney

"Memorial service?" Brando said.

I could see Brando looking surprised as if this type of event had never occurred to him. "Yes, celebrating Mom's life was always part of the plan."

"What are the choices?" asked Brando. "Does this mean going to church?" he groaned.

"Don't worry," I said. "The church is out. Mom stopped going years ago, although she remained friends with the minister, Arthur Bently. He'll do the service for us if we find another venue."

"Where?" said Mona.

"Two choices," I said holding up two fingers, hoping it wouldn't turn into a big debate. "We have Whispering Pines, a modern, franchise funeral home with low ceilings, folding chairs, fake flowers and pastel décor that looks like a dental office from the 1980s. Or McIsaac's traditional older home, with heavy velvet drapery, excess tassels and soft lighting everywhere."

"Christ, both are depressing," said Brando. "Jack Bilby at the Pines is a jerk who won't return my calls and

McIsaac's looks like the film set from the Addams Family. In fact, the missus is starting to look like Morticia."

"Not nice," said Mona. "Besides, it's irrelevant. If it's a franchise versus an independent, I'd vote for McIsaac's," said Mona.

"Price?" said Brando. "What's the difference?"

"Similar." I didn't want to get bogged down by minutiae with this group. "Funeral services are expensive; we're going to get a good stiffing either way. I've sat on a couple of committees with Mrs. McIsaac and she's very community-oriented. Their customer service is much better too. Shall we go with them?" To my surprise, they all agreed, so I noted that decision. It reminded me of taking notes at my company's board meetings. I learned when people agree quickly, to note it and hustle to the next item before they start rehashing things.

"That's done," said Brando, looking relieved.

Leave it to Brando to assume we were finished when we'd barely started. "Well, there are several things that we need to look after," I said before people started packing up their things.

"What exactly, Courtney?" said Brandi.

"We need someone to contact Reverend Bently. We need to pick out an urn for Mom's ashes and decide on the service and the songs. Plus, there's catering and notifying people—"

"Enough, Courtney," said Brando, waving his hand like a regal king who couldn't believe he was mired in such trivial details. "I thought you were supposed to look after this, Queen Bea. You're the executor."

I so wanted to fling one of the markers his way. But I had to keep my cool. "I am the executor and I have overall responsibility for the estate, but it doesn't mean I do all the tasks." I took a breath and held up two pages of my to-do list. "See this? I have a hundred and twenty-four items, so far." Brando grabbed the two sheets out of my hand and scanned through them as if he didn't believe what I was saying. He slid the pages back to me.

"So how do we divide and conquer?" he said.

"I think people should play to their strengths. Brandi, you're in hospitality, would you look after the catering?"

Brandi nodded. "Sure, you tell me how many guests there will be and what food you want, and I'll look after it."

I didn't know any more than she did. *Why was she asking me?* But I didn't want to lose her support. "I can pull the guest list from Mom's contacts and notify them. I can tee up the venue," I said, knowing that part was going to take the most time. "Does anybody want to work on the service with me, or help write the obituary?"

Mona piped up, "I can help with the service planning, but I don't know how to write an obit."

"Don't look at us," said Brando.

Like I knew anything about writing an obituary. I figured I'd get stuck with it anyway, so I might as well sign on for it before I got upset. I jotted it on the list. But my brother was not getting away without any tasks. "Brando, what would you like to do?"

"No idea. How's that for honesty?" He looked pleased with himself for taking a swing at our values so early in the game. Then he must have realized he was being a jerk. "What do you want me to do?"

"Well, when the cremains come back from the crematorium, we need someone to pick them up and buy an urn to store them."

"That's creepy," he replied. "What else you got?"

"You could be the family contact with the funeral home," I suggested, knowing he'd never go for it.

"Even creepier if we are going with the Addams Family."

I'd forgotten how immature Brando could be. All his life, he'd weaseled out of assigned tasks if he thought he could get away with it. If I gave in too soon, he'd be walking over everybody. "So, you'll do the urn and the ashes, then," I said, blurring the line between stating and asking. He nodded subtly like a billionaire bidding at an art auction who didn't want to draw attention to himself. I figured that mini-nod was as close to a commitment as I would get. I reviewed the list and could see that the time commitment was minimal for everyone except me.

"Right then. Now we need to pick a date," I said, knowing that would trigger endless discussion. "Could everybody get out their calendars?" After hearing about everybody's schedules for the next month, we finally landed on the last Saturday in June.

"We done here?" said Brando.

Not even close. "Just a few more things. I did ask you to block off ninety minutes." I felt the need to remind them since we'd only been an hour. "I have a question about Mom's bank account that I don't understand." I saw the Brandies sit up. Whenever money was involved, they'd be right in there like dirty socks on laundry day. Mona leaned her head on her left hand and doodled with the other.

"As you know, Mom's account was frozen as soon as the bank was told she'd passed away. That's standard. As executor, I'm the only one who can do any transactions with her account. I checked Mom's bank statements the other day and saw something unusual. Each month her Canada Pension and Survivor's Pension went into the bank, and the entire amount came out in cash the next day. Does anybody know what that's about?" I saw Mona's doodling hand halt for a microsecond, then start up again.

"Beats us," said Brando, exchanging an agreement glance with Brandi. "She never talked to us about how she spent her money."

"How much was she taking out?" said Mona.

I flipped open my file and read to the group, "Seven hundred and thirty-two dollars, every month. That's a sizable chunk of change."

"Maybe she paid her groceries and bills in cash," said Mona. "You know she wasn't big on technology or online banking."

"Possibly, Mona. But her groceries went on her Visa, and she had pre-authorized debit for her power, phone and internet bills."

"Maybe it was just a couple of times," added Mona.

I pulled out the file with the bank statements. "I went through the last two years when she started getting her pension and it's the same every month. Sometimes on the day it was deposited or the next day."

"And this is important because—?" said Mona, stopping in the middle of her starchy reply. "I mean, this is in the past. It doesn't seem right to trawl through her bank statements and judge her on how she spent her money."

"There's no judgment, Mona. I was just doing my job as the executor."

"So does this mean less money for us?" Brando asked.

Leave it to my brother to bring it all back to him. God, he was annoying. "Well, in the overall scheme of things, yes. But it was her choice how she spent her money before she passed away."

"That's right," said Mona. "So why are you pushing so hard about this? It was her money, her choice."

I wondered what Mona's problem was. Shouldn't she be happy that as executor, I was keeping an eye on things? "I need to know in case it's a monthly debt that I have to look after."

"Well, I can't help you," said Mona.

Brando sat up. "I agree with Courtney. We need to figure this out." He looked at Brandi, and she nodded.

"Noted," I said. But this wasn't something to be voted on. "Anything else?"

The Brandies exchanged a look. "We have something, don't we, Brandi?" said Brando, stating the obvious. Brandi nodded.

"Okay," I said, as in, *Let's get to the point*.

"We had a quick boo at the garage and house, and it's nuts. It's all second-hand crap and the place is wall-to-ceiling with worthless stuff," said Brando, with Brandi nodding. "We say, dump it all."

I glanced over at Mona. She looked up, suddenly engaged with the twins' statement. "Wait a minute," she said, sitting up, with a big pout on her face like a spoiled child watching someone loading up all her favorite toys and taking them to a charity shop. "We're so not doing that!"

A storm was brewing in everybody's head but for different reasons. I needed to get a handle on this. "Mona, hang on. Let's let Brando and Brandi explain what they mean by this. Everybody should have a chance to speak their mind."

"Good one, Queen Bea," said Brando. "Well, as you know, we want this done quick and the stuff here is of no value. We say, bring in my friend Marty from Junk-Be-Gone. He'll drop off a dumpster and we'll fill it. Then he'll haul it away to the dump for a reasonable fee."

"Not an option," Mona said, her doodles getting bigger and angrier.

"Brando and Brandi, I hear you," I said in my best "dealing with confrontation" voice. "You are busy; we are all busy. Yet, I feel like there's money tied up in this inventory—thousands possibly." I could see Brando slapping his knee like it was the funniest thing he ever heard.

"Not a chance, Sis. This is worthless junk."

"Brando?" said Mona, pointing to the glass cabinet. "That group of figurines alone would fetch over a thousand bucks."

Brando looked slightly surprised, then dubious. "Well, I doubt you'd get that amount flogging them online, but good luck to you."

"Hang on, everybody," I said, looking at the Brandies since things were getting stupid. "We aren't going to pay someone to throw all this in dumpster. We can have a big estate sale. We can all pitch in with the sale and see what happens."

"Nope," he shot back. "You want your big-ass yard sale, you two can do the work."

"Okay, and we'll keep the money," said Mona calmly. "That would be my preference."

Brando sucked in a short breath and glanced at Brandi. "No, you don't, Moan. It gets shared four ways."

It was time to cut in. "Let's calm down, everybody. I think we should take a breather on this and come back to it later. I'd prefer us all to agree on this one because it is a big issue. Now, is there anything else?" I looked around. Nobody said a word. "Okay, I have one more thing. Before things get too hectic, or sales start happening, I'd like each of us to find an item that reminds us of Mom. Let's take a walk around."

Brando sighed. "I don't do second-hand, so I don't see anything I want. I could take that TV Mom had in the living room. DeeDee's been inviting friends to hang out in the basement rec room, so I'm kitting it out and putting out the welcome mat. That sure beats them hanging out at the mall."

"Well, that's fine, I'm sure we can arrange that," I said. "And in addition, maybe you could find something of sentimental value, Brando." I could see a blank stare on his face. "Find something that has a special memory for you—it could be a framed photo, or a gift she gave you, or something you gave her. What about this serving tray you made her in your industrial arts class? You got the highest mark in the class, didn't you?" I said, pointing to the tray on the end table.

"Well, that's butt ugly. She only kept it because I made it. Nah, don't want it." Brando said. "Brandi, do you want anything?"

"I'd take a few photos, but I don't need any older stuff," said Brandi, reviewing the table full of family photos. "I'll take a couple for you, Brando, and we can divvy them up later," she added.

"Mona? Anything suit your fancy?" I asked her, as I watched her pick things up, turn them over and set them down. She stumbled around with a look on her face like a weirdo at a yard sale who had arrived at the end and was determined to find the buried treasure.

"Yeah, I'd like something for sure. But I'm a little tired. Do we have to do it today?" Mona asked, with a sigh.

"Okay, fine, but I'd like to pick something today because I know things can get crazy." I wandered around the living room, but it felt like there was too much to choose from—and much of it was from Mom's collecting, rather than an item that had sentimental value for me. I wandered into the kitchen and looked at the glassed-in cabinet full of china items. Then I spotted the sugar bowl from my childhood. I gasped because I hadn't thought of it in years, yet I loved it so much. It was a small octagonal container with a matching lid and a round hole to hold a tiny spoon. There were eight panels, outlined in black, with designs alternating between pink and blue flowers, like lupines and bluebells.

The bowl was special to me because Mom only brought it out on occasions when she'd allow us to sprinkle brown sugar on our oatmeal. She made it sound thrilling to have brown sugar that was soft and so sweet when mixed with the porridge. She controlled the spoon (or we would have eaten the whole bowl) and sang to us as she heaped on the sugar with a spoon that was a fraction of a teaspoon. She was brilliant, and I teared up thinking about how imaginative she was to make it feel so special. Yup, that was the item for me. I didn't care about anything else.

I walked back into the living room with it in my hand. "I found what I want," I said, proudly holding out the sugar bowl. Silence. "What?" I asked, looking at the three of them.

"Oh wow, it's Mom's sugar bowl!" gasped Brando. "I thought that was long gone."

"Where on earth did you find that?" Brandi asked, looking shocked.

I turned and pointed to the kitchen. "Right there on display in the glass cabinet, along with all the other pieces."

"Remember how Mom would ask if we wanted two or three spoons of brown sugar?" said Brando. "Of course, we always said three, but it was like, a miniature spoon. We thought she was being generous."

Brandi piped up. "Remember she sang a song about sugar for us? Ours was the Rolling Stones' 'Brown Sugar', right, Brando?"

"You got it," he smiled, turning the moment into a karaoke session, singing into a narrow vase on the table that substituted for a mic.

"Yes, and mine was The Archies singing 'Sugar, Sugar,'" I added. This was cool, reminiscing with the Brandies about old times with Mom. "And how about you, Mona? Did Mom sing to you with the sugar bowl?"

Mona looked mildly confused. "Yeah, uhm, it was Mary Poppins singing 'A Spoonful of Sugar.'"

"Cool. Well, I'm glad it's still around. I will treasure it always," I said. Brando and Brandi swapped a secret expression.

"On second thought, I'd like that," Brando said.

"No, I've claimed it," I stated calmly. "I gave you all first dibs on everything, and nobody showed any interest. And this is special to me." I always felt a strong connection to Mom with the sugar bowl. The Brandies wouldn't even remember I took over sprinkling duties when I was six because Mom could trust me not to eat all the contents. The twins would have eaten all of it.

"That's before we knew it was there," said Brandi.

"Yes, and you were invited to look through the house and choose it earlier and you didn't. You snooze, you lose."

"Nope. We're starting over, girl. And I want it," said Brando.

"So do I," said Brandi. I don't ask for much around here, so it's the least you can do to let me have it. I think Mom said it was her favorite Asian bowl."

I saw Mona jump when she heard the description, "Asian bowl." It was odd; one minute she was asleep at the wheel, then at full alert. I didn't give it much thought; I was too busy focused on the Brandies who only wanted it once they saw that I claimed it. "Look, fair is fair. You had your chance and didn't bother. We're done here."

"Well, I think you better hit rewind on this selection thing, because I'd like it too, Courtney," said Mona. "So put it back in the china cabinet until we decide who gets it," she stated calmly.

I was burning inside but determined it was now going to be mine, no matter what. I'd play nice for now, but they had no idea how hard I'd play to get it. I walked back into the kitchen and placed it on the top shelf. "Fine. I'll do this to move on, but make no mistake, this is mine." I sputtered out a sigh to show my displeasure. "Okay, anything else?"

"Yes," said Mona. "I have a much bigger burning issue."

Chapter 15

Mona

"Look, I know we'll sort out the little issue about Mom's sugar bowl," Mona said, waving her hand like a magician trying to make it disappear. Inside, she was freaking out, because she had zoned out while the three of them wandered down nostalgia lane discussing the bowl. It didn't look like an item from the Ming dynasty, but she needed time to do research. And even if it wasn't Ming, what if *that* was the item Mom had told her was super valuable and hidden in plain sight?

She had no memory of her Mom and the sugar bowl when she was growing up. When she wanted brown sugar on her cereal, she'd walk to the pantry and pull out the jar packed with brown sugar. There was no limit to the amount of sugar she scooped out. And her mother had not sung songs about sugar. She had to scramble to come up with "A Spoonful of Sugar" to make it sound like she had a fond memory of sugar rationing. Always the outlier with the siblings, she had no shared memories and therefore zero attachment to that bowl. However, if Courtney had walked off with it that day, that could have been a problem. She wondered if she should tell the group about its potential value, or just do a stealth price check on her own.

What if she won the battle for the sugar bowl? It could be worth a fortune, and they wouldn't even know. She could keep it for a year, then eventually sell it without anybody noticing. She decided to check on the approximate value as a first step because the rest of them knowing the price would only add fuel to the fire.

"What's the burning issue, Mona?" Courtney asked, her face still red from the previous conversation.

"Right, yes," Mona said pulling herself back into the group dynamic. She tapped the marker on one end, slid it down her fingers, then tapped on the other end. "We need to find a new apartment."

"What do *you* mean by 'we,' Mona?" said Brando.

"I'm being renovicted by Bruce and his wife," Mona blurted. "They gave me three weeks' notice to move out. That's just wrong."

"That doesn't sound like Bruce," Courtney said. "I knew him from high school, and he was a pretty good guy."

"I've been a stellar tenant for three years and this is the thanks I get," said Mona, her voice laced with hurt. Normally Mona would ask her Mom to help figure it out, but her support system was gone. She needed to rally sympathy with this crowd.

"I'm sorry, Mona, that's tough news," Brandi said. "What's the renovation for?"

"He's making it wheelchair accessible, then moving his mother back into the apartment."

"The nerve!" Brando feigned outrage.

"Mona, that's not exactly renovicting. Legally, that's a valid reason," Courtney said. "However, as I recall, Mom said you're on a month-to-month lease. So, he has to give you two months' notice. Point it out to him and I'm sure he'll revise it."

"He claims he gave me notice six months ago," said Mona. Now she was scrambling to make her story sound airtight.

"Did he?" asked Brando, getting into his courtroom style of questioning. "You do have a reputation for beefing up your side of a story."

Mona let out a sigh. She didn't like where the questions were going, but she had already pried open the cellar door and now she had to face whatever mess was down below. "He gave me an envelope a while ago, but I didn't read it. So as far as I'm concerned, it doesn't count."

"Right," sneered Brando. "If I tried that with income tax, do you think they'd accept that excuse?"

"No idea," said Mona. She was behind on her income tax as well, so she had no clue about how it worked. She'd best keep that one to herself.

"Was the letter registered?" Courtney asked.

Mona shrugged. "If that means I had to sign for it, I guess so." She hoped to sound as ill-informed as possible about the mysteries of the postal system.

"Do you owe any rent, by chance?" Brando sniped.

Mona paused; everybody was staring at her. They'd find out one way or the other. "A couple of months." Mona's eyelids trembled. "Why the interrogation? I thought you would help me find a new apartment."

"Mona," said Brando. "Remind me: how old are you?"

"Thirty."

Brando laughed. "Did you know that when our mother was twenty-one, she had three kids to look after?"

Mona squirmed. "Your point being?"

"Honesty is your 'value'," he said with air quotes. "Here's some honesty: you need to take responsibility. You owe your landlord money. He's got bills to pay and an aging mother to look after—he can't wait around for you to pay your back rent. The solution is simple: either find a roommate, shack up with your boyfriend, or get a job like the rest of us. *Jeezus*, Moan."

Mona shifted. This wasn't going the way she pictured at all.

"Mona, I'm sorry that you are dealing with it and I'm sure you'll sort it out. But we could leave that issue for now. Unless it relates to the estate," Courtney said.

"It does," Mona stated sitting up. Without her Mom, there was nobody who had her back. The best thing was to just fess up. "Look, I have no money. I owe Bruce six months' rent and there are no apartments available. So, I will need to stay at Mom's house for a short stay, just until you give me the money the estate owes me, then I'm gone." Mona said, scanning the expressions of the three siblings. Shock times three.

"I don't like it," said Brando. "No offense, Mona... well maybe a bit."

"What's your problem?"

"How can I put it nicely, girl?" Brando said, looking out the window. "Fifty bucks says you'll move in, and never move out."

"Yeah, but—" said Mona.

"No yabbuts, Mona," he continued. "Don't ask why, but I have this nagging image of you refusing to leave the house. Then we'd have to pay Tony the Bailiff a fat sum to remove you from our house, while a posse of your outraged girlfriends chain themselves to the front steps. And then, you'd have one more girlfriend shooting a video and posting it to social media. Did I miss anything?"

"One to bring lattés," Mona added. Nobody saw the humor; she needed a new tactic. She went for a concerned citizen look. "Listen, there's a bigger social issue at play here, Brando. Affordable housing. There's almost none, and any available is not affordable."

"I know how dedicated you are to social activism," said Brando.

She looked at him, wondering what was brewing in his little peanut brain. "Yeah, from a guy who wouldn't know a social issue if it poked him in the eye."

He grinned like he had a twenty-nine-point cribbage hand and couldn't wait to flip his cards. "I heard about your last social activist idea. You pushed all the major dictionaries to change the spelling of *dictator* to d-i-c-k-t-a-t-o-r," he said spelling it out. "What was your deep thinking on that one, Moan?"

"Well, it is a male-dominated profession," she said, watching Brando's face scrunch into a puzzled look, his head tilted like a dog who heard its master say something important yet had no idea what it meant. Mona could see his brain in motion searching for another attack angle.

"Right. And how many of your friends did you convince to sign it—ten? Or are you up to eleven now?" Brando taunted.

"Just over two million, the last time I checked."

"What?" he gasped, glancing at Brandi and Courtney.

"The meme went viral," Mona said, showing no signs of surprise or hubris. She liked his look of disbelief because she knew how little Brando respected her.

"Bully for you, Moan, with your global activism success. But just to bring you back to earth with a thud, you can't stay at Mom's house. This is not an affordable housing crisis, it's a personal crisis because you won't get off the sofa to get a job and pay your rent."

"Did you know you're an A**hole, Brando?" said Mona.

"Who me?" he said, smirking. "Can you prove it?"

Mona grabbed her phone and clicked furiously. "Yes, I'll send you a link to a forum called *"Am I an A**hole?"* You describe what you did and present your case to the group, and then the court of public opinion decides if you are or aren't."

"Nah." Brando rocked back and forth on his chair, taking it right to the edge. "I don't need to ask some group if I am. You should ask about yourself. At least I earn a living, provide for my family and pay my mortgage."

She wanted to poke him in the eye, but she'd save that for later. However, she noticed he'd jotted down the info which made her smile.

For now, she needed to stay positive and focused. "Don't worry," she said, "I was just messing with you, Brando." Looking at the three of them and sporting the special smile she wheeled out when she was trying to charm naysayers on a topic, she said, "We can work this out. As you business types would say, it's a win-win situation—I have a big, no-fail plan."

Chapter 16

Mona

Mona called out to Shiva as she walked out of her mother's house. Suddenly she felt weighed down by so much, on top of her grieving that wouldn't quit. She'd have to reach out to her girlfriends for a support circle because she couldn't carry the sadness alone. She texted but found out they couldn't meet until the following week, so Mona had to carry the burden on her own for now.

Courtney's question about their mother's bank account rattled her the last time they met. She didn't know why, because her mother—*their* mother—had every right to do what she wanted with her money while she was alive. She was of sound mind right up until the end, so there was no issue. And yet, Mona didn't speak up and own it during the conversation. She couldn't say why, other than she felt judged by Courtney and Brando for everything she did. Courtney showed judgment through her sharp questioning which implied that Mona was lacking either character, fortitude or strategy. Brando loved to point out what a loser she was in every conversation. He'd been like that since day one. Brandi didn't say much; she was sweet, but clearly she was in the shadow of Brando, and he was both bossy and opinionated about everything. Brandi simply went along with him.

She hoped Courtney would not figure out her mother's monthly payout so that she wouldn't have to deal with it. Still, she needed an explanation in case she did. Mona got out her erasable board and markers to map out her situation. She stared at the board, but nothing came up for her. She petted Shiva over and over, which usually got her creative juices flowing, but this time, nothing. She moved to a yoga position and sat quietly for twenty minutes to see what bubbled up.

Eventually, a message wafted into her head telling her she didn't need to worry about it all. She didn't need to explain it or even apologize for the payments. The three others could just deal with it. In the meantime, though, she still needed a place to live and a source of income to keep her going until she could get back on her feet. The thought of both massive issues overwhelmed her.

Raj would happily help her out and had even invited her to move in with him. However, he had a small apartment, and it wasn't a pet-friendly building, so she'd have to give Shiva away. They argued about it a few times until she realized he didn't understand that it was a non-negotiable for her. She dropped the topic.

She thought again about her idea to move into her mother's place. The more she thought about it, the more appealing it could be for her. No furniture to buy, no rent to pay and it felt remarkably familiar—in fact, her old bedroom was just as she left it when she moved out. Of course, when she'd suggested it, Brando had jumped all over her, but that was his usual response. Courtney sounded like the typical executor; she didn't want any new hassles to deal with, but too bad. If she kept chipping away at the idea, each time she saw them, they'd eventually give in out of sheer exhaustion. She just had to focus her energy on achieving what she wanted.

The next time she saw the sibs, she could present an additional selling point: she could sell all the valuable stuff in the house and garage that shouldn't be part of the estate sale. She knew the general pricing for the items or could wing it. She could charge the siblings a modest fee for each sale and that would solve her money problems, temporarily. And more importantly, it would buy her time until she could find the super valuable pieces. Yes, she decided—that was the ticket. It solved all her issues. For the first time in weeks, she felt like she had hope and more importantly, a solution. There was another family meeting scheduled for next Saturday to continue with the plans for liquidating the house contents and the estate. Based on the rambling pace of settling an estate she would have plenty of time to get herself sorted out.

Now all she needed to do was get Courtney and the Brandies to buy into the idea.

Chapter 17

Courtney

Jamie and I chatted in the kitchen while we chopped veggies and chicken for dinner. We were making a stir fry, and I was excited at the thought of sitting down to a meal with the whole family. With recent traveling for work and the endless list of estate stuff piling up, I hadn't kept the best connection with my husband and family. That had to change.

My cell rang and buzzed on the marble counter. I was in the middle of chopping, so I didn't want to stop to take a call. Jamie glanced at the call display for me.

"You might want to get this; it's from the law firm," he said, sliding the phone to me with the back of his hand. I wiped my hands and pressed the speaker phone with my pinkie finger, trying not to slime up the phone.

"Hello, Megan."

"Hi, Courtney. Got ten minutes?"

I glanced at Jamie, who nodded okay. "Sure, Megan. I'm chopping stuff for dinner, and Jamie is here, but I'm sure it won't take long." I glanced at the clock and noted it was twenty-two minutes past five. Later, I would check the time against what we were billed. I already felt like we were stoking this enormous machine full of money going directly to lawyers and accountants, and we had barely started. But I also knew not using a lawyer could cost us way more in big mistakes.

"Question..." Megan said while flipping through her papers. "Did your mother own any land?"

I shrugged and looked at Jamie. He looked puzzled and shrugged back. "Not that I'm aware of. What's the address?"

"Sixteen Robbins Road. Near Bonny Lake," she said.

Then it clicked. *Of course, I knew it.* I stopped slicing because I was holding a big knife and felt my stomach flip. "That was the land with the trailer on it that Mr. Vincente left to my mother when we were kids. I totally forgot about that. Why?"

"Something came up when we ran the legal notice in the *Gazette*. The municipality got in touch. There are back taxes owing on it," she said. "Going back decades."

"That doesn't sound like Mom. She paid her bills." I said, sounding defensive. Mom took pride in looking after her affairs. She wasn't ashamed of being poor, but she didn't look for special treatment in life. Yet as I thought back to our dire financial situation as kids, she barely had enough to cover food and clothing for us. My mind was already calculating late fees and penalties. "So why would they wait this long to collect unpaid taxes?"

"Good question. I got a copy of Mr. Vincente's will. I decided to dig around and ask questions at the property tax office. It looks like they weren't diligent about the land transfer and the property files in general. They were sending the tax bills to a Marilla Vincente in Sudbury,

Ontario. She was next-of-kin. A niece, they thought. Does that ring a bell?"

"I remember Mom saying he didn't have any kids, but that's all I know. If the niece had been getting invoices from the municipality that weren't hers, why wouldn't she call them?"

Megan tapped her pen. "Who knows? Maybe because she wasn't given the assets in the will, therefore she ignored them. We see property admin mistakes all the time because it was done manually back then. Until there is a sale or an event like this, nobody notices."

I didn't like where this might be going. All I could see was a huge tax bill and lawyer fees piling up. "What does this mean for us, Megan?"

"Couple of things. First, there will be taxes owing. Now maybe you can make a case for avoiding interest and penalties because they sent them to the wrong owner. And I'm sure you know that land has gone up in value since your mother acquired it in the 1980s."

"Maybe we could sell it to raise some money," I said, teeing up the veggies in a straight line.

"Yes. However, you will have to pay the taxes first. And don't forget, since it wasn't her principal residence there could be capital gains if you sell it."

"Like how much?"

"Well, that depends. Let's not get overwhelmed just yet. Either way, there's going to be a tax bill on your mother's estate this year. When somebody passes away, the government gets its claws into as much as possible. There will be probate tax, income tax and possibly capital gains," said Megan in rapid-fire syllables, as if she was just warming up. "Keep in mind, too, that tax bills are paid ahead of absolutely everything—even lawyers," she chuckled. "In case you don't know this, Courtney: do not distribute any money to the beneficiaries until you have your bills paid. As executor, you are legally responsible if you distribute money to beneficiaries before the tax people. There is a priority for payments, which I will review with you when we meet. Got it?"

"Okay," I said, but I wasn't really. It was becoming apparent this estate stuff was about to expand like a hot-air balloon that hung like a question mark overhead. "Megan, we are working on the estate inventory that you asked me to prepare. I'll get on it, and then maybe you can meet with us to go over everything we need to know."

"That's fine, Courtney. I'll wait to hear from you," she said and hung up.

Dread crawled through my body. That reality check from Megan meant several things: we would need money in the short to medium term, and it wouldn't arrive in the right order to pay bills. I'd have to tell all the beneficiaries that they wouldn't be getting a cent for some time. I could just imagine how that was going to go over with the siblings and Doris. Somehow it would be my fault. I brushed tears away.

"Honey," Jamie said gently wrapping his arms around me. "What is it?"

I placed my head on his shoulder as tears poured out. He let me cry and didn't attempt to move or speak for five minutes. He simply rocked me quietly, and it felt like such a relief to be in his arms. Finally, I lifted my head, and he handed me a tissue.

"You can tell me."

"I... I don't know if I can do this," I said, gulping a breath. "On top of our lives and work, this estate feels overwhelming. Each time I get a call or email, something new comes up."

"I get it. But you don't have to carry all of this on your shoulders," said Jamie, holding both my hands.

"I feel like it's going to be a battle with the Brandies and Mona, no matter what I do or how hard I try. They even complain about me spending money on a lawyer."

"Too bad, that's their problem. Yes, you are the executor, but you don't know law. You have to get legal help, no matter what your siblings say."

"Why me? Maybe I should quit as executor. I don't know what I'm doing."

Jamie laughed. "Are you kidding me? Can you imagine any of the others in that role? Brando would bulldoze his way through to terrible effect. Brandi's sweet and honest, but she wouldn't have a chance taking on Brando. And Mona, well, even if she got around to doing a fraction of the tasks, she'd be arranging things to benefit her."

I wiped my face with a big tissue. "I guess."

"Besides," he continued. "I know how conscientious you are. If you gave your word to your Mom, you couldn't live with yourself not to keep it."

I felt a little jolt in my body. "You're right," I said, pulling myself together.

"That's more like it, hon," Jamie said smiling at me. "Promise me one thing."

"Okay. What?"

"I know how committed you are to your projects and how much you care, but remember, it's fine to ask for help and pay for the experts as needed."

"Thanks, hon."

"Let me know if I can help, right? Even if it's just to vent or cry on my shoulder. And I promise," he said with his Scouts' honor salute, "not to tell anybody else you are afraid of failure."

I laughed. He knew me too well. He hugged me one more time and everything felt better.

Once we finished preparing the dinner, Jamie walked to the bottom of the stairs and shouted, "KIDS, dinner!" He walked back and carried the meal to the kitchen table, where the kids liked to eat.

He poured two glasses of wine a third of the way full, and then added a little more to my glass, winking at me. I felt so lucky to have him on my side. "Let's just enjoy our time with the kids tonight," I said.

"Right on," he replied, clinking my glass.

Footsteps thundered on the stairs. Ava and Jake raced each other across the tiled floor in their sock feet, laughing and sliding into place at the last minute. It was a ritual that I loved—it showed me they were still enthusiastic about gathering as a family. My friends urged me to enjoy them while I could because best friends, projects and hormones would soon kick in and they'd be rejecting everything. I had the urge to sweep them up in my arms and hug them because they made me so happy, but I worried sentimental hugs with a teen like Ava might ruin everything.

Even though I was savoring the moment, I knew the first thing I'd be doing in the morning was rushing to the bank to find out where we stood with Mom's accounts and finances.

***

On my way to work the next day, I went into the bank and was relieved to see Heather working. She knew the situation with our mother, so we could cut to the chase with stuff.

"Hi, Heather, how's it going?" I said, punching my PIN in as fast as possible.

"Great, how about you?"

I nodded and smiled, then got down to business. That was one thing I liked about Heather: she knew not to gossip with me like she did with others. "I would like to get a printout of Mom's bank accounts, verify the beneficiaries and whatever else I need to do on her accounts."

"No problem," she said typing so fast it looked like she was faking it. "She only had a few." In minutes she had everything printed out and I scanned through them to see if I had everything I needed. "There is one thing I'd like to find out about, Heather, and I'm not sure how to do it. It's the cash withdrawals of Mom's pensions the day after they arrived. That's been going on for years."

"Easy, that was Mona. She had a bank card issued on this account, so she was allowed to deposit and withdraw—but she only withdrew, never deposited," she added with a smirk. "She arrived promptly the day after the pension arrived and took out the equivalent in cash."

"Mona was the one withdrawing the cash?" My heart thumped.

Heather nodded and slid a receipt under the glass for the transaction. "When she came in last week to get this month's payment, I explained it wasn't a joint account, so when your Mom passed away, we froze the account. As executor, you are now the only one authorized to do anything with this account. Didn't she mention it?"

No, she did not. Worse, she lied to me and the Brandies when I asked everyone about it. But I couldn't say that to Heather because I didn't want to hang out family laundry, even though I was furious with Mona.

"Thanks, Heather," I said, gathering the papers and shoving them into a folder. I didn't even attempt to organize them; I'd do it at home. I hoped she couldn't see my anger. I could see her eyebrows lifted, as if she were interested to find out about Mona's activities. I hustled out of the bank before she had a chance to ask me more questions.

OMG, what was that about? And what about the first value, honesty, that Mona proposed? What a farce! But what was even more disturbing is that Mona believed her own story. Legally, I knew she was allowed to withdraw the money from Mom's account. The Brandies and I might have been a bit peeved with Mom about it, but mostly I was angry at her for not telling us. That meant both Mom and Mona knew it was "kinda, sorta" wrong to favor one child over the others. It wasn't so much about not getting the money—Jamie and I earned a good living—it was the secret the two of them were keeping, even when I asked Mona directly about the missing money at the meeting. I remember her sounding hedgy, but she lied by hiding it. Worse, our mother was enabling a child who needed to grow up and not rely on her for money and support. No wonder Mona stumbled around from one drama to the next in life. She was perfectly capable of getting a job like the rest of us; she just chose not to because Mom provided a basic income guarantee. Who wouldn't love that?

Now, along with news about outstanding tax bills, I had Mona's crap to address. Should I meet one-on-one with Mona before revealing her secret to the Brandies? Or should I just go for the fireworks as a group and watch Brando's reaction? I decided to tuck the Mona–Mom conspiracy away for safekeeping, in case Mona got out of line and I needed something big to leverage.

Chapter 18

Doris

Five days after her disappointing trip to the suburbs, Doris decided enough time had passed with Courtney not getting back to her about her payment for cleaning. At the very least, she needed her final wages, and she wanted her gifts from Babs' estate. If she waited until Courtney got around to it, who knew how long that could be? Doris figured she had to take matters into her own hands and "set some boundaries," as her daughter often nagged her to do.

She had called her friend Maria, a hairdresser who had a small business, and asked if she knew how to create an invoice. Maria invited her over to show her how. When Doris walked into the salon, Maria showed her an example of a simple invoice and gave Doris a piece of paper. She had a computer but no printer, so she handwrote the invoice with Maria's help.

After that, Maria offered her a free cut and set, which was the exact lift she needed. She could only afford to go to Maria once a year, and she was overdue for a trim by a couple of months. A month earlier she had put her hair in two braids, then chopped and hacked away at the bottom to trim it. She figured it must have looked bad if Maria offered to do it for free.

When she was finished, she walked over to Courtney's house. Her knee still ached, but her bank account ached more. She felt like a pegleg walking up the steps to the front door. Courtney's daughter Ava answered with barely a hello. Doris asked if she could talk to her mother.

Doris waited for several minutes, then finally sat down on the front steps. She was fed up with Courtney showing little concern for her financial situation. After about ten minutes, Doris pushed the doorbell one more time. Courtney arrived at the door. There was no apology for taking so long. She looked preoccupied as usual.

"Hi, Doris, what can I do for you?"

Oh, we're going to do this nonsense each time, are we? Why was she making Doris beg for what was rightfully hers? She knew Babs wanted her to have the things. She fumbled around in her purse and unfolded a piece of paper. "Here's the invoice for last week's bill and I'd like to get my gifts as soon as possible," she added. She had practiced that sentence all night in her sleep. She was tired and wanted to get it over with.

Courtney waved her hand. "I'll have to stop you right there, Doris. The lawyer said I can't give out any gifts until we pay all the taxes. Sorry, but it's the law," she said, easing the door closed.

Something came over Doris, and she pushed her hand in the door to stop Courtney's action—even if it meant jamming her hand. Startled, Courtney stopped closing the door. Now Doris steamed. She was Babs' best friend and couldn't believe she'd been dismissed like that. It was so disrespectful.

"I don't understand, Courtney. It's right there in the will in black and white that I am being given the cash and the knick-knacks."

Courtney sighed "Look Doris, I talked to the lawyer last night and she said I cannot give out any gifts until all the bills are paid; I could be held legally responsible for doing so. Do you want me to get into trouble?

Doris didn't give a rat's butt if Courtney got into legal trouble. At that moment, she felt humiliated, like a child being scolded by an exasperated parent. She was worried that Courtney might not pay her or hand over the gifts. She knew Babs would have been horrified at this turn of events and would have encouraged her to get feisty, even if it was with her daughter. Babs said that her daughter sometimes became a little too authoritarian in these situations. Babs would always add that Courtney meant well, and she was obsessed with doing everything perfectly, but sometimes, perfect wasn't the best solution. Doris knew that Babs was trying to protect her daughter, but she wasn't buying that explanation—Courtney had a personality flaw. And the only way to deal with her was head-on.

"Well, the invoice isn't a gift, it is payment for cleaning I did for your mother," she said in a "take-that" tone.

Courtney's eyes darted around as if she was thinking about what Doris said. She paused and said, "Okay, you're right. I can pay your bill, but I can't give you the gift money until all debts are paid."

"What about the knick-knacks? It's not like you'll be paying the tax man in ceramic thingies," Doris added, trying to poke holes in the big story that Courtney had spun.

"I'll ask the lawyer about the non-cash items at the house and let you know. If I have the cash in my wallet, I will pay you for the invoice. You're sure you didn't already get cash from Mom?"

Doris stared directly at her as if to say, "What an insult." It worked. Courtney excused herself and told her to hang on. She closed the door, making Doris wait on the front steps again. Her knees hurt, so she sat down. She'd wait hours if she had to; she wasn't leaving without her payment. Deep down, Doris understood the problem: Courtney saw her as white trash, like she'd been treated as a kid. That's why she was rejecting Doris—she reminded her too much of her childhood. Yes, Babs' kids had worked hard to lift themselves out of poverty and now lacked for nothing in their lives. And that was fine, except they had forgotten their roots—and that others had helped them out when they were kids. And worse, they showed no compassion for others who were still poor. Courtney physically distanced herself from Doris, as if she were afraid that she might catch poverty again like it was a contagious disease.

The door swung open. Courtney said, "Here you go, Doris. That's one hundred and forty dollars. I am just going to get you to sign that you were paid. No offense, eh?"

"None taken," said Doris, as if she had a choice. She didn't care that she had to sign, but it felt like a sucker punch from Miss Perfect and yet another "I don't trust you" moment. She signed and handed the paper to her;

Courtney passed over the cash. "Thanks. I'll just count it, no offense," she said, snapping each twenty.

"I'll get back to you about the other gifts once I know," Courtney said, closing the door. A slow-boiling energy surged through Doris, pushing through her every limb. She hadn't felt this shamed in years. The temper that had earned her the high school nickname "Hot-head Doris" rushed back. These exchanges with Courtney brought out the scrappiness in her and the urge to exact revenge on those who treated her wrong. She was never violent with her revenge, but everything else was on the table. Except this time, she didn't have Babs telling her when she was taking things too far. Babs was like ballast for her—keeping her from doing something stupid. She walked out of the neighborhood, favoring her knee. Seething fumes wafted from her body. Each step hurt, but she barely noticed it.

She checked her purse to see if the key to Babs' house was still in the zipped pocket. She clamped her fingers around it, turning it over and over as she walked and schemed.

As she let herself into the garage and walked to the inside entrance of Babs' house, she had a flash of inspiration—and it was a good, old-fashioned, trashy idea.

Chapter 19

Courtney

When I contacted the municipality and found out about the tax bill, I knew I had to tell the siblings right away. After providing endless paperwork, the municipality waived the penalties and interest because I could prove they had made the error in sending the tax bill to the wrong person for all those years. Still, twenty-one thousand was a lot of cash. I needed to discuss the matter with the Brandies and Mona. I pulled out my phone and texted.

Courtney: *Hi all. We need to meet for the estate.*

Brando: *What about?*

Courtney: *Money.*

As soon as I said the word *money*, they all agreed to meet. I knew it wasn't going to be a pleasant conversation when they found out.

When Mona and the Brandies arrived at Mom's house, I hustled everyone into the dining room. I got right to the point and explained about the land that Mom had been bequeathed from Mr. Vincente and then reminded Mona about us three living in the tiny trailer for years until Mom could afford to buy her current home. Mom never got a tax bill because it went to Mr. Vincente's niece who ignored the bills.

Brando twitched in his seat. "Let's cut to the car crash: what do we owe?"

"The good news is that I talked to the municipality, and we don't have to pay penalties and interest because it was their mistake—"

"How much?" Brando snapped.

"Well, the original was thirty-eight thousand, but with the penalties and interest removed, it's just over twenty-one thousand dollars." The silence was eerie.

"OMG," said Mona looking visibly shaken. "Where will we get the money?"

"Easy," said Brando. "Sell the land."

To my eye, Brando looked like a greyhound on a racetrack trying to bust out of the starting block, ready to catch the never-to-be-caught hare on the track. I had to hose him down before he got too far off-track.

"Hang on, there's an order to clear up this mess. We will have to pay the taxes before we can sell it. I'll bet we'll have to remove that trailer on-site. It's old and falling apart, and that will cost something." I could see looks of discouragement creeping over faces, but I needed to lay the cards on the table. "And don't forget this is a piece of land left to the four of us, so we'll all have to agree to sell it."

"Well, that's not an issue," said Brando. "But first, we need twenty-one grand in change."

"There are a couple of options. We could each chip in five thousand each..." I began.

"Not a chance," said Mona, her face pale. "Unless you sell the house."

I wasn't surprised that Mona was broke. "Right. And we can't sell the house until we pay the taxes." I glanced at the Brandies who looked almost as shocked. While they loved the appearance of looking well off, I wondered if they were both up to their ears in credit card debt. Besides, on principle, none of us would want to front Mona's share of the bill.

"How much money is in Mom's bank accounts?" asked Brando.

I glanced at Mom's bank statements. "Just over two thousand dollars in total." I wondered if I should bring up Mona's siphoning Mom's bank accounts but decided it could lead to an even bigger brawl. "Also, we have her car, which will net a couple of grand. But keep in mind we have the ace up our sleeve: the Maud Lewis painting."

"What's that worth?" asked Brando.

"Depends," I said. "I spoke to a couple of art galleries and auction houses." I wanted them to know I was working my butt off for the estate. I could see Brando miming with his hands to pick up the tempo. "They said, depending on the scene, the condition of the painting and confirming if it's real—there are tons of fakes out there—anywhere from five grand to forty grand. But appraising it will take a fair amount of time; there's a lot of work involved. And if we want to go with a big auction house, we have to wait until they have an auction. It could take months."

"That's great, but it seems like a long way off," said Brandi. "In the meantime, do we have other options?"

Things went quiet. I looked around. I could see wheels turning in everybody's head. I thought I'd let them stew for a minute.

Mona looked up from her doodling. "Let's revisit the estate sale. As I mentioned, there are some real gems in Mom's shop and home. If we reach the right people, we could raise lots of cash."

"How much?" Brando asked.

"I'm guessing ten to fifteen thousand, depending on the day, the weather and who comes out to buy," Mona said.

I looked at Mona and wondered if that amount was based on anything at all, or if she just pulled it out of her crocheted beanie. Out of all the options, this seemed like the best. "I think that's a great idea. Brando, Brandi, want to revisit this?"

Silence. Then they both nodded.

"Great. But I want to make one thing clear: Mona and I are not doing this alone," I said, before anybody got ideas. "If you and Brandi want to pitch in, we'll put the money toward the tax bill. We're in this together, and the faster we solve the challenges, the faster I can distribute the estate."

The Brandies leaned in like they were two lawyers at a trial trying to stay out of earshot of the judge. "Okay, but one day only," announced Brando, as if he had to win this argument.

"Sure," I said, not sure why he had such strict guidelines, but saying yes to shut him up. Suddenly, I felt relief. We were all on the same page, figuring out selling dates, logistics and rain dates. We talked about roles. Mona said she had some ideas for the event and she would do the social media. Brandi would help get things set up to look more appealing. Then we talked about cash and floats, pricing and dealing with eTransfers.

"I've decided what my role will be," said Brando.

"What's that?" I asked, feeling like we were making progress.

"I'll do exit security."

"Say what?"

"I'll plant myself near the exit to make sure none of those little Christers from the neighborhood steals anything. I can look mean and tough when I want," he said folding his big arms in front of his chest with an ugly look on his mug as if to prove his tough look.

"Brando, that's of no concern to me," I said, wondering how he dreamed up such a stupid thing to worry about. "Sure, there might be a couple of light-fingered folks in town, but most people are honest."

"Besides, if someone is stealing a few items, maybe it means they can't afford to buy something they need, so we'll just help them out a bit," said Mona.

"Nice spin on local thieving," said Brando. "Seriously, we need to protect our stuff."

"Says the man who wanted to throw everything into a dumpster a few weeks ago," Mona joked, with an edge to her voice.

It had been going so well. Suddenly Brando and Mona were snapping at each other, back and forth. Insult, response, insult, response. I rapped my knuckles on the table. "KIDS, DO I HAVE TO STOP THIS CAR?" I shouted in my best Mom voice. Everyone stopped talking.

"That's good, Courtney," said Brando. "Kind of funny, even."

I giggled, a bit surprised by my success at breaking them up. I wasn't trying to be funny, but if it stopped the bickering, I was all for it.

Mona looked puzzled. "What does that mean, Courtney?"

"Of course, that wouldn't mean much to you, Mona," I laughed. "Mom used to shout that at us when she was driving the car, and we were all fighting in the back seat. You were like an only child, so you had nobody to argue with." I looked at the twins. "Brando, we need you in the selling role, that's your strength. Besides, you'll make it fun and lively. Can we count on you to do that?" I crossed my fingers and hoped he'd agree to it.

"I see right through you, Miss Suck-up. But I guess I could manage the sales and I do have a voice that carries. And I'll decide who gets to beat us down in price or not. There are certain items where we will not be beaten down."

In these situations, I knew the best thing was to let him think he was running the show. He was no multi-tasker, more of a hyper-focused, one-thing-at-a-time type of guy. But I'd let him think that he was fully in charge. At least he got off his silly idea of imitating a security guard at a big box store exit, staring down honest people as if they were nicking items.

Relieved, I started clearing up the papers. I'd had enough for the day. "Thanks, everyone. We have an opportunity to raise a tidy sum for the estate. We'll look to Mona to guide us on the sale." I could see a slight look of worry on Mona's face, but it felt good to have one sibling take on a major task for once.

"I'll do my best, but there are no guarantees," Mona said.

"Our next task is to visit the land and trailer at Robbins Road. Brando and Brandi, when was the last time you were there?"

They both went quiet. "The night we moved from there into Mom's house in town," said Brando, his face clouding over. "I swore I'd never go back there. Who wants a reminder of grinding poverty? It was an armpit of a place to live, right Brandi?"

I knew that it had been a sad time for Brando, and he was still angry. I didn't love the trailer era, but I understood that Mom was doing her best for us, and I just accepted it at face value. Not only was he embarrassed to live there, but he also had no father to support us. "Crazy, but I don't think I've been back either since we moved out. Mona, did Mom ever take you there?"

"No, she never mentioned it to me at all," Mona said.

I tried to recall the years we were there; it was a fog. "That means about thirty years since we were there. And I don't remember Mom talking about visiting there. We'll have to prepare ourselves for a place that's entirely grown over—I can hardly picture it."

"Well, it will be a right mess, no matter what. We may have to hire Lensky's Excavation and Backhoe to clear it out," said Brando. "If we clean it up, it will sell for more. Be sure to get three quotes, Queen Bea."

Right. I was about to ask Brando to take that on, but of course, he delegated the task to me to make sure he didn't have to take on any extra work. Rather than argue with him, I'd get the lay of the land first. Then I'd ask so many stupid questions, he'd get fed up and say he'd take over. That's the way we rolled in our family.

Chapter 20

Mona

Mona packed up her knapsack, water bottle and dog treats for the trip to the land they hoped to sell. It wasn't far away, only ten kilometers, but it felt like a big adventure. Brando wanted to take his truck with a cab that could hold four people, plus Shiva.

On Saturday, the sun appeared in full bloom with no clouds, and a gentle wind stirred the air like a slow-moving ceiling fan. Mona was surprised to learn about the place where her siblings had grown up. While it meant nothing to her, she liked that it might be worth enough to plump up the estate coffers. She couldn't figure out why her mother had never mentioned it; she tended to compartmentalize her life. She seemed to tell her three older siblings certain things, and Mona other bits of information, but nobody had the full picture of her life. Was that on purpose? Or was it simply a matter of dealing with what was in front of her? She wasn't a manipulative or agenda-type mother, so Mona wondered why the secrecy.

Brando picked everybody up and barreled down the streets until he drove out of the town limits. Even though winter was long past and summer was kicking in, the roads looked bumpy and uneven on Robbins Road. Brando drove like he was a stunt driver on a TV car ad dodging puddles, potholes and other setbacks that would challenge even the toughest truck.

His speed caused them to drive right past the hidden driveway until Courtney shouted, "There's sixteen!" from the civic number on a sign by the ditch. Brando braked and backed up, fishtailing his way back to the driveway. Mona was relieved when he finally stopped. She didn't drive with him often and hoped to keep it that way.

"Should we walk in?" asked Courtney. "The road is full of ash trees and thickets—it could scratch up your truck."

"Makes sense," said Brando, pulling over and parking on the side of the road. They got out and stared at the surroundings. The three siblings looked puzzled. "That's odd," said Brando. Brandi and Courtney nodded. Mona had no idea what caused it to look weird.

"It looks like the road has been cleared," Courtney added. As they walked around the bend, the property morphed into an attractive and well-maintained driveway. The edges were cleared and shrubs were growing in bursts of green. Off in the distance, a group of portable solar panels lined up neatly, with a finishing touch of fairy lights strung along the trailer. Courtney squinted and said "Holy cow, it looks like—"

"Somebody is squatting here," Brando interjected, looking toward the old trailer. Instinctively, the three sisters and Shiva moved closer to Brando, silently nominating him as leader of the pack. They stepped gingerly. There were gardens, a clothesline and a trailer in decent condition. "What is this?" said Brando, pointing to the lived-in space. He grabbed a sturdy broken branch and yanked off the small twigs.

Mona's heart pounded. She wasn't familiar with the land or what to expect, but it was clear the others didn't know what was going on either.

"What's that?" Mona asked, looking at the baseball bat of a branch he now wielded in his right hand.

"My insurance policy," Brando replied.

"Is it necessary?"

"Probably not, unless it's the Morgan brothers."

"Who are they?"

"Local drug dealers and all-around nasties," said Brando. Puffing up, Brando bellowed "Hey!" His voice echoed through the trees. "You're on private land!"

A door opened slowly and a group of four piled out of the trailer. From Mona's angle, she could see what looked like a family—a mother in her thirties, a father and two teenage boys.

The mother raised both hands in the air and cried as if surrendering. "Please, please don't hurt my boys," she wailed, stepping in front of her children to protect them.

Brando stopped in his tracks. "Whoa, sister," he called out, his voice sounding less menacing as he lowered his big stick. "You've been watching too much television. This is Danbyville."

Mona was moved by the woman's bravery; she was barely taller than a yardstick and her sons with their arms folded—one on either side—looked like a pair of

Goliaths guarding her. Yet maternal instincts made her look fearless as she pulled them close to her and moved towards her husband. Mona felt sick that someone was that frightened. And while Brando looked mean with a stick in his hand, she knew he wasn't violent. Stupid maybe, but not violent. She focused on the group until they came into focus.

"Maria. Juan?" Mona said, placing her hand on Brando's arm to tell him to stand down. "OMG, and Luis and Bayani. It's the Santos family!"

"Mona, is that you?" Maria shouted, relief sweeping her face.

"Yes. Don't worry, we won't hurt you!" Mona shouted. She ran to Maria and hugged her, while the woman wept. Mona rocked her gently back and forth to calm her down.

Brando eased up on the menacing look, yet still didn't look impressed. "Who's this and what are you doing here?"

"Maria and Juan are Continuing Care Assistants at the hospital. They were so good to Mom over the past year," she said, returning her gaze to the Santos family. "How are you, anyway?"

"Good, good, thank you, Mona dear," Maria said. "We were so sorry to hear about your mother."

"Well, I don't remember them," sniffed Brando.

Of course you wouldn't. Mona thought. *You barely came to the hospital, and the few times you did, you wouldn't have noticed the two workers from the Philippines helping our mother.*

"Juan kept the room sparkling clean and told Mom a joke every day," Mona said. "And Maria helped with Mom's medical care. So gentle and compassionate."

Courtney walked over to the two boys, both teens. "Hi, Luis. Aren't you in my daughter Ava's class at school?" He nodded but looked embarrassed by the situation. "I thought so," she added. "You and Bayani are incredible soccer players."

"Your place looks fantastic," said Mona. "Look at the garden! You've got produce and flowers, it's incredible. And you've cleared out so much brush." She looked at Maria and Juan, who were beaming.

Brando rolled his eyes. "Okay, thanks Miss Hug-a-Tree. It's officially a lovefest. But I want to know why they're living on Mom's land."

Maria and Juan exchanged glances. Maria stepped forward lightly. "Your mother offered it to us when we arrived from the Philippines and started working at the hospital. The four of us were living in one tiny hotel room with only a mini-fridge and microwave. She knew there is very little accommodation in Danbyville."

Juan nodded and added, "We're raising hungry teens to be top athletes. This place allows us to grow healthy vegetables. And it helps keep our costs down. Maria is also studying to become a nurse, to get a better job at the hospital." Juan put his arm around Maria and kissed the top of her head.

Mona beamed and turned to her brother, who still had a slight snarl on his face. "See, Brando? There's no problem. Mom was holding space for them and honoring the whole family while Maria betters herself so they can live a good life here in Canada."

Brando pulled his phone out of his pocket and mimed keying in text. "Mona, could you hang on while I run that through Google Translator? I don't speak Flake."

Mona shot him a look but at least she felt confident that Brando wasn't going to turf them out of their home. "This is exactly like something Mom would do, so I think it's great." She looked at Courtney, who looked a little uncomfortable, while Brandi looked blank.

Brando calmed down a bit, but it was clear he had things on his mind. "Let's say for argument's sake my Mom said you could stay here. How long?"

Juan smiled. "She said until we had our own place sorted out. And we are working extremely hard to do that. We don't want to take advantage of her generosity."

"Right, it's not like it's a rush," said Mona, wanting to point out the irony. "For a place that's been sitting empty for decades."

"Enough, Mona," said Brando, pointing at her. He returned his gaze to the couple. "Maybe she did say you could stay here, but do you have any proof?"

"I have an email," said Maria, walking into the trailer. She came back out with her phone, scrolling and flipping quickly. Finally, she stopped and handed Brando the phone. "Here it is if you want to read it. I can send it to you as well."

Courtney stepped forward. "Hi, Maria and Juan, I'm Courtney, the oldest daughter and executor."

"Oh yes, we remember you at the hospital and your mother talked about you and your families. She was so proud of you all."

Mona could tell Courtney felt a little embarrassed because she had obviously never noticed Maria and Juan, yet they knew about her.

"Thanks. And yes, I would like a copy of the email," she said, asserting her authority. "I must say, you've done a decent job here. We thought the place would be a mess."

"It was," joked Maria and Juan together. "We promised your mother we would bring it back to life," added Maria.

"We put in a lot of weekends with our boys clearing it out and hauling everything away," added Juan. "We are saving every penny, and we hope to buy a place within the next six months."

"Thank heavens for your dear mother!" said Maria, tears in her eyes. "I just forwarded the email. And I'm sorry we all scared each other so much."

"Well, I guess we need to talk as a family," said Brando, turning to point out to the others it was time to leave.

Mona hugged Maria, Juan and the two boys. She had a deep admiration for a family that had sacrificed so much to come to Canada. Living in a tin can of a trailer wasn't appealing to her, but she could see they took pride in making the place livable. She knew Nova Scotia was desperate for good healthcare professionals and they all needed to make them feel welcome here. She would text her craft circle to start knitting caps, mitts and scarves for a deserving family that would need them this winter.

The four siblings and Shiva turned around and headed back down the lane toward the truck.

"This changes the water on the beans," sighed Brando.

Mona had no idea what that meant. Knowing Brando and his tone, it wasn't good. She tried to understand him, but he was an intense soul. She figured he had karma to work out. "Look how much they've improved the land," she said. "All carried out by hand, I might add. It would have cost us thousands of dollars."

"Yeah, but the timing sure sucks," said Brando. "We've got a big tax bill to pay."

Mona didn't care about his first-world problems. They were now supporting a family who needed a leg up. In celebration, she slipped a little doggie treat to Shiva, who looked at her fondly. This morning she had almost bailed on going because she wanted to sleep in. Now she was relieved that she was there to prevent a terrible scene. While Brando wouldn't have hurt them, he would have raced in, all guns blazing, without even asking if they had permission to be there. At least they left on a positive note.

Silently, the four siblings piled into the truck. "Just give me a minute," said Brando as he pulled a Bic lighter and a small pipe out of his pocket. He flicked the lighter wheel until he got a steady flame, then turned it downward to light the cannabis. He sucked in deeply and leaned his head back, releasing smoke, followed by a short *ah* as it took effect. He then passed the pipe to Brandi, who did the same.

Courtney shifted on the bench seat. "Brando, could you and Brandi please open your windows? I can't stand the smell of weed."

Both opened their windows halfway. "Better?" he asked.

"A bit," Courtney replied, staring out the back window. "I'll survive." Then she leaned toward the front. "Maybe you should smoke a little less dope, guys."

"And maybe you should smoke a little more. Might make you less of a Queen Bea." Brando retorted.

"If we get stopped by the cops, I'm not part of this dope-smoking stuff," Courtney sniffed.

"Last I heard, cannabis was legal in Canada."

"Not while you're driving," Courtney shot back.

"The ignition is off. Relax. Besides, we went to school with all the cops," said Brando. He turned around to Mona, offering her the pipe. "Want a puff, Mona?"

"Is it organic?"

Brando laughed. "Hang on, I'll check the package from the government store." He held it up and read from it. "Let's see... it's called 'Standard Shit,'" he joked. "Now tell me, how can a barely-working gal like you afford premium organic dope?" he said, passing the pipe back to Brandi.

"I don't buy it; my friend grows it," she said in a matter-of-fact tone. "It's clean and very potent, with no chemicals."

"Right, Mona the Moocher. Always bartering, but never paying her way through life," said Brando.

"Whatever. Can we get going? I have things to do this afternoon." Mona didn't have plans, but hanging out with this jerk wasn't her idea of fun.

Brando took another puff and blew it out the window. Mona could see him now relaxing. *Thank God for small mercies.*

Brando looked at Courtney. "Before we take off, I want to say one thing. Courtney, on Monday, I want you to call Megan to start the process of evicting the Santa Claus family. Since she's charging us three hundred and fifty dollars an hour, she might as well earn her keep."

Mona tensed up. "Hang on there. First, it's the Santos family, and we told them it was okay to stay there."

"Noooo," he said, dragging out the word for impact. "You told them that. That's why I shut you down. What I said was, 'We will have to discuss this as a family,' which is code for 'Stay tuned; things might change.'"

Mona could feel a churning inside. "That's not fair. Mom said they could stay there until they found a place."

Brando tapped the dashboard to hold attention. "Yes, she did. But rest her soul, she's gone now. This land is going to the four of us and we need to liquidate it to pay our tax bill. Right, Queen Bea?"

Courtney shifted slightly. "Brando's got a point, Mona. While they seem like a nice family, they've had a good run there. We need to sell the land. They'll just have to pivot," she added.

Aside from disliking that buzzword *pivot*, Mona was furious. "That's not fair. We're reneging on Mom's promise. I won't be part of this."

"Well, we'll just have to take a vote, and majority rules. All those in favor say 'aye,'" said Brando, raising his hand to the roof of the cab. Brandi and Courtney added theirs. "Against, nay."

Mona shot her arm in the air.

Brando smiled. "Three for it, one against. Motion something or other. What is it, Queen Bea?" Brando said, sucking in another drag.

"Motion carried," she said, scribbling in her estate notebook.

"Not quite," said Mona. "Majority doesn't rule in this instance. Mom left the four of us the land. That means if we sell it, all four of us must sign the documents. I'm not signing."

Brando turned toward the back. "Mona, I know you like to think there's a mythical creature running one step ahead of you sprinkling pixie dust to make your problems go away. News flash: there are no pixies in your corner. That was Mom—but she's gone. And now you have a new reality."

"Too bad," she said. "I'm still not signing. Yes, the scenario complicates the family estate. But I have a feeling if we honor Mom's promise to this wonderful family, the universe will work it out so that everybody wins. Wait and see."

Brando and Brandi laughed. Brando's eyes were glassy, and he had an amused look on his face. "And what kind of timeline has the cosmos given you for this warm and fuzzy real estate deal?"

Mona didn't care what he thought. She closed her eyes and pictured a scenario with everybody smiling and the Santos family excited about the outcome. They were all hugging; it was a happy celebration. She sat back in the seat with a sunny smile on her face. "I don't know about a timeline. You'll just have to trust, and the universe will deliver."

Chapter 21

Brando

Brando hung up from his call with the funeral home. When they told him the cremains were ready, his stomach tightened. He could barely focus when Mrs. McIsaac talked about urns, asking him what he was looking for and inviting him to look at what was in stock. He didn't want to offend her, but he sure as hell couldn't go browsing in the urns aisle at the local funeral home. He lobbed it back into her court by asking what she recommended. She said there weren't many to choose from because of supply chain issues during Covid. She went on and on about glass versus china and endless patterns which he didn't care about. As soon as she mentioned decorated enamel, he said, "Enamel is perfect. Less chance of dropping and breaking it at the wrong moment." She said she had a lovely flower pattern that she knew Babs would like.

Relieved that one part of his task was complete without touch involved, he thanked her and said one of the family would be by to pick up the package. He knew it wouldn't be him, so he'd have to find someone to do the deed.

He couldn't tell Courtney he would be getting someone else to pick the ashes up because she'd bust his chops—he could hear her high and mighty "blah-dee-dah" that would make him feel two inches high. He couldn't ask Brandi. They had already discussed it and she was equally grossed out by the thought of it. That left Mona. How he wished he didn't have to make this call to her. If there was one thing Brando hated, it was groveling. He neither wanted to receive groveling—too pathetic—nor do the groveling—even worse. Except now he needed her help. He'd need to think of a reward to convince her to take the burden off his plate without revealing his reasons to her.

He vaped a couple of puffs, then called her number. It rang a bunch of times. He expected it would go to voicemail, then she picked up.

"Well, the dead arose and spoke to us all," Mona said in a lazy tone.

Funny you should mention that topic. But he needed to ease into it. "Look, Mona, I may have been a bit harsh the other day when you asked to stay at Mom's place. I'm sure you can understand my position," he added.

"No, actually, I can't," she said. "Perhaps you could enlighten me as to why you wouldn't want to help a family member in her time of need."

"Well..." he started but faltered. He wasn't sure if it was her comment or that he was a bit stoned, but he couldn't remember why he was against it. The only reason he could think of was that Mona created chaos out of thin air. She didn't do it on purpose, but she still did it. He figured that's what she'd do in this situation, and it would delay the estate process. But he couldn't say that to her. "I was a tad quick to say no to it without further thought." He was dangerously close to an apology and it nearly killed him, but he was on a mission.

"What do you need, Brando?"

"Huh?"

"I know when someone is trying to butter me up. I'd rather you just come right out and ask than do your slinky dance and slip in the request at the last possible second."

Normally, his irritation level would start climbing, but he couldn't lash out at her. "Okay, I could use your help with one thing." He could picture her arms folded in full defiance about whatever he said. He waited to see if she was going to tell him off.

"I'm listening."

Brando was encouraged because she didn't sound as threatening as Courtney did in this situation. "Well... this whole bullshit Courtney's thrown my way about taking care of Fluffy. And then there's the cremains business at the Addams Family funeral home."

"That's two things," she said.

Right. He got carried away trying to offload his assignments. "Got me."

"Look, I hear you, it's tough stuff for someone like yourself who's not in touch with his emotions," she said. "However, I've been clear from the start; I just can't look after Fluffy, end of discussion."

There was a long silent pause. "Okay," he said, wondering what was coming.

"But with the cremains, I can help you."

"You can?" he said, sitting up. He had almost zoned out but was now glad he hung in there. That's what he was dreading the most.

"For me, the ashes are just what's left of her energy. She no longer has a physical presence on this earth. But her spirit and energy are all around us. I still feel some kind of connection with her. Do you know what I mean?"

Well, whack-a-doodle-do. Not feeling a thing there, girlfriend. He wondered how he could wiggle out of this one. If he agreed with her, she'd know he was lying. Maybe she was just messing with him and waiting to hear how he behaved. He decided it was better to be honest but hold the side order of sarcasm that he normally served. "Sorry, Mona. I'm not feeling the spirit. But if you say so." If she were willing to do this task, he swore to himself that he wouldn't make fun of her.

"That's okay, Brando. I get it," she said. "You aren't used to this kind of thing. So, yes, I would be honored to look after Mom's ashes. But on one condition."

"What?" he asked, assuming it would be a ball-crushing deal breaker.

"You have to drive me to McIsaac's to pick up the ashes and the urn and take them to my place. And ditto on the day of the service, especially if it's a muggy day. You can pick me up at home and take me to the funeral home."

"You got it!" He almost high-fived the air and yelped out of sheer joy, but he short-circuited it at the last second. Brando was starting to realize she was genuinely caring in these types of situations; he'd give her that. Yet he was still worried she might flake out and not follow through on her promise. He didn't want to *unseize* the day if there were such a thing. "Can we go now and pick up the package?" he asked.

"Okay. See you in ten."

He jumped in his truck and raced across town. It was a warm and muggy day, so he ran the AC in the truck before he picked her up. She was outdoors with Shiva waiting for him. The two climbed into his truck and he didn't even complain when Shiva leaned forward from the back seat and licked his face. It took only minutes to get to the funeral home.

"Be right back," said Mona, turning to Shiva. "Stay here with Brando," she said, slamming the door. Shiva stuck her head out the window and barked up a storm, paying no attention to Brando as he tried to calm her.

Ten minutes later, Mona walked toward the truck with a carrying bag in her arms. It looked heavy, and she was tiny. Since Brando had no idea how big or heavy it might be, he got out to walk around and open the door. Shiva started whining and barking; she couldn't stand being apart from Mona. She called for her to settle down from outside the truck, a request that Shiva totally ignored. Brando opened the door, and she climbed in with the package. "Wow, it's heavier than I thought," she said.

"That so?" Brando said. He had no idea what it should or shouldn't weigh. All he knew was that he didn't have to store the ashes in his home and worry that his mother might reach out and tap him on the shoulder at night. He was being ridiculous, but he knew his Mom (and now Mona) were really into that stuff. He didn't believe in it at all, or maybe he did but didn't want proof of it while he was sleeping.

She looked inside the bag. "I like the urn," she said, peeling back tissue paper. "Looks like a nice flower garden against a deep green background. Well done."

"I did my best," he said. Mrs. McIsaac had done all the work. But he approved it, so he figured that was his contribution. He swung into the driveway of Mona's apartment. "And thank you, Mona." This time it came from the bottom of his heart, with no insults tacked on at the end of the sentence.

"No problem," she said smiling as she fished out her keys and picked up the package. "Oh, and thanks for your full support for my short-term stay at Mom's place."

The sound effect in his head was like someone dragging the needle across a vinyl album on the turntable which suddenly came to a screeching halt. He didn't recall stating his full support, but when you gave Mona an inch, she'd return with a backhoe and drive it forward for a hundred miles. That was Mona in a nutshell.

Still, relief flooded through him. He had no idea how heavily picking up the ashes was weighing on his mind. He drove over to the lake and parked his truck in the little hideaway spot. To celebrate, he lit up his pipe. He was glad none of the women in his family were there to remind him he was smoking too much pot. Courtney was especially annoying. Lately, Brandi was turning down offers to smoke with him, which was her way of saying he was smoking too much. Even his party-friendly girlfriend Roxy made noises about it now and then, so he switched to paying cash for his dope so that it didn't show up on their credit card. Yet it was his daughter, DeeDee, who hurt him the most. She had joked about her Dad being a stoner. He didn't like that because he wasn't being a good role model.

When he thought about it, it was true. He had picked up the tempo with his dope habit. He thought about when that had started, and realized it was during the blur of the last months of his mother's life. He felt terribly guilty that he hadn't visited her as much as he should have, something everyone pointed out to him. There were no excuses; he didn't visit her enough at home or in the hospital. Mostly it was because he couldn't bear to see his mother so ill. It just sucked the life out of him, and it made him feel useless.

He was normally the fixer in the family for his Mom: gluing broken chairs, resetting the remote, bringing in her groceries and shifting heavy items (oh the endless moving of furniture at home and in the garage!) Didn't matter what needed doing, he did it, complaining and joking at the same time. Then he'd sit down and shoot the breeze with her over a coffee—she always had a pot of brew on the go. That's what he loved. It wasn't the big events with his Mom, like the staged family dinners—it was the one-on-one moments that he missed.

Brando knew he could be a little abrasive. He was like his father, when he was being a jerk or a doofus his Mom explained. When he asked what the difference was, she explained when he was being a jerk, he knew better but was doing something annoying anyway. And when he was a doofus, well, he was more innocent and just a little dense. Then she added, "Either way, I love you." That always got a laugh. She'd also tell him the good things he did that were nothing like his father.

One time near the end of her life, he mumbled something about not visiting enough. She held his hand and told him not to worry. She said she knew exactly why he found it so hard to visit. His Mom understood him and loved him unconditionally. He hadn't cried since his Mom died and had no idea why, except the tears wouldn't come. But he also felt like he was letting his mother's spirit down by not showing his deep grief.

As he took another puff on his pipe, he realized he had nobody to talk to about this. As the family tough guy, he just didn't feel comfortable discussing it with anyone, not even Brandi. His buddies at work mostly joked and insulted each other as their main form of communication. And when someone was going through a tough time, they had an unwritten rule to avoid the topic altogether. They had been doing it so long, he didn't feel comfortable breaking the code.

For now, he promised himself after he got through the estate sale and his mother's service, he'd ease up on the dope. He fired up the truck and drove back home.

Chapter 22

Courtney

There were endless tasks to sort out for the estate sale, so I asked everyone to come to Mom's house on the Saturday before. Things were tense over the sugar bowl, and we put it on simmer for the time being. We agreed it wouldn't be sold in the estate sale, yet the thought of stowing it in a cupboard with keen buyers lurking around made me nervous. I could just picture a collector spotting it and convincing one of our kids to let them buy it when the siblings weren't around. Now I was wishing I'd put my foot down and moved it to my place for safekeeping. When I had a second, I would wrap it and hide it at the back of a top shelf.

In a strange twist of events, Brando told me he could live with Mona staying at Mom's place, which didn't sound like him. While I didn't like it, Mona had a way of getting the outcome she wanted. Besides, I couldn't let a sibling suffer without a roof over their head. If too much time passed and she refused to leave, I'd find a way to tempt her out of the house with a promise of money.

When we told her it was okay, she was packed and ready to move in a couple of days. She had convinced Raj and her friends to help her—he even rented a cube van for her—which meant she supervised the move. Right up her alley. She looked happy to be back in Mom's house, but who wouldn't enjoy a rent-free home? Meanwhile, the estate was stiffed with paying the utilities and taxes—although I had to admit it wasn't a bad idea to have someone living there. I was worried some town teens might get ideas about poking around the house with nobody home.

Sometimes Mona surprised me. Just when I thought she was the laziest sloth on the planet about work, she kicked into full gear on the estate sale. In two weeks, she had organized the house and garage, setting aside the most valuable pieces, although fretting about them non-stop. And she was running a major social media campaign, throttle on high. She created a photo gallery with the most exciting pieces highlighted, and she mobilized her girlfriends to post and repost everything. There was a buzz around town and beyond Danbyville. I realized one thing: when Mona put her mind to something, she could set the world on fire. The problem was, it didn't happen very often.

The four of us gathered in Mom's living room the day before the sale, and it was clear Mona was going to run the show.

"Okay, everyone, here's a marker and a roll of masking tape. We are going to mark the pricing on as much stuff as possible. Since I know about pricing, I will work with each of you to tell you the price and you can mark it. It will help us to get the most out of the sale."

"That sounds like a lot of work, Mona," said Brando. "I was picturing more of a free-for-all and telling people to make an offer."

"How many yard and estate sales have you attended in the past five years?" asked Mona.

Brando mimed a zero.

Mona held up a small vase, rounded and cloudy white with flowers on it. "And what if someone said to you, 'I'll give you five bucks for that.' How would you respond?"

"I'd counteroffer ten," he said. "Not a penny less."

"Congratulations. This is a Lalique vase that would get between eight hundred and a thousand dollars. In fact, I'm holding it for the online sale," she said, walking it to a cabinet that was locked with a "not for sale" sign on it.

"Really? I was thinking about what I'd pay for something like this."

We had tons to do, and I couldn't have him hijacking an event. "Brando, let's play to our strengths here. Mona knows what she's talking about. And unless I'm wrong, you, Brandi and I haven't spent any time at yard sales."

"So where were we?" said Mona, looking around the room.

Out of the corner of my eye, I could see a woman in a garish outfit outside in the driveway heading toward the steps. She had a limp. "Here comes Doris, the alleged cleaner. Guess what she's coming to collect?"

"Her knick-knacks, which was the official term in the will," laughed Brandi.

"I just remembered; I didn't get back to her after I spoke to Megan. I was allowed to give her the knick-knacks, but not the cash gift." I dreaded a conversation with Doris. Aside from being an endless talker when she got on a roll, she was also stubborn. She'd been to my place a couple of times, and I had been a bit short with her.

"She looks like she's on a mission," Mona said.

"Maybe she forgot her broomstick here after her last cleaning," said Brando.

Mona stomped her foot and Shiva barked. Everybody went quiet, with surprise on their faces. "Not nice, you guys. Did it ever occur to you that Doris brought Mom joy and kept her company on days when we weren't here? I know she wasn't the best cleaner, but that wasn't the point. She was broke and Mom liked helping her out financially. I know that she loved giving her money with no expectation of anything in return."

"Yeah, Mom was good at giving away cash for nothing in return, wasn't she?" I said. Mona glared at me. I could see the Brandies exchanging looks, wanting to know what my comment was about.

Doris rapped on the door. Shiva barked until she recognized Doris, then jumped up in glee.

"Be nice, for heaven's sake," said Mona. "She's got a lot of issues to deal with."

Mona was right, not that I was going to acknowledge that. "I'll get it," I said, walking to the front door. "Hi, Doris, come in. I just remembered I owe you a call. The good news is that I talked to the lawyer, and I can give you your items today."

"Thanks, Courtney," said Doris, limping over the threshold. "I don't want to take too much of your time," she added, pushing her way inside.

"Well then, don't," muttered Brando, winking at Brandi. I could see Mona giving him a rancid glare.

"So, it's the figurines in the glass cabinet," I said, walking toward the spot. "And there are sticky notes with your name on them. I see you've got a good-sized carrying bag." I handed her some newspapers to help wrap them.

"That's right," Doris said, pulling on the cabinet door. And when it stuck a little, she yanked the handle rather than seeing what was wrong.

"Here, let me help," I said, trying to sound patient but making sure nothing got broken. Aside from having no cleaning skills, Doris was clumsy and often dropped items during her cleaning gig with Mom. I eased the door open, revealing a group of ten colorful figurines huddled together like runaways from an estate sale. I lifted each one looking for a sticky note on the bottom. A layer of dust outlined every one of them revealing that they hadn't been dusted for years. "Here's one. I'll set this on the table for you." I kept turning them over, but only found a second sticky note out of the ten. "That's odd," I said, "I'm sure she said there were three figurines for you."

Doris turned and said, "Oh, sorry, the third item is over here." She walked to the painting on the wall and said, "This is the other knick-knack."

"The Maud Lewis painting?" I gasped and watched as everyone joined in the chorus of shock as if the room had suddenly filled with toxic gas.

"Is that a Maud Lewis?" she asked, her voice sounding naïve and surprised. "I didn't know what her paintings looked like."

Suddenly I felt woozy, like everything was going sideways. "Oh my God, no, Doris," I laughed, sounding giddy.

"I am so sorry. You must have made a mistake. Mom was clear that the painting was going to us kids. That's the bulk of the estate right there." I shot a look of "Help me out here" to the other three but for the first time in their lives, they were speechless.

"Well, there's one way to confirm it," she said, walking toward the painting. "I remember it was the one in the corner because I watched her put a sticky on the back." Doris wobbled over and picked up the painting, turning it over to reveal a sticky note with their mother's initials and Doris's name. Like a thrilled judge in an international figure skating competition, she held it proudly in front of her, turning to each child to make sure they'd see it.

The Maud Lewis painting was only about eight by ten inches, yet worth a fortune. I knew there was no way Mom had left something that valuable to Doris. Babs had missed seeing this conniving woman in action, who was not only desperate and delusional, but convinced that she deserved the painting more than Babs' children did. "No Doris, this isn't yours and you are not taking it," I said, removing it from her hands and placing it back on the nail.

"It's mine," Doris spoke loudly.

Brando leaped up and put himself in between the painting and Doris. "Back off, Doris. You are not walking out the door with it. There is some kind of mistake that we need to sort out." He stood with his arms folded in front of him looking as solid as a barn.

Doris puffed and panted, then paused, her anger rising. "I'll leave now, but I'm getting what's due to me. You're nothing but a greedy bunch who want for nothing, while the rest of us barely get by," she said, stuffing the two figurines into her carrying bag and hobbling to the door. She let it slam behind her.

"What the hell was that?" I squeaked, wondering if we had just lost out on our big cash payout.

"That's nuts. She's up to something," said the Brandies in unison.

"I agree, but we just have to figure out how she did that little sleight-of-handwriting on the sticky note," I said.

"Maybe she's tampered with it," said Mona.

"Have any of you picked this up, or moved it while Mom was around?" I asked. Everybody shook their heads no. "Okay, good, because I haven't either."

"This is a crime scene!" barked Brando, sounding a little dramatic, as if quoting one of his favorite TV detectives.

Mona looked worried. "What if she has keys and comes back? You know what she's like."

"I wouldn't worry about that," said Brando. "She's nuts, but she's not crazy. This is a small town she knows better."

"I disagree, Brando; I'm getting the locks changed, Mona," I said. "This painting is worth a fortune and for some reason, Doris thinks she's entitled to it. Nobody touches this painting until I talk to Megan."

Damn. My task list now included a call to the lawyer and a potential court case. Everybody in town knew Doris was a pit bull, who would not give in, especially when she was wrong. She might not have ripped off our mother, but the minute Mom was gone, the gloves came off.

The last thing I felt like doing was preparing for the estate sale, but it was the next day, and the locomotive was turning into a runaway train. While Mona, Brando and Brandi talked about other items, I slipped into the pantry, stood on a chair and brought down the sugar bowl. I was still wound up about Doris's visit and worried something might happen to the bowl. Looking around, I spotted leftover newspaper and wrapped the lid separately from the bowl. Since the basement was a no-go area for the sale, I walked down the treacherous vertical stairs and stored it on a shelf with Mom's preserves. I would tell the others about it when I went back upstairs, except Shiva was barking and pacing because some people had come to the door hoping to buy ahead of the sale. Mona was pleasant but firm with them, sending them away empty-handed.

"Okay, I think that's everything for tonight," said Mona, looking around. "The weather looks good for tomorrow. The sale starts at nine in the morning, which means they'll start arriving by eight. If anybody wants to arrive early to help me move stuff or do crowd control, I'd appreciate it."

"I'll do my best, Mona, but I'm bagged," I said. I couldn't imagine what kind of work she needed to do so early in the morning.

"Ditto," said the Brandies. "See you in the morning."

Chapter 23

Mona

After everybody left, Mona moved around the house, picking up items that were too valuable for the sale. Yard and estate sale buyers were looking for bargains. For the true collector items, she needed time to research pricing and find buyers who were willing to pay what she wanted. She noted that her mood felt a little brighter over the last week—it was fun to pour energy into a positive project. She'd been bummed out over her mother and realized that she couldn't continue to just mope around being sad.

She was also upset about Doris's deceitful scheme. Mona found a bottle of Malbec in her mother's kitchen cupboard and a wine glass on the counter. After pouring herself a generous serving, she opened her Mom's reference book and started browsing the catalog, fascinated by the items she read about, along with her mother's handwritten notes. As she was flipping, Mona spotted a listing for a covered bowl like the sugar bowl, but she couldn't remember the details. She wasn't attached to it like her siblings were, but she still wanted it in case it was valuable.

Mona hadn't found any pricing yet for the sugar bowl, and she was worried Courtney was going to turn into a bit of a nut case over it. But if this book proved it was worth a lot, they had to stop her. She debated discussing it with the Brandies but knew Brando couldn't keep quiet about something like that, so she'd keep looking on the sly. She was curious to study it a little further to see if it had to do with the Ming Dynasty. The colors didn't look right, nor did the shape; she was stymied and wasn't going to let it go to Courtney until she'd done her homework.

She decided to take a picture of the sugar bowl for reference. She walked over to the cabinet and looked on the shelf. It wasn't there. Surprised, she got out the little step ladder and started to climb it, but realized she was on her second glass of wine and wasn't feeling steady. It must have been in another spot anyway. She climbed back down and returned to the sofa.

At midnight, she dragged herself to her room, regretting having drunk so much wine. She fell into a deep sleep but woke up around 4:00 a.m. Her mind was busy organizing the event. At 5:00 a.m., she got up and started getting things ready for the sale in a few hours.

Chapter 24

Courtney

I went to bed early so that I'd be rested for the sale the next morning. All the craziness of the estate was taking its toll on me. It felt like every spare minute was dedicated to paperwork, phone calls and follow-up. One problem would resolve itself, then another would replace it.

I lay in bed and slowly fell into a restless sleep. I dreamed all night about Mom's land and the Santos family living there, preparing for the sale and Doris's crazy grifter scheme.

There was no way Mom promised that painting to her and she wasn't getting it. I knew she had scammed us somehow. We just had to figure it out. It could cost us to get it sorted out, but we couldn't let her take us for a ride. It was as if she became envious that our mother was leaving us money and convinced herself that she deserved it more than us kids. Ever since Mom passed away, it felt like there was a shakedown going on, an endless assembly line of lawyers, accountants, banks, taxes, siblings and now friends with their hands out taking a piece of the action.

I woke up early and couldn't get back to sleep. I decided I might as well go to the house and help Mona get set up. I left a note for Jamie and the kids to come over for the starting time of 9:00 a.m.; it felt unfair on a Saturday when the kids would sleep until noon if left undisturbed. I packed the family cooler with food and refreshments, then my knapsack with water, snacks, sunblock and a hat. It promised to be a warm day, so I wanted the family to be ready for everything.

When I turned onto Mom's street, a bright red fire truck was parked in front of the house. Brando's truck was there too. My heart ping-ponged in my chest. What happened? Did Mona forget something on the stove? Suddenly I wondered if Mom's house insurance was paid up and cursed myself for not knowing that detail. I turned off the car, barely closing the door and bolting to the house. As I got closer, I could see Mona, the Brandies and David McClary, the fire chief laughing and talking.

"What's going on?" I gasped.

"Hey, Courtney," said Mona. "We're just getting set up for the sale."

"There's no fire?" I said, panting.

"No, the volunteer firefighters are getting ready for their fundraising booth," she said, smiling and moving us away from the action. "Come over here and I'll brief you guys on the plan."

I didn't know about a firefighters' fundraiser. I looked around and was shocked by how organized the place looked. A lineup was forming, and people were following rules. What were the odds? I said, "Wow, Mona, this looks great." Admittedly a smooth-running event was not what I pictured with her, but sometimes people surprise you.

"Thanks," Mona said. "Here's how it will work: the cash and admin table over there is for us when people exit. The paved driveway is set up for seniors so that they can wander around with walkers, canes and wheelchairs on even ground. And I've put out the things they like buying—lower-priced trinkets, china and costume jewelry. And there's a box marked *FREE* for unsellable items that somebody will love."

"What else?" Brando asked, already restless to get going.

"The front lawn is the fundraising and distraction zone. The fire crew have a booth and they're selling coffee, tea and sweets. This is for the people who arrive early; they'll have to take a number and wait to be let into the house at 9:00 a.m." She nodded toward people setting up another table. "That's the food bank folks. In all the ads, it said free entry, but I asked people to bring food or a cash donation for them. We got the firefighters to bring out a large kitchen pantry unit from Mom's stuff and we are encouraging people to 'Fill the Cupboard.'"

Then she looked to her right where there was a stand of trees. "In the shade, the SPCA is setting up a table for a 'Pet and Cuddles' fundraiser starring Shiva. For a buck, kids or adults can pet and hug Shiva. She's great with everybody, especially kids," she added.

"That's brilliant," I said.

"Yup, I don't have to worry about looking after Shiva all day and they're raising money," said Mona, smiling. "And then there's a kid drop-off zone with tons of activities, run by the day-care staff. They charge people five dollars to drop off their kids while they shop. And it raises money for the day-care. Among Mom's stuff, I found an inflatable pool, old costumes, antique toys and a cooler I filled with water for bobbing with apples. They will hold contests with prizes every hour."

"I'm sure it will do really well," I said. My eyes darted randomly; it felt like Mona had waved her magic wand and a circus was blossoming. I had no idea she'd think up all this stuff. Cars were pulling up by the minute and it was still an hour before the sale started. "Mona, I'm a little worried about how busy it's getting already, and people are parking everywhere. It may upset the neighbors."

"Don't worry. I held a meeting on Tuesday evening and invited everyone in the cul-de-sac to brief them and hear their concerns. They're fine. I promised to let them in the back door fifteen minutes before everybody else." She handed out aprons with big pockets for those selling items. "Courtney, you and Jamie are responsible for finance today. I've got the cash box with a float for you stationed at the exit point. Everybody leaving will be funneled to walk by you two, so you can take their cash. Jacob could be a runner if you need to find me. Brandi, can you work inside with Olivia, Ava and DeeDee?"

Brandi nodded. "Yes, but I'm not sure what to do."

Mona shrugged. "Answer questions, keep people out of the private areas in the house, price things, guide them to the washroom."

"What about me?" Brando sounded offended.

"I was getting there, dude," Mona joked. "You have the key role and the most fun, I might add. Think of yourself as the barker to lure people in and do crowd control. Be nice to people, guide them to the right spot, break up clumps of people causing gridlock and most of all, make them laugh. No pressure."

Brando's smile brightened. "I can do that!" He wandered off and started chatting with people from town and accompanied them into the garage.

Mona looked at Courtney and Brandi. "He'll do a fantastic job. That means I can now manage the event. So, if you need to ask me anything, call or text me, or flag me down."

Just then, Brando re-emerged from the garage, wearing a top hat, and white spats over his running shoes, carrying a cane and a monocle squished into his left eye. "Look what I found in Mom's shop," he beamed. He tossed his cane into the air and caught it, then spun in a circle like a dancer in an old movie. "Do I remind you of anybody?"

"Mr. Monopoly?" asked Brandi.

"Well, I suppose if you were thinking I looked like a rich man," he joked.

"I was thinking Mr. Peanut," I said.

"No, you dimwits," he said spinning his cane like he was born with it attached to his hand. "P.T. Barnum, from the Barnum and Bailey Circus. And let's hope there's a sucker born every minute who is willing to buy this stuff today," he said, lightly tapping his cane on Mona's shoulder. He walked over to his truck which had a souped-up stereo system and plugged in his phone. "Instant party," he said as lively music kicked in.

"Nice one, Mr. Barnum," I said watching Brando transform as if he had been waiting all his life to play the role. Why not? He had all the right stuff: a big mouth, pushiness, insensitivity and an obsession with money. He was also a shameless goofball who would do anything for a laugh. Mona had found the perfect role for each one of us. Given that Danbyville was a small town without much going on, she understood the sale would be the marquee event today. I was amazed by her talent for special events.

With thirty minutes to go before starting, the lineup was snaking down the street and the firefighters were delivering coffee. Brando was entertaining the crowd, keeping people laughing and curbing their restlessness. He started picking out teaser pieces that would be up for sale, making comments and showing them to people in the line-up. The more he hammed it up, the happier he looked.

"Okay people, here's a blast from the past," Brando yelled, picking up a tray with four tumblers and walking toward the line-up. "Does anybody remember Schwartz's Mustard glasses from the 1960s? Yes sir! The mustard came in glasses with lids. Sturdy as all get out. The design was card suits: hearts, clubs, spades and diamonds. Once the mustard was gone, they became Nova Scotian cocktail glasses."

Several people leaned close to see them, smiling and saying their parents and grannies had them. Several took pictures.

"What's the provenance?" someone shouted from the crowd.

"Prova-say-what?" Brando shot back.

"The source or origin of the glasses."

"Why didn't you say that?" Brando joked. "They were my mother's, of course. She used them every Saturday night for her cribbage games. She and her buddies would have drinks— always rum and Pop Shop cola. Right Doris?" Brando said, looking at her in the line-up.

Doris nodded. "You forgot the snacks: there was always a plate of Ritz crackers, stacked with baloney or cheese or both."

"Classy, an early charcuterie board," cracked Brando which made Doris laugh.

"Give you fifty bucks, right now," shouted a guy in the crowd.

"Seventy-five," sang a woman further back.

"Really, Marion?" asked Brando, shocked.

"I texted a pic to Nancy in Toronto," said Marion. "She wants them, bad."

Brando looked over to Mona for guidance, she discretely shook her head no.

"Afraid not," he joked. "You tell your sister that she refused to date me in high school, so no mustard glasses for her. Unless she'll trade her home in TO for these." The crowd chuckled.

"Seriously, folks. For those interested, please go see my sister Mona and she'll tell you the price—which, by the sound of things, could turn into an auction."

Mona nodded appreciatively. She clapped her hands at the siblings and their families and said, "Ready or not, let's do this sale!"

I watched Mona walk to the middle of the driveway where she had placed a large ship's bell on the table. She handed it to Brando and told him to go for it.

Brando grinned, replacing his top hat with a tattered tricorn hat and rang the bell hard, like he was the town crier, shouting, "Oyez, oyez, oyez! And for my Jewish friends, "Oi vay, oi vay, oi vay!"

Laughter rippled from the front to the end of the lineup. He reveled in the playful insults lobbed back to him. I had to hand it to him: he knew how to work a crowd.

He had DeeDee pull a crepe paper streamer across the driveway, which he then pretended to cut with a giant pair of cardboard scissors. "Ladies and gents, boys and girls, we are open!"

**

Chaos, giggles, kids running rampant, money changing hands, Shiva and Brando barking and larking about in unison. The estate sale was in full swing. I had never held a yard sale or worked on one before, so I soon realized once the doors open, it takes on a life of its own.

Brando, ever the salesperson motivated by goal-oriented antics, had decided to ring the ship's bell whenever there was a sale over five hundred dollars. And with Mom's shop packed with multiple dining sets, furniture and collectibles, it felt like I was hearing the bell regularly. I had to admit, it added to the merriment.

In addition to the constant ping of my cellphone notifying me about eTransfers, the cash box filled quickly. I stuffed wads of bills into a carrying bag to take to the basement for safekeeping. I made at least a dozen trips, so I knew we were doing well.

The sale was scheduled to end at 1:00 p.m. but there were still people mingling and nobody looked in a hurry to wrap up. All the family workers were wearing sun hats, and I had Jacob offering food and drinks all day, so nobody appeared to be keeling over from the heat or exhaustion. While a ton of stuff had sold, there was still a wide selection of stock. Mona told Brando to announce fifty percent off, which prompted him to ring the bell one more time and shout at the top of his lungs for the whole town to hear.

An hour later, Mona walked over to me and said we were officially closing the sale. People still lingered, but they were mostly talking; sales had dried up. She asked me to go with her to the basement to count the money. We had a folding table set up and we pulled out the two moving boxes full of cash. There was so much, I got Ava and Jacob to help sort the bills. We teased Jacob saying he needed extra training because he wasn't used to looking at cash, but he was soon sorting each denomination by color and putting them into hundred-dollar stacks. I had a spreadsheet set up where I entered all the bank transfers, then a column for each denomination. When I hit the final tally, Mona and I gasped. We couldn't believe it.

"Let's go outside and gather the family to announce it," said Mona.

"Great idea, Mona. Let's go, kids!" We rushed up the stairs and went out to the lawn.

Mona waved to the family who had worked that day. "Okay, everyone, we have the total for the sale. First, I'd like to thank all of you for helping today. It was an incredible effort on everybody's part, and we even had fun. Goes to show, that when we put our minds to it, the Martin and Nichols family can make things happen."

"What's the total?" Brando joked from the side.

Mona paused for effect and waited for everyone to lean in a bit. "We made fourteen thousand, one hundred and thirty-two dollars." Cheers went up all around.

Mona smiled. "Thanks, but I'm not finished yet. The firefighters made five hundred bucks, the SPCA two hundred and fifty, the daycare two hundred and ten, and the food bank has three hundred dollars cash and boxes of canned and dry goods," she said beaming. "And I committed a one percent donation from our sale, so we will share another hundred and forty bucks among the groups here.

"Great job, Mona," I said. She hadn't mentioned the donation to us, but given how successful the sale was, I wasn't going to complain. This was a time to celebrate. "Everybody, give it up for a spectacular event that Mona organized." A round of applause and whistles bubbled for a good ten seconds.

As soon as the applause died down, Brando's stereo started blasting Blue Rodeo's "We are Lost Together." Memories flooded back of times when Mom played this song and got all of us to sing when things were a little bleak, but she wanted us to hang in there as a family. We'd sway with our arms linked and at the end of the song, she'd say, "Never lose hope." We all loved it so much; we were still playing it when Mona was born so she knew it too. Somehow it had morphed into our family song. Even if people didn't know all the lyrics, everybody knew the chorus.

I looked at the Brandies and Mona, and everybody was grinning. It was like Mom had swooped in and selected that song to remind us that we could achieve so much more when we worked together.

"Did you tee up this song, Brando?" I asked.

He shook his head. "Totally random."

"Why?" asked DeeDee. "I know this song, but I'm not sure why."

"This was a song Mom played when she was trying to get us to hang in there together," I said.

With the chorus about to kick in, Mona shouted, "Okay everybody, in honor of Babs Martin Nichols, our dear Mom, grandmother and mother-in-law, I want everyone to link arms and sing along."

While there was momentary awkwardness as everybody linked arms and settled in, I was surprised that every one of us did, including the siblings, our kids and our spouses. That even included Milo, who was usually negative about anything that might prevent him from looking cool and aloof. For me, I was singing out of relief and celebration that the day went so well.

I looked at Brando. His top hat was at a jaunty angle, and he was waving his cane like a symphony conductor after a beer or three. Although he was singing at the top of his lungs, and off-key with the otherwise gorgeous harmonies, it in no way diminished the moment because that's what it usually sounded like in stadiums with everybody singing.

Brandi exchanged glances with Brando and chuckled, singing with less gusto than her brother, but still into it. I could see she enjoyed linking arms with Olivia and Milo.

She was happy because... well... she was always happy. It didn't take much, and I wished I were more like that.

Mona, the delicate little flaxen-haired beauty sang surprisingly well—holding the notes, blending perfectly with the harmonies and keeping us all on track during the song.

"Can you believe this song came on?" I shouted at Mona as we swayed.

"That was a special delivery from Mom," she grinned, quickly returning to the song.

I couldn't say for sure why Mona looked so happy, but I guessed that she had proved herself to be an impressive event leader and the key contributing member of the family on this day. And, for once, she wasn't the butt of endless millennial jokes. It made me think that we should stop being so hard on her.

I looked around at the family. The song had taken on new meaning—we were a rag-tag bunch of totally lost people who were only connected as a family by one tiny thread: Babs Martin Nichols. And yes, we were a curious collection, but we were still family. I couldn't explain why we acted up at family dinners—a bad habit, I suppose. But this song was reminding us that we were in this first family get-together without Mom, and hell, we were even having an enjoyable time. Who knew?

Whether Mona was right, and it was Mom's magic that had twiddled the knob to land on the perfect song, or it was a total coincidence, it didn't matter. It had served its purpose. Yet at the end of the song, I could swear I felt her presence and her message was clear to me: "Never lose hope." *Well done, Mom. Well done.*

Chapter 25

Mona

Mona noted the lovefest that had just brought the family together in blissful harmony had lasted only four minutes and forty-two seconds—the length of the song. With the spouses and kids sent home after a solid day's work, Courtney and the Brandies stayed behind to help clean up, return unsold items to the house and talk about the next steps with the estate.

Mona buzzed with energy. Shiva was passed out on her dog bed in the corner, happily worn out from a day of cuddles. Once everything was tidied, Mona served snacks and drinks in the living room. "Okay, you guys, given the outcome of the sale I'd like to discuss my next project which is to sell the smaller stash of more valuable items. I plan to put them online with the local marketplace, as well as other specialty online sellers."

"Sounds great, Mona," said Brando, tearing into a bag of nacho chips, dip and beer as if he was in an eating contest. His top hat had finally come off, and there was a band of sweat and flattened hair on the top of his head. His left eye looked a little tortured from sporting a monocle. "How long do you think it will take to sell the stuff?"

"No idea," Mona said. "You put them up for sale and someone could contact you in ten minutes, or you could wait ten months." She felt like she needed to manage expectations and set boundaries before things got rolling. "As you can imagine, it's hard work to research this stuff, post photos, run the ads, answer questions and make the sale. Then there's shipping."

"Agreed," Courtney said. "I had no inkling how much work this selling lark would be."

Mona smiled. "I'm glad to hear you say that, Courtney, because I would like to get a fee for doing this work." She could see Courtney and the Brandies wince. She decided to go in for the kill. "I'd like thirty percent of everything I sell."

"Oh please, Mona, we aren't charging for our time and we're all doing a lot of work," Brando said, shoveling in more nachos.

"And that work is...?" Mona said looking directly at him. She was prepared to wait this one out. She knew that Brando had barely lifted a finger until today, and even then, he focused on entertaining buyers. He did it well, but the sale would have done well with or without him. But she didn't want to spoil the moment.

"Well, there was this sale. We went out to the land, and we've attended endless meetings," he said, grabbing a group of tissues to wipe his forehead, then slam dunking the balled-up tissues into the garbage.

"Three," said Courtney.

Brando turned his head looking puzzled. "Three what, Queen Bea?"

"Meetings."

"That's all?" Brando looked surprised.

"And we all did," Mona added, looking directly at Brando. "What about you and Brandi?" She decided to let that simmer before negotiating. Brando took a swig of beer.

"Since nobody asked me, I thought I should remind you what I've done so far," Courtney said, pulling out her paperwork. She held up her estate task list and waved it at everyone. "I'm now at one hundred and sixty-two tasks and every day, new ones are added. Some things take ten minutes, other tasks take hours or days."

"Yeah, but you're the executor, Courtney," said Brando, with a look on his face that explained everything.

"Well, I wasn't planning to take an executor's fee, but maybe I will if we are going to base it on measured output."

Brando nudged Brandi. They shared a puzzled look. "What's an executor's fee?"

Courtney rustled around her bag and pulled out a copy of the will. "It's in here. I can claim up to five percent of the value of the estate for the executor's work I complete."

"For what?" said Brando. "You make a couple of calls and badger us into coming to meetings and that's going to net you ten to fifteen grand? I don't think so."

"Come on," barked Courtney, "it's a lot more work than that."

Brando turned to Mona. "And you are living at Mom's house rent-free. Now you want to skim thirty percent off the top. That leaves Brandi and me out of any compensation."

Mona could see the bear had been poked. "Now hang on, Brando. We're all getting money from the estate. But Courtney does have a time-consuming role and mine is too."

"Nope. We all have to agree on it, and we say no," Brando said sitting down.

Mona knew it was time for the trump card. "Fine. If you two want to take on this next phase, selling valuable antiques and you believe that no compensation is required, then go right ahead."

Brando looked up, his nostrils flaring. "And what will that bring in?"

Mona pointed to the cabinet full of items. "There are thirty-five items here, worth anywhere from eight to ten thousand if done right."

Brando and Brandi whispered briefly. "Looks like a lot of work to me."

Mona wanted to take the cane and give him a good smack upside the head. "Duh, that's why I want my fee." But she knew she had him. "On the positive side, that would raise most of what we need to pay off the property tax bill."

"Ten percent of the sales," he blurted out. "None of this thirty percent shit."

"Hang on," said Courtney. "We shouldn't have to pay Mona anything to help on the estate. Besides, it looks like Mom already gave you plenty of money."

Oh boy, thought Mona. She knew Courtney was just waiting to throw it in her face. "Stop it," she shot back.

The Brandies looked confused but leaned in closely. "What do you mean, Courtney?"

"Remember the mystery when I noticed somebody was withdrawing Mom's monthly pension the day after it was deposited?"

Mona adjusted herself in the soft easy chair. She wished she could sink deep into it and disappear. *Yet she had to fight back.* "That is totally irrelevant," she gasped.

"The hell it is," said Brando. "So let me get this straight: you were the one siphoning Mom's money out of her account. And even when Courtney raised it, you didn't own up?"

"I didn't 'steal' it," she said, using aggressive air quotes. "Mom offered me money to help me out. It was her choice and it all happened before she passed away."

"Yeah, well, you chipped away at our inheritance over two years," said Brando. "How much did you say it was per month, Courtney?"

Courtney flipped through the files and pulled out a paper. "Seven hundred and thirty-two dollars." She picked up her smartphone with her calculator. "Let's see... multiplied by twenty-four months... that's over seventeen thousand dollars."

"What?" the Brandies gasped. "That should be deducted from your share of the estate."

"No way," shouted Mona. "Mom was of sound mind when she chose to give me the money."

"I'm starting to wonder about that, Moan," sniped Brando.

"It is NOT part of the estate," she continued, "I have nothing to hide." She turned to Courtney, "Call Megan and she will confirm that."

Mona could see Courtney sigh.

"Mona's right," said Courtney. "We may not like it, but it was Mom's choice while she was alive. I will ask Megan. But Mona, what bothers me is that you hid it. If you were so sure, why wouldn't you own it back when I first raised it?"

Mona wiggled. "I figured you would judge me or argue about it."

"Got that right," said Brando.

"And now we have trust issues, Mona," added Courtney.

"Forget about the money I received from Mom," she said. "Let's move on. And I'm still taking a percentage of the online sales, or I'm not doing the work." Mona sat back and waited for them to puff and pant.

"We don't have much choice," said Courtney, looking at the twins.

Mona could tell by their irritated faces that she had won. For those three, money was everything—it was how they measured their success. Her winning that round, she knew, would irk them to no end. "Tell you what. I'm not an unreasonable person and not as obsessed about money, so I would agree to fifteen percent instead of thirty."

"Ten, not a percentage more," said Brando. The three sat quietly, glancing like anxious players at a poker game who weren't getting the signals. He gulped more beer and set the can down. "All those in favor of ten percent raise your hand."

Mona watched as Brando and Brandi slowly raised their hands in the air and eventually, Courtney added her hand as well.

"Motion carried. Got that, Queen Bea?" he sniped.

***

Mona almost smiled. Brando had played right into her hands. She had started with thirty percent to spark outrage, so his ten percent suggestion would look like a big win for him. But she wasn't done yet. "And I want to include the sugar bowl in my research, to find out if it's valuable," she said walking over to the cabinet and stepping on the ladder, knowing it wasn't there. She got to the top and opened the cabinet. "OMG, the sugar bowl isn't here!" she shouted.

Brando and Brandi jumped up and started looking furiously. "What the hell?" said Brando. "I wanted that sugar bowl! Did somebody sell it? I will personally pummel them."

Courtney looked up from her paperwork, startled, once she registered what Mona was saying. "Oh, hang on, I moved that for the estate sale," she said.

"Why would you do that?" Mona asked. "We agreed that nothing would be sold from this cabinet, and we taped it up."

Courtney blushed. "I worried someone might badger one of the kids to sell it for five bucks and then it's gone forever. I couldn't risk it," she added.

"Now we don't trust you, Courtney."

"That's ridiculous."

"Maybe. Maybe not. Where is it?" Mona asked.

"In the basement, for safekeeping."

"Oh, I get it," said Brando, now pacing the room. "You move it down to the basement and hope we don't notice, then let time go by. When we're not looking, you slip it out of the house unnoticed, and six months later act surprised that it's gone. And we would have all believed it was sold accidentally at the sale. Nice try."

"Brando, your top hat was on too tight today," shouted Courtney. "If I were trying to steal it, I would have pretended it had sold accidentally in the estate sale today."

"Still, it doesn't look good," said Brandi. "We all want the bowl, so we can't have someone trying to smuggle it out of the house."

"That's crazy talk," gasped Courtney. "Yes, I want it, but I wouldn't steal it. I'll get it—"

"No!" Mona and the Brandies cried.

"I will get it," said Mona, walking to the basement steps. "This is my home. I will keep it here, under lock and key until I do my research."

Mona could hear the outrage from Courtney and the Brandies at her calling it her home. Too bad. She couldn't afford to let Courtney take possession if it were valuable. Yet she couldn't even imagine what would happen if that were the case. How would they decide who got it? Up in the living room, the other three sounded busy digging their heels in. She walked under a beam in the basement and found the package on a shelf. After removing the paper, she held it up to the light and studied it, wishing she could remember what her mother said. Did it belong once to a prince or a pauper? She didn't have a clue.

As she walked up the stairs, she thought about the sugar bowl and the effect it was having on the siblings. While it wasn't the biggest estate ever, there could be thousands of dollars for each of them once the bills were paid, all to be divided equally. Yet all she could picture was the tension brewing over a sugar bowl that was not divisible by four. There would be one winner and three losers. And for different reasons, none of them appeared ready to back down.

Mona could picture a family bun fight in the works.

Chapter 26

Courtney

I was sitting on the bleachers at the school soccer game watching Ava play. The score was nil–nil, and the exhausted girls looked like they had just finished a marathon and were then asked to tack on a soccer game after they crossed the finish line.

My phone rang; normally I'd be glued to the game and send the call to voicemail. I checked the display and didn't recognize either the area code 867 or the number, so it was probably a telemarketer. But then I thought about all the messages I'd left about the estate. Since it was difficult to reach certain people and businesses, I decided to answer.

"Hello," I said, half watching the game and half waiting for a robot to start its scam.

"Courtney?" said a man's voice I didn't recognize.

"Yes, who's this?"

"Dad."

I froze. A short, sharp pain shot through my temple. If this was my birth father, I found Dad a very odd identifier. When I think of the word *Dad*, it sounds very informal, friendly and happy. He was none of these. And given that I hadn't spoken to him since the age of two, I had no desire for a tender father-and-daughter moment.

"Dad who?"

"Your father," he said, with a tinge of impatience.

My butt was tired of sitting on the bleacher for an hour, and my patience wearing thin. I decided to make him work harder. "No, I don't know. I need more detail," I said, taking a slug of water.

"It's your father. Dirk Martin."

"Oh, forgive me. The last time we met, I was two. You offered to go to the store for stuff and never came back."

"Yeah, well, that was over forty years ago. Things change."

My stomach started to curdle as if I'd just downed a glass of milk and realized it was sour. I refused to respond to that absurd statement. Was I supposed to just let bygones be bygones? I switched to official mode. "What can I do for you?"

"I heard your mother died."

"Uh, huh," I shot back. "I guess Aunt Eileen got in touch, eh?'

"Something like that," he said. "I'm sorry. How are you, Brando and Brandi holding up?"

"Look, Dirk," I said. "I know you don't give a rat's ass about your children. So how about telling me what you want." There was a long dangling pause and I refused to fill the space.

"Uhm," he started. "I loaned your mother money in the eighties after we split up. She was desperate and somehow tracked me down. It was five grand. I'm short of money now, so I'd like to get it back."

I stepped away from the game and walked towards the woods. "You've got to be kidding me," I said in a calm, yet aggressive tone.

"I'm in a bind and I need it back."

Now all the things that I swore I'd say to him if I ever got the chance welled up in my head. I didn't know where to start. Suddenly a gem popped into my head. "You know, I was at Mom's house the other day and guess what I found in her desk?"

"What?" he asked.

"I found a Hilroy scribbler started in 1979 and running until just before the millennium..."

"Okay...," he said, butting in.

"Let me finish," I lobbed back. "It noted the monthly alimony that you were supposed to pay Mom for twenty years, which you never did. Not a cent. And even if you did loan her five grand, which I highly doubt, it doesn't come close to what you owe her."

"I can explain."

"I have no interest in excuses. You hurt my mother terribly, you hurt your three children by not providing for them. You left her high and dry as a single mother, while you larked away your money in the Yukon on drinking, gambling and God knows what else." She had no proof for her accusations, but her Mom had told her stories. "So, Dirk. I'll make you an offer."

"What?"

"Although I don't believe for one second that you gave Mom money, I will pay back your 'loan' when you send us all the money you owe in alimony." I waited for the fallout.

"You're a ball-buster just like Babs," he shot back.

"I'll take that as a compliment. And really, all it means is that I'm strong enough to stand up to the likes of you." Now I was getting angry and knew I needed to calm down. "And if you have anything else to discuss, call our lawyer, Megan Blume. Her number is in the book."

He hung up before I had a chance to say anything else. That was good because I was just getting started. I turned my attention back to the game just in time for Ava's team to score a goal and end the stalemate. Thank God that had finally wrapped up.

I texted Brando because I knew he'd want to know about the call from our father and he'd update Brandi. Mona wouldn't care because she wasn't related to him. Brando was furious about the call, and we talked at a hundred miles an hour until we ran out of steam and calmed each other down. We even forgot the battle royale that was brewing over the sugar bowl. But that was Brando—a hothead one minute, then oblivious to the outburst five minutes later.

After I'd spoken to Brando, I sent Megan an email describing the call with my father, his demand, and my response. She said it was the right thing to send him to her for any further conversations. Great. Now I could return my attention to Mom's land being occupied, outstanding debts, taxes, a fraudulent cleaner and the tug-of-war over the family sugar bowl. Good times, indeed.

Chapter 27

Brando

After Courtney's call about their father attempting to squeeze the estate, Brando walked out to the patio with a beer. Every day brought something new, and he was fed up with the roller coaster around the estate stuff. He and Brandi had simple plans: they wanted their money, and they wanted the thing wrapped up, neither of which was happening. He was suspicious of Courtney who seemed to delight in dragging this whole thing out for as long as possible.

He couldn't figure out why she wanted the sugar bowl so much. He wondered if it was valuable and if she was just trying to pull it out from the other siblings for her gain. She seemed so attached to it that he immediately thought she was up to something. That's why he was going to hold tight, like a bulldog with a meaty bone and he'd instruct Brandi to do the same. Nobody was going to touch it.

Then there was the memorial service looming in a couple of weeks. He couldn't figure out how he'd get through it; the thought of it stressed him out. He knew it was important to say goodbye to their mother, but doing it made everything final. He hated the creepy funeral home, and it depressed him. If it were up to him, he'd take his mother's ashes to the nearby river with the family, and each could take a turn saying something about her. Then they could sprinkle some ashes along the shore. Instead, it was this big spectacle with a service, a retired minister and a bunch of people who loved to talk. After the service, they'd have to go to the burial plot and yak further. Courtney would be bossing everybody around—especially him—to make it perfect... for her. He wished he could call in sick.

Worse, there was nobody he could talk to, not even Brandi. While they were close, Brando knew she relied on him to be the big brother and pillar of support. That's what everybody expected, so he couldn't say anything that would make him look weak and helpless. He'd just have to soldier on and get through it.

Chapter 28

Courtney

I opened the door to the police station and said hello to everyone. Given the simmering problem with Doris and the Maud Lewis painting, I had cornered Cliff Murphy after the town's Chase the Ace fundraiser to ask him about my situation. He was the most senior officer, and he knew Doris. Briefly, I explained what had happened and asked if he could advise me on the next steps. Doris irritated me to no end for trying this on and I dreaded what it could cost us in lawyer fees to sort out. I was convinced she had no claim to the painting. I remembered from years ago, Mom saying it would be a great nest egg for her or "you kids."

"Hi, Courtney," said Crystal at reception. "Go right in, Cliff is waiting for you."

"Thanks." I realized everyone in this office knew what was going on; if not, they'd find out soon enough. I walked to Cliff's office and knocked lightly on the open door.

"Come on in, Courtney," he said, smiling. "Have a seat," he added, pulling out his spiral notebook and grabbing a pen. "Let's start at the beginning."

"I think Doris has tried to defraud us with the Maud Lewis. Mom left a few so-called 'knick-knacks' to Doris in her will, and a gift of two thousand dollars, which she's yet to receive," I said, pulling out the will in case he needed it. He scribbled quickly on the page.

"Keep going."

"The will said that Mom had placed yellow sticky notes on the figurines for Doris. Admittedly, I was a little slow getting around to delivering the items. I've been busy," I added, just so that he knew I was working hard on the estate. "A few weeks ago, Brando, Brandi, Mona and I were at Mom's house, getting ready for the estate sale."

"Okay," he said, flipping a page over.

"So—Doris comes to the door—"

"Did you invite her?"

"No, we were busy," I said. "Doris asks if she could have her items; she needs the money. I had checked with Megan, our lawyer, and she said it was okay to give her the figurines, but not the cash gift."

"Then what happened?"

"Doris goes to the china cabinet and pulls out the two figurines. I mentioned there were three for her. And she says, 'No, the other knick-knack is over there,' and points to the Maud Lewis painting. We nearly fainted. I told her she made a mistake. But she insists that she saw Babs put a sticker on there. She says, 'There's one way to find out,' and lifts the painting off the hook and turns it around for us to see."

"Did you give the painting to her that day?"

"No way," I said in a tone that may have sounded annoyed, as in, *How stupid do you think I am?* I calmed myself down. "I was clear: I told her there must be some mistake and I'd have to look into it."

"Okay, good. You haven't been swindled... yet," he noted. "That means we might be able to sort this out without taking legal action."

I knew Cliff was a calm officer who aimed to minimize confrontations. And I supported that idea unless it meant giving up the painting. "She immediately said that she watched Mom put the sticky on it, but I don't believe her. Something sounds weird."

Cliff wrote furiously. When he finished, he looked up and said, "I'd like to look at the area around your Mom's place. Can we do that?"

"Sure. I will let Mona know. She's now a tenant in Mom's house," I said.

"A tenant?"

"That's another story, but there's no crime, just family manipulation," I joked. He showed no response. I then texted Mona and she was fine with us dropping by.

***

When we got to Mom's house, we walked into the living room area. I showed him the china cabinet and he took pictures from every angle. Figurines were jammed in the cabinet, set on glass shelves with dust surrounding each one. On one shelf, two figurines were gone except for the dust outline. One was left.

"Is this the shelf that held the two figures that you gave to Doris?" Cliff asked.

"Yes," I said. "By the lack of dust on this shelf, it looks like they've been recently handled."

"Those were the most valuable figurines," said Mona. "I think that's why Mom gave them to her."

"But she didn't take the third one?" Cliff asked.

"No," I said, inspecting the shelf in question without touching anything. "There was a third sticky, but *I think* Doris moved it from the figurine over to the painting. Doris called it a knick-knack, but there's no way Mom would have used that term for a valuable painting. Nothing is adding up," I added.

Cliff wandered over to the painting, took some pictures, then put his gloves on. He lifted it off the wall and clicked pictures of the back. "Hmmm, there's a piece of Scotch tape on top of the sticky note."

"Yeah," I said. "Mom insisted on using bargain sticky notes that don't stick, so it doesn't surprise me."

Cliff snapped a close-up picture of the sticky note and the piece of tape. "There's a nice fingerprint on this piece of tape. Did Doris tell you Babs stuck it on there?"

"YES!" both Mona and I blurted in unison. "All four of us were here, and she said that," I added.

"Okay, this could be helpful," he said. "We have both Doris' and Babs' prints on file."

"Really?" My eyebrows shot up.

"A break and enter charge when they were eighteen."

Mona and I exchanged looks. She looked shocked, but I knew Mom had a history of minor offenses in her teens. "I vaguely remember her talking about that. It was revenge on some guy... what was his name...Rodney?"

Cliff smiled. "Yes, Rodney Hogan. They called him Hot Rod. But 'he done them wrong' as they say, so they went into his place, and let's say... redecorated. His house wasn't even locked, but Rodney wanted the book thrown at them."

"That Doris must have been a bad influence on Mom," I said, thinking about the trouble that bubbled up when Doris was around.

"Actually, Courtney, they were two peas in a pod, and they egged each other on. I don't like to speak ill of your Mom, but it's the truth. And in the bigger scheme of things, Doris isn't such a bad person. She's scammy but it's usually when she's low on cash," said Cliff.

"I get it. She's broke and angry about losing her friend," I said, worrying that he might be softening his attitude. "But it still doesn't excuse her from trying to pull off a heist."

Cliff nodded. "I understand, but nothing has happened yet. My goal is to clear this up without a big fuss. For now, there's a couple of important things to keep in mind."

"What's that?"

"First, nobody should handle this painting. We don't want any more fingerprints on it. Second, after I've done my work, you'll need to get this appraised. It will guide us on how to proceed."

"Okay," I said.

"One last thing, Courtney: I want to be with you when we meet the appraiser, in case I have questions."

That meant more estate money to be spent hiring a professional appraiser and another item on my to-do list. But I imagined we'd have to do that anyway if we were going to sell it.

"Got it. I'll be in touch as soon as I get an appraiser."

***

I discovered one of the foremost appraisers of Maud Lewis's work was Mr. Mansell in Halifax. He didn't seem like he had a first name. Due to his reputation, he was busy—so I had to wait to get the appraisal done. After Cliff finished his investigative work, I dropped the painting off in person at the Mansell Gallery. A few weeks later, Mr. Mansell called to set up a meeting for me and Cliff. Despite my pleading for news, he refused to release any information over the phone, so Cliff and I had to drive to the city.

Cliff and I found a parking spot a few streets away from the gallery and chatted non-stop on our walk over. On a busy street in Halifax, cars and motorcycles whizzed by and trucks rumbled along, in and out of potholes. When we stepped inside, the space was eerily quiet. A young couple stood in front of a large painting in the middle room, quietly discussing its merits. Mr. Mansell noted us out of the corner of his eye and nodded discreetly in our direction, indicating he'd be right with us. Cliff and I pretended to be looking at the artwork, but really, I had no idea what I was looking at.

Minutes later, the appraiser came over and shook our hands. Though it was a warm day, Mr. Mansell was decidedly old school: he wore a suit and tie, and leather shoes. He gave us his background and explained that he had authenticated hundreds of pieces in the last few decades. He and Cliff chatted lightly, but I wanted him to cut to the chase.

"Winter Sleigh Ride," Mr. Mansell said, smiling at the Lewis painting with happy bright colors, frosty whites, sky blues, and a red sleigh and barn, with evergreen trees on one side and a house in the distance. "Such a heart-warming subject, isn't it?" He put on his reading glasses and a pair of gloves.

I held my breath.

Finally, he turned to us and said, "I have good and bad news. What would you like first?"

"Good news," I said.

"Well, it's not a fake," he said, his tone saying there was more to the story.

"Okay," I said, heart pounding. Maybe it wasn't the most popular subject and would sell for less—everybody had their favorites. "What's the bad news?"

"It's not an original Maud Lewis painting. Rather, it's a silk-screen print from an original."

"What does that mean?"

"Back in the sixties and seventies, the owner of the Ten Mile House Gallery, Bill Ferguson, got permission from Maud and Everett to create silk-screen paintings of her artwork. He wanted to help Maud to earn a little more money." He paused briefly as if to let everything sink in before continuing.

"How were they created?" I asked.

He leaned his head sideways to get more detail from the painting. "It's an incredibly laborious process. A silk-screen artist had to paint each stencil, one layer at a time—and there were nine. Then they had to wait for each layer to dry. There were only a few hundred created, and they are as close as you can get to an original. As the prices of originals skyrocket to twenty, thirty, fifty thousand dollars, the silk-screen prints are becoming popular because they are more affordable."

I figured the word *affordable* must be the bad news. "I gather it's not worth as much."

He shook his head. "While they are collectible, they could sell anywhere from eight hundred to a couple of thousand dollars. It depends on who's interested, the price you are asking, the subject of the artwork and a variety of other factors."

Another blow for the estate, I thought, tearing up. We had just lost out on thirty to fifty thousand dollars. We stood around talking for another fifteen minutes, and Mr. Mansell described the market for silk-screens and the options for how we might go about selling it. He said he'd email an official appraisal and an invoice. I nodded, but nothing registered.

"That sucks," I said to Cliff after we left the gallery, knowing that our nest egg was not going to cure our bills and debts. It felt like we'd won on the estate sale, only to have the rug yanked out from under us on something else—exactly as Megan described.

On the way back to Danbyville, Cliff said he'd talk to Doris. I asked about the fingerprint on the Scotch tape. Then I cracked a joke that the painting might not be of interest to her now that it was only worth a grand.

"Well, it could be the litmus test for the case," said Cliff. "If she believes it belongs to her, she'll be outraged wanting to pursue it legally. If not, well... that will tell us something different."

"I'll call the Brandies and Mona to tell them the news." I dialed their numbers on conference call and linked them on speaker phone, describing the outcome of the meeting.

"Are you sure it's a fake?" Brando said, crackling through the phone. "I mean, does this clown actually know what he's talking about?"

"It's not a fake, Brando. If it were, it'd be worth zero. It's a silk-screen and it could be worth a thousand dollars or so."

"It ain't thirty grand," he said. "Thanks for getting our hopes up there, Courtney."

"It's not my fault. We all chose to believe it. Did Mom ever say it was an original, or did we assume it?" I said, my nerves on a low simmer with the accusations flying. "Mona, did she ever tell you?"

Mona coughed as if she were buying time. "She only ever called it 'the Maud Lewis.'"

"Well, another one bites the dust. Way to go, ladies." Brando said, hanging up. At least Brandi said goodbye before hanging up.

I didn't take it personally. It was a typical response from Brando when things didn't go his way. While I was upset too about the price the piece would fetch, it still wasn't over for me. I had lots of mopping up to do on this project, including trying to get Doris to grow up and stop trying to get something that didn't belong to her. On top of that, there was the memorial service for Mom. With tensions rising between siblings, that was the next situation that made me nervous.

Chapter 29

Mona

Mona's project to sell the premium items stumbled along. She had put her mother's valuables for sale online and with the local Buy and Sell. It was an exercise in dealing with flaky people who messaged but didn't show up, scammers who wanted her to mail items to a destination and then not pay her ("not my first rodeo," she'd reply) and tire kickers, *el cheapos* who wanted something for nothing. She had sold only four items and taken her percentage off the top. Life was easier since she no longer had rent to pay at her Mom's place. She hoped Courtney wouldn't put the place up for sale too soon.

Her mother's landline rang, and Mona jumped. Shiva woofed. The phone hadn't rung in a long time. She didn't know if she should pick it up or not; it was an old-school phone with no call display. After five rings, she lifted the receiver. "Hello?" she said, sounding frightened, as if someone was going to leap through the phoneline to get her.

"Mona?" A friendly voice belted out the greeting. She sounded like Mona's Mom, except with a voice like crushed gravel, as if she had just belted back a cocktail and smoked a carton of unfiltered cigarettes. It was her Mom's sister, Darlene, who lived in Cape Breton. Darlene was also into buy, trade and sell stuff, but it was mostly cheap crap because "that's what people buy around here," as she described it.

Mona remembered long conversations her Mom and her sister used to have on the phone. When Babs heard Darlene's voice, she'd tell her to hang on while she poured herself a rum and coke and then she'd climb into the easy chair. They'd talk forever, laughing, swapping stories and egging each other on. Mona knew how much they both treasured those calls.

"Hi, Aunt Darlene," Mona said, her spirits lifting. "It's good to hear your voice." Her aunt always made her laugh. Mona and her parents had only visited a few times because Cape Breton was a five-hour drive away, and it was a hard trip to fit in. Mom would only go if she could stay long enough to make it worth her while. Aunt Darlene was usually dealing with health issues and couldn't travel much.

"You too, Mona," she said, a little wistfully and then paused. "By the Jesus, I sure miss your Mom."

"Me too. So, how are you?"

"Good, dear, good," Darlene said in a Cape Breton accent. Even though she grew up in Danbyville, she'd run off and gotten married when she was eighteen and had lived in Cape Breton since then. "I hope to come to your mother's service."

"Really? That would be awesome. When will you know for sure?"

"As soon as I hear from Mickey and Minnie," said Darlene.

"Wait, is Mickey a man or a mouse?"

"Good one, darlin'," she laughed. "We get so used to nicknames that we forget they sound funny beyond the island. Mickey got his name for his habit of carrying a mickey of rum in high school. Then he met Margie. She was short and tiny back then, so everybody started calling them Mickey and Minnie, and it stuck."

"Well, the service is coming up, so I hope Mickey can do the drive."

"Me too. But listen, hon, it's a long shot. He's got big lung problems—they're filled with fluid, so he's wheezing and coughing up—"

"Yeah, Mom told me," said Mona, cutting in before Darlene could finish her sentence. In her Mom's family, who were all a certain age and older, they didn't "mansplain," they "medsplained"—that pathological need to describe every single medical issue that afflicted all family, friends and neighbors. And no matter where they started on the body—whether it was a blocked carotid artery, a burst appendix, or gout in the left toe—they always ended up idling at the intersection of the upper and lower intestine. It grossed out Mona and her Dad. She recalled her father's face souring as he tried to enjoy an evening snack while Babs gabbed with her sister two feet away.

"Anyhoo," said Darlene. "How's that crazy brother of yours?"

"Brando is good," Mona said. She hoped Darlene wasn't looking for an update because she didn't have anything.

"He's some funny, eh?"

"He's a joke alright," Mona said, wondering if her aunt would notice that she had just insulted him. In Darlene's eyes, he was the golden boy who could do no wrong.

"Tell him I said he'd better do that stand-up comedy sketch about how to fart at a family gathering and blame the dog," she said, laughing with her scratchy throat. "He's been talking about it for years. I think he'd be a real hit on amateur night at the Chuckles Club in Halifax."

Don't encourage him, Mona wanted to say, but figured if her aunt liked his material that much, she shouldn't sound negative. "I think he's still practicing his sketch on the family. He needs to get it perfect before he goes for the big time."

"Right on. He needs to keep working on his material. I won't keep you, my dear, and I'll let you know a couple of days before if I can come."

"I sure hope so, Aunt Darlene. We'd all love to see you." She hung up the phone. It felt weird to hear someone sound so much like her mom. While she was happy at the thought of her aunt attending her mother's service, she also liked the idea because Darlene might have insight into the items she was trying to sell.

Chapter 30

Courtney

When I saw Cliff Murphy's number on the call display, I was both happy *and* worried. He had interviewed Doris about the Maud Lewis piece—and Doris had either admitted to her con game, or we were going to war.

"Hey, Cliff," I said trying to sound upbeat. "How did your meeting go with Doris?"

"Well, I pushed hard on specifics about who placed the sticky note on the Maud Lewis. Once she repeated the story, I pointed out the inconsistencies with her first version from weeks earlier—and the consequences of lying. And for the punchline, I reminded her that we have both her and your Mom's fingerprints on file from their antics years ago," he said.

I knew Doris, and she was as stubborn as they got. So, I was bracing myself for the worst. "What was her response?"

"She could have won a bicycle race she was backpedaling so fast."

That was music to my ears. "So, what do we do?"

"That depends on you and your siblings. She did try to steal from the estate and wasted everybody's time and energy."

"I know—we had to make a special trip together to the gallery in Halifax. That took a whole day."

Cliff snickered. "Well... I also picked up my auto parts on the way. Plus, we ate at The Chickenburger and played a tune on the jukebox, so it was a fun day for me."

"I'm glad somebody had a grand day out," I joked. "I had to take time off work. So, what's next?"

"I told Doris, now that she's admitted to it, your family could take action against her. What are your plans?"

I could hear Cliff clicking his pen waiting for my response. "Did she show any remorse?"

"Between you and me, she cried. She said she was finding it hard to earn enough money to live on. She also felt disrespected by you and your siblings when she tried to pick up her items. And she's angry about her lot in life while you guys have so much."

I felt sorry for Doris, even though I wanted to throttle her. I knew if I asked the Brandies, they'd want to take action. Mona might have a different response. While they didn't get along, Mona had a soft heart, and she appreciated that Doris and Mom were best friends.

"What would you recommend, Cliff?"

He paused. "Given that the painting was only worth a fraction of what you thought and the fact that she's broke and scared, I'd like to cut her some slack. But it's up to you."

I thought about Mom and knew exactly what she would have done. She would have torn a strip off Doris and made her apologize—then she would have forgiven her. While it wasn't our fault Doris was broke, she was a good friend who would have done anything for Mom. "Well, if she promises not to try any more shenanigans, we can end this now."

"Good on you, Courtney," he said. "My goal is to settle things before everybody gets all riled up and wants to prove a point. Keep in mind, that she's just trying to stumble through life like the rest of us. I'll tell her the good news."

"Thanks, Cliff," I said, hanging up. I checked it off my list and entered the fifteen-minute call into my time app. I had already racked up ten hours with Doris, Cliff and paperwork. So, who knows how long I would have spent on it if we had "tried to prove a point," like Cliff said. Frankly, it was a relief to close this chapter.

I decided I'd tell the others that it got settled and leave it at that. I felt bad for being so short with Doris when she tried to pick up her items—Mom would not have been impressed. I committed to getting the gift to Doris as soon as I could, even if I had to loan her the money.

Chapter 31

Brando

With only a week to go before their mother's service, Brando's stress level edged upward. He found himself zoning out at work and meetings, thinking about his life, his Mom and other details that were swirling around him. He was standing at the golf course with his workmates, yet his head was elsewhere. Aside from not sleeping well, he had awoken from a dream this morning, and couldn't shake it, even though it was now afternoon. He rarely remembered dreams, yet when he did, they were so stupid, he couldn't tell anyone about them.

The latest was a recurring dream about his mother's memorial service. He was standing in the creepy funeral home and there was a bulging piñata full of weighty items following him wherever he walked. He was blindfolded and waving the piñata stick like a madman, knowing that it was ready to burst and land on his head.

"Your turn, Buddy," said Jeffrey, giving Brando a nudge with his golf club. "Time to hit your ball into the sand trap."

"Or maybe into the woods," said Conrad. "You remember how our golf coach told us to visualize before hitting."

"Thanks for nothing, Big Con," Brando quipped. Not exactly his finest searing comeback, but for some reason he didn't have the energy to think of anything better. He worried about what was happening to him lately. Here he was on a premium golf course by the ocean, having a perfectly fun time for being "at work." There was no reason to feel anything but lucky to have his job. Yet he kept flashing back to times in his life when he was mean or unreasonable about his mother.

Sports were a sore point with him from his youth. He was told constantly by teachers that he was a natural athlete, which was good because he wasn't academically inclined. He loved all kinds of sports, except his mother couldn't afford to pay for gear or registration fees. That led to arguments with his mother and later, feelings of sadness or guilt about things he had done.

Brando's first strong memory was from when he was in elementary school. He remembered bounding home from school, telling his Mom about a new hockey league for kids and announcing he wanted to play. He'd talked about it non-stop for weeks and couldn't understand why she didn't say much in response. *Shouldn't a mother be encouraging her son to play sports?*

A few weeks later when his nagging didn't stop, she sat down and explained hockey was a sport for well-off people, not them. Aside from the cost of registration, she explained, there was weekly travel, plus food and lodging on the road. And there was expensive gear and skates, which he'd grow out of in a year, and she'd have to start all over again. His Mom finished by saying that she was terribly sorry, but she couldn't afford it. His reply? "Not good enough, Mom! Every kid except me gets to play. It's not fair." Then he stomped off and didn't speak to his family for days. He was so fed up with not having a two-parent household with enough money to play sports. He swore he'd never get into that position when he was an adult.

The next few evenings, he heard her making calls and whispering in hushed tones, changing the subject when he entered the room. He pretended not to notice, but he knew it involved him—and at that age, it usually meant something embarrassing.

When he came home from school the next day, she proudly showed him a carrying bag with mismatched, second-hand gear and a pair of bashed-up skates. It looked like a sale bin at the charity shop. Horror rippled through his system. The thought of playing hockey with kids and wearing their cast-offs was too much. The teasing would be endless.

Beaming, she rattled on about the kind-hearted hockey coach offering to pay for registration, and he said Brando could travel with his family to games. She went on and on, and when she finally stopped for a breath, she sprung her arms wide in triumph. Instead of thanking and hugging her, he walked out of the house slamming every door he could, some of them twice. As he brushed past her, he could see shock on her face and tears trickling down. The memory was almost physical as if he were receiving a fresh sucker punch directly to the stomach. For such a stalwart woman, rarely had he seen his mother shed a tear. She had barely cried when he accidentally closed the car door on her hand earlier that summer. Yet, decades later he still felt the shame as if he'd accepted discarded gear from neighbors.

What he had learned from the deep poverty they lived daily was that embarrassment was a brief blush of discomfort for doing something that made him look silly or even stupid. Shame was another level up. It was full-on humiliation baked right into every cell of his body—and that's what he couldn't deal with at the hockey arena. People stared at him with pity that his mother couldn't even buy him a round of new gear that didn't smell like Jordy Hansen's armpits. The fact that he was in a family with a single mother who was constantly broke and two steps shy of bankruptcy, dogged him. As an adult, he never bought second-hand items. It had to be new or nothing.

While he had never considered his mother's feelings before, he started thinking about what it must have been like for her, not being able to provide any extras for her kids. She felt shame too, but for different reasons. Brando wondered what it would feel like to tell DeeDee that she couldn't have something that she deeply desired. Of course, in response to his childhood, he had never turned down a single request from his daughter. And she acted like an entitled kid, barely acknowledging his generosity, often ignoring what he bought her as if it didn't quite meet her picky little standards. She too, was ungrateful but only because she got everything she ever asked for. How did it all work with kids?

Then he remembered a lengthy inventory of minor stupid things he'd done, or more importantly, not done. As an adult, he rarely returned his mother's voicemail messages, and when he'd finally call or visit, she acted excited, as if he hadn't behaved like a jerk. There were tasks she asked him to do like fixing the remote control ("Jesus, how many times do I have to fix this?" he'd complain as he untangled the digital mess). "Jesus has nothing to do with it," she'd joke back, which only made him fume until she'd finally apologize for being hopeless with the remote.

It didn't stop there: there were also sticky windows, a lawn to mow and clotheslines to repair. Things he scribbled on his palm, but never quite got around to doing. She'd end up asking a neighbor for help. What was his problem? He thought about it and decided that he was truly a terrible son.

That's why, when he saw the sugar bowl, he realized how important it was to him. It brought back the good times with his mother when she was happy singing to them all and doing something she could afford (what's a little brown sugar?) and showing her unconditional love. Yes, Courtney brought up the sugar bowl first, but he would have gone there eventually, so it was no big deal that she was first. He was surprised that Brandi showed interest in it; usually, she backed off when Brando wanted something. That's why he loved her way more than Courtney, and well, Mona barely got a like from him. Besides, he knew Mona only wanted the bowl in case it was valuable. He could tell she had to make up a song when they were talking about it. She could easily be eliminated from the discussion, and he knew he could persuade Brandi to take something else. What it meant was a battle with Courtney, who would never back down from a brawl with him. She would *not* get that sugar bowl.

"Dude, wake up!" Con gave him another nudge. "Gotta reel you in, Buddy," he said, pretending he was holding a fishing line and bringing in a gigantic fish.

Brando jolted back to the golf game in progress. He normally enjoyed his friends Jeffrey and Conrad, who had been clients and friends for years. In the summer, they booked monthly games on a Friday to wind down the week and spent most of their time exchanging insults with each other.

He stumbled through the rest of the game but couldn't wait to finish. His mind was on the bigger things about to unfold in his life. Yet there was one thing he knew for sure: he had to have that sugar bowl.

Chapter 32

Brandi

The week ahead loomed large for Brandi. She knew Brando was tense about the funeral service for their Mom, and she was nervous too. While Courtney was the obvious choice as executor and organizer of the service, that didn't mean Brandi enjoyed working with her. All that meant to Brandi was that Courtney was bossing them around even more than usual. She spent half her time rhyming off the number of things on the estate to-do list and calculating the time it took. It was hard to imagine the work on the estate consumed as much time as Courtney described. Wasn't it just a bunch of form-filling? She and Brando wondered if Courtney was actually working that hard, and they figured she'd complain whether it was hard work or not.

Part of the problem with Courtney in charge and their mother not around was the shaky dynamic in the family and recurring childhood roles that continued for years. Technically, becoming adults should have brought their old roles to a screeching halt. Yet they all seemed locked into their assigned behaviors. Habits were hard to change. It's like each person behaved one way in their households, then reverted into immature siblings at family events.

Growing up, Brandi had always watched from a distance, with Courtney and Brando at loggerheads. They both complained they had the worst lot in life, and they were wildly competitive about getting Mom's attention. When they were kids, Courtney got the attention because she was the oldest girl. Brando got more attention because he was the only boy and while their Mom didn't say it, they all knew he was the golden boy—which allowed him to get away with more things. Meanwhile, Brandi saw herself as the filler in the middle of a sibling sandwich. It was assumed that she would side with Brando, so that's what she did. Nobody ever thought to ask her opinion and the few times she tried to speak up, she was shut down. That summed up the frustrating life of a middle child with nowhere to go in the family pecking order.

Then when Mona arrived on the scene, twelve years later, she assumed the role of the youngest and most spoiled child. Based on her place in the family pecking order, Brandi felt like she was the "nothing-est." She also couldn't join in any conversations with Courtney and Brando squabbling; they took all the oxygen in the room. Their Mom was always so tired of prying apart the warriors. During those times, Brandi felt like she shouldn't bother her mother with her own needs. She understood it was a big relief for her Mom not to have to worry about Brandi—in fact, she remarked how much she appreciated her little girl's calm demeanor. That short-circuited Brandi wanting to act up; it would have been odd to behave like the others. She never had the chance to sound bossy, cranky, or demanding because she didn't own that role. Still, she spent many nights replaying scenarios of how she should have responded to the others but lacked the courage to do so.

She had continued in her selfless role with Milo, as the supporter, while he and his daughter Olivia got settled in Canada as refugees. She also helped him to launch his career as an artist. He had arrived broken and penniless from a war-torn part of Eastern Europe and refused to talk about it. His first wife, also an artist, had died in the war, and he was left to look after Olivia.

Brandi had met him when she was training in hotel hospitality in Halifax, and he was staying at the hotel where she was working. She went the extra step for him and Olivia several times, and suddenly romance blossomed. Brandi was never sure if he really loved her, or if she had simply arrived at a time in his life when he needed stability. They traveled in such different worlds. He'd been a successful artist in Europe. She knew nothing about art but fell madly in love with him and scrambled to learn about it. She never really felt comfortable in galleries and at exhibitions the way he and Olivia did; they came across as a bit snobby and stand-offish. Brandi felt awkward—she felt like she was either overly friendly or trying too hard to fit into that world. Sometimes she wondered what they even had in common.

The unifying fear they shared was a lack of abundance. During childhood, her family was perpetually broke. As an adult, she vowed to never suffer from poverty again. He had everything before the war: fame, money, and opportunities to travel. Then they lost it all—and when he came to Canada, he swore he'd become a successful artist again. When Brandi and Milo met, they recognized their mutual fear of having nothing. Together, they worked hard to create a prosperous life. Yet she had given up much to be with him. She wanted children, but from the get-go he said he didn't want any more. Olivia was enough—and based on her strong personality, she understood why. Brandi wondered if he had even wanted a child; perhaps it was his wife's dream, not his. But she never dared ask that question. What was done, was done. Still, his refusal to have more children left her feeling a bit empty in her life, though she did her best to bring Olivia up as her own.

After Brandi's Mom died, she started thinking about her life, where she was going and her level of general happiness. She had never dared to consider whether she was happy in life or not; she simply did what she needed to do. As a result, she assumed she was happy and *acted* that way. Now she wondered if she was just so good at acting that she believed it herself.

Those thoughts snuck into her head here and there, and she didn't know how to deal with them. She had nobody to talk to. Yes, she had friends, but they were based on school activities and volunteer work. She had built her social life around her family and doing what they wanted.

Milo was always around successful artists, and lately, Brandi started to question what he saw in her. When she asked him, he sighed and shot her a "What kind of stupid question is that?" look. Then he replied, "You are my rock. I'm around people who gravitate towards artists, but it's just a show. They'll move on to newer and more exciting artists because it's not about me. With you, I feel safe and secure."

That was a relief to her because she didn't feel the least bit artsy. She felt like an imposter. Deep inside, she was just a plain Jane, a small-town girl from Danbyville who was more comfortable in her snug jeans with heels, a sweater, and a ponytail held in place with her favorite scrunchie—she still had a case full of scrunchies that her Mom had given her on her fifteenth birthday which she cherished. Maybe she could wear this outfit to the next exhibition and pretend she was being ironic. Scrunchies were considered tacky, so she might just pull it off.

Something else had changed when her Mom passed away—Brandi no longer wanted to be the perfect child who never made a fuss. Now she could be anything. She wanted to establish boundaries. And for once in her life, she wanted to be heard—even demanding about what she wanted. She was sick of being the "good sport" and coming last in every family situation.

The sugar bowl was her chance. She wasn't about to let her interest drop just because the others all wanted the same thing. She was even willing to take on Brando. Since he'd gotten his way for his entire life, she hoped that Brando would step aside to make his twin sister happy. While she'd love the sugar bowl to be valuable, she was more interested in being the one to own it. That would freak everybody out because she'd be the last person anyone expected to walk away with the family's crown jewel. And that's exactly why she would fight for it.

Chapter 33

Courtney

My phone buzzed. The call display was *Pet Vet*, which meant Tim Robinson was on the line. To help Mom out, I'd taken Fluffy there for shots, so we were used to working together.

"Hi, Tim, how's it going?"

There was a pause. "Well, I'm not sure." He paused again.

My heart fluttered. "Is Fluffy okay?

"Yes, she is. But something weird is going on. I don't know where to start."

Tim was a brilliant and gentle vet who worked miracles with all creatures. From our school days, I knew people were more of a challenge to him than his beloved patients.

"How about at the beginning, Tim?"

Tim cleared his throat. "Brando came by this morning with Fluffy in a carrier. He was in quite a state of agitation. He wanted to see me. I was with a client, so Erma tried to help him. He told her he wanted me to 'take care of Fluffy.' When she asked for details, he said, 'Tim will know,' and left the clinic."

I couldn't imagine what was wrong with Fluffy. She was fine when I took her to Brando's. "Then what, Tim?"

"I tried to call a bunch of times, but he wouldn't take my call. Finally, he texted me and instructed me to put Fluffy down."

"What?" I croaked. *What the hell is Brando up to?*

"I was shocked because she's a healthy three-year-old cat. I told him, first of all, I wouldn't do anything until he came into the clinic."

Thank heavens Tim is sensible. A wave of fear swept my body. "Did he come in?"

"Yes. He told me that Babs requested in her will that Fluffy be buried with her."

"She what? Oh my God, Tim. Of course, she didn't."

"That's what I thought. I said I found that hard to believe. She loved Fluffy. Besides, I told him, we don't just put a pet down. When a cat is perfectly healthy, we pursue options like putting them up for adoption, or getting help from the animal shelter."

"He said that I should ask you because as executor, you stiffed him with a job he didn't want to do, but it was in the will. What's going on, Courtney?"

I could barely catch my breath and blurted, "He totally misunderstood. What Mom said was, 'When the time comes, I'd like Fluffy to be buried with me.' She meant that when Fluffy passes away, she wants the cat to be added to her gravesite. In fact, I was going to call you to ask about how long cats live on average, so I can calculate how much money to put aside for her ongoing care and her passing."

"That's a relief, Courtney. I guess it was all a big mis-understanding. But he was pretty wound up, so I said I'd talk to you. I didn't want to get into a tussle with him. Remember grade school?"

"Yes, I know he bullied you a bit."

"A lot."

I thought back to grade four when Brando was going through an angry phase and he had picked on a few kids, including Tim, who wasn't built for fighting. "I know, Tim. He gave you a wedgie, didn't he?" I said, trying to sound sympathetic.

"A Super Wedgie, actually."

"Right," I said, restraining an inappropriate laugh be-cause I was freaked out about the cat and Tim was clar-ifying Brando's bullying tactics from grade four. *Lordy.* "Okay, Tim. Don't do a thing; one of us will be over to pick up Fluffy. And I assure you, she will be looked after with great love and respect."

"That brings me great comfort," Tim said.

I hung up, my body buzzing. It was noon; I announced to my boss I was heading out for lunch. I jumped into the car and drove by Brando's office just as he was coming out. He looked exhausted and angry. But so was I. When his colleagues saw us facing each other, they said hi quickly and jumped into a car.

"Tim just called me. What the hell, Brando?"

"What do you mean?" he barked.

"He said you tried to have Fluffy put down."

"I did exactly what you told me to do."

Feeling dizzy, I grasped the edge of the car. I needed to hear his interpretation of what I said. "Which was what, Brando?"

"You know.... like Mom said in her will," he said.

"What do you think I asked you?" I said, gasping for breath and trying to sound calm.

Brando shifted slightly; he kicked the dirt. "You know... 'take care of her.'" he said with air quotes.

"*Sweet Jesus,* Brando. I asked you to take care of her pet Fluffy—as in feed her, provide shelter, play with her, and love her. What did you think I meant?"

"Bury her with Mom's ashes," he said with diminishing confidence.

"We're not a crime family. I didn't order a hit on Fluffy!"

Shock rippled across Brando's face, as if the instructions had been crystal clear to him right up to that point, but now he had the sinking feeling he had screwed up. "I guess I mixed up what Mom meant."

"You idiot!" I shrieked. "Why do you think I offered you a year's supply of premium cat food?"

He shrugged. "I kind of wondered about that."

I wanted to pound him senseless, but that wouldn't help anything. "So, did it not occur to you to question or clarify anything that seemed odd to you?"

"I could say the same to you," he shot back.

"Here's the thing, dude—it was always clear to me that someone had to adopt and look after Fluffy. You were the only person in the family who could do that task right now—Jake is allergic, Mona has Shiva and Brandi has Bastet. Do you get that?"

"I do now."

"So, are you willing to adopt Fluffy, as in keeping her alive with food, shelter, love and attention?"

"Yes, that was always my preference."

I sighed. There was no point rehashing things; it was mop-up time. "Listen, can we call a truce? I'm sorry it wasn't clear to you and whatever I did or didn't do to make it obvious."

He nodded.

"From now on, let's agree that we will both ask questions if either one of us isn't sure about something. Deal, Buddy?"

"Yup," he said, barely looking at me. "And I would appreciate it if you don't mention this to Brandi and Mona."

I was surprised he raised it, but then again, if I had nearly done something that stupid, I wouldn't want others to know about it. "All righty," I said, looking at my watch, trying to move things along. "I'll call Tim. I already told him there was a misunderstanding. Can you pick up Fluffy later today at Tim's? If there is a bill for the vet time, we will pay it out of the estate."

"Got it. Pick up Fluffy from the vet. Love and care for her. We done?" he said, confirming that he had got the instructions right.

"Right, thanks. See you later."

Without a word, he turned and walked toward the office.

Chapter 34

Courtney

With the Fluffy debacle behind us, I could now turn my attention to Mom's service. In between loading the dishwasher and popping the muffins in the oven for Ava's bake sale at school, I grabbed a coffee and stood at the kitchen island to plan my day. Each day, the list for the estate mushroomed with a lengthy list of short tasks and bigger projects which then multiplied into more work. I started jotting and in fifteen minutes, I had scribbled enough items to feel discouraged. But then my learnings from the time management workshop kicked in: start by taking three deep breaths (check), then list everything you can think of including small wins. Label them one of four ways: urgent and important; not urgent but important; not important, but urgent; and finally, not important and not urgent. I took it one step further by highlighting in yellow the ones that were important and urgent.

1. Funeral service for Mom. Make sure Mom is honored properly. Avoid turning the whole thing into a circus.

2. Estate sale, follow-up. Sell remaining items, give away unsold items and pay down debts. Find out how Mona is doing with the sales of Mom's items.

3. Prepare all the estate documents for probate and pay probate tax.

4. Do Mom's personal and business taxes.

5. Finish all the paperwork with Doris and her attempts to steal our inheritance!

6. Figure out how to pay the property taxes. Get Mona to agree to sell the land. Ask the Santos family to move on.

7. Find a ten-foot pole and pry Mona out of Mom's house.

8. GET THE SUGAR BOWL, come hell or high water.

I had just started the list when my cell rang. It was the funeral home, and since it was just after eight in the morning, I figured something needed fixing. "Hello, this is Courtney."

"Hi," said the gentle voice. "This is Vera McIsaac. From McIsaac's Funeral Home."

Yup, got it. I had no idea why she did that every time she called; it was like a nervous tick as if I wouldn't remember she was from the funeral home. "Hi, Vera, what's up?"

"Well, we've got a bit of a complication," she said, then stopped.

That was the other thing I found annoying about her. Not only was she introducing something that didn't sound good, but she also presented every sentence individually, then paused. And I had to coax her to continue. "What's going on?"

"Our air conditioner broke down today."

Sigh. "Okay, so are you going to call Benny's Heating and Cooling to get it fixed?"

"I did. But the problem is that he has to order a part."

Duh. "And what does that mean for us?"

"There are supply chain issues because of Covid. We won't get the part for six weeks," she said.

"Well, that sucks," I said, unable to hold back my frustration. All I could think about was the warm and muggy weekend in the forecast. I could picture everybody puffing and panting indoors in the sweltering afternoon temperature. Nova Scotia was getting hotter each summer, and we weren't used to super hot and muggy days.

"I just wanted to tell you in advance," she said. "We try to avoid surprises. You have enough on your mind."

Got that right. It wasn't her fault, but it was still annoying. I was so tired of hearing about the fallout from Covid. It had slowed down, changed, or ruined everything for the past year. I wondered if Whispering Pines could take us at the last minute. It would mean more money, dozens of phone calls to alert people and endless tasks, but it could work.

"I called Whispering Pines," she said.

It was like she read my mind, but I suppose it was the logical next step in a one-horse town with only two funeral homes. "And?"

"They have a service on Saturday."

"Well, it is what it is."

"My sincere apologies. The good news is that we have two large ceiling fans in the service room. It will help," she said.

Sure, two fans moving air that feels like an industrial furnace blowing around hot air in an enclosed space. I glanced at my watch; I was now running five minutes late.

"Thanks for letting me know, Vera. We'll just have to muddle through. I mean, the service is only about half an hour. How hard can that be?" I hung up and jotted down that I now needed to update the siblings. But right now, there were kids to be ferried to school activities.

***

"This is all your fault," said Brando.

"That the funeral home has a broken air conditioner?" I looked to Mona and Brandi to help me out. I had cornered the Brandies at the school parking and flagged down Mona who happened to be cycling by. Mona pretended to be interested but was checking her texts. Brandi had one eye on the conversation, the other on Milo who was at the soccer field watching Olivia release her frustrations on an unsuspecting soccer ball.

"I wanted to go with Whispering Pines," said Brando.

"No," I said, flipping through my notebook until I found the highlighted note for the funeral home. "You said Jack Bilby was a jerk who didn't return your calls."

"No need to get into a big blame game, Queen Bea," said Brando. "Let's focus on solutions here, instead of regrinding the past."

That's only when you are wrong about something, otherwise you'd drive it into the ground. "Okay, so we'll stick with the plan as is at McIsaac's?" I asked all who barely managed to hang in for the conversation. "Can you show me a sign?" Finally, the three of them nodded, which I jotted down, only to get a scowl from Brando for doing so.

"That it?" said Brando.

That was becoming Brando's favorite question. Given how hard it was to gather everybody, I figured I might as well ask for more. "Since the service is on Saturday, can we do a check-in to make sure everything is okay?"

"Yup. Nothing new to report," said Brando.

"Do you have the ashes all sorted out?"

Brando kicked the dirt. "Why do you ask something like that? It's just insulting."

I could see Brando and Mona exchange glances, which made me wonder what was up. "Sorry, Bud, but it's a big day and I want everything to go well." I turned to Mona, "It's going to be super hot on Saturday, so I hope you have arrangements for Shiva to stay at Mom's home in the cooler air." I added our mother's name in there to remind Mona she didn't own the house, even though she certainly made herself at home there.

"My girlfriend Rochella is going to look after Shiva for the day," said Mona, her voice pinched. "Don't worry, it's all under control."

"And the catering is confirmed," said Brandi. They are dropping it off just before the service to minimize the amount of time it's out on the tables."

"Great, thanks. And here's my update," I said, taking a breath to carry on, even though nobody looked the least bit interested. "So, I checked back with the minister; he's all set for the service at the funeral home and the gravesite. We have about thirty guests who have mentioned they're coming, as well as Aunt Darlene."

"Aunt Darlene's coming?" Brando suddenly perked up. "Right on. Love that old doll."

Of course you do; she idolizes you. "Yes, as long as her ride materializes."

"Well, keep me posted. I'd go pick her up in Cape Breton if need be. She's Mom's closest relative and friend."

I was surprised by Brando's willingness to step up. "Great, thank you, Brando. I will let her know that. She'll be delighted."

"Guess I better stock up on dope for her; she likes to toke. And she can't afford to buy it, so I will treat her."

"Okay, so the service is at two, can everybody be there by one?" I looked around; everybody looked morose. "There's a special room for family at the back. We gather there first."

"Sure, Queen Bea," said Brando. "I'd love to take an indoor sauna for an hour before the service."

I knew if I said thirty minutes, they'd aim for fifteen. "Well, do your best, please. This is important for Mom."

"Got it. I'm out of here," he said lifting his coffee mug in a toast. Mona shouted, "See ya!" as she jumped on her bike and took off, while Brandi returned to the soccer match on the field.

"Right, see you all. Have a nice day," I said to thin air. I knew the drill. When Brando was asked to do something and sounded agreeable, I knew he had no intention of doing it. Some days it was hard to be a serious adult, but I had a job to do for my mother and nothing would stop me.

Chapter 35

Mona

Saturday morning. Mona thought about the day ahead of her. The sun blasted through the light curtains in the bedroom window, boosting the temperature in the room. Fever gripped her as she struggled to wake herself up. She placed her hand on her forehead and dabbed the sweat with her sheets. Her lips were parched as if she had fallen asleep outside in the sun.

She felt a shift under the sheets and noticed that Shiva had joined her for an early morning snuggle, on the left side of her body. Waking up to a warm pooch worked wonders in the winter, but clearly, Shiva hadn't learned to ease up in the summer. To the dog, more heat was better. Mona leaned over and gulped a glass of tepid water on the nightstand, then laid back on the pillow to wake herself up.

It was the day of her mother's service, and Mona couldn't have felt worse. Her night was a patchwork of tossing, waking, listening to sleep music and crazy dreaming. She felt disoriented and covered her head with the sheet as if it would help to make the looming day disappear. Shiva, who had waited patiently to go outside three hours earlier, was now pacing. Mona groaned and slapped on a T-shirt and shorts. "Let's go, Shiva," she said, trying to sound upbeat. Shiva licked her hand but as soon as she noticed Mona moving, she bolted towards the door. Mona sat on a lawn chair near the door, letting Shiva run rampant in exchange for behaving so well while she slept.

Mona picked up her phone; texts were piling up. It was only 10 a.m., but she could tell it was going to be a long and tortuous day. In her mind, she reviewed the things she was responsible for today: one, have Brando pick her up and bring the box with the ashes and urn to the funeral home. Two, make sure Shiva was being cared for this afternoon. All doable. Of course, she had to have a shower, dress appropriately and get her head around attending a service that was another step in the loss of her mother. While it was ceremonial, once the service was over and her mother's ashes went into the ground, that ended the physical part of her Mom's presence in her life.

She wished she were closer to Courtney and the Brandies because nothing could replace having a family. But this wasn't a day where she could suddenly reach out for help. Yes, she could contact her large circle of girlfriends and they'd come right away, but only if she asked. Couldn't one of them drop by to see how she was doing?

She sensed Courtney would be especially tense today. In addition to the farewell to their Mom, Courtney always behaved like the rest of them were hopeless and only she could do things perfectly. It was ridiculous, but that's how Courtney rolled. Mona decided she wouldn't be the one to cause any anxiety with Courtney or the family today. She would not even take the bait when Brando behaved stupidly, as she knew he would. In preparation, she texted Brando to ask what time he'd be there to pick her up in the truck, only to get a snarky reply: *on time*. Then she texted Rochella to reconfirm that she was taking Shiva for the afternoon. There was no response immediately, but she knew Rochella would get back to her when she could. Even though she knew everything would work out, she felt off-kilter. Shiva came over and licked her hand as if to comfort her and convey that she wouldn't cause any problems today. Mona buried her face in Shiva's furry collar and cried her eyes out.

Chapter 36

Courtney

Turning off the alarm before it rang at 6:00 a.m., I got up quietly to avoid waking Jamie. If I was going to deal with this day, I needed a run and wanted to fit it in before it got too hot. I hadn't slept well last night. All through the night, I reviewed plans and thought about what could go wrong. I had notified all the seniors who might be heat sensitive to tell them about the breakdown of air conditioning in case they wanted to bail. Nobody did. Then I rechecked with the caterers and was pleasantly surprised that Brandi had done what she had promised. Brando said he'd picked up the ashes and urn last week, so at least he couldn't mess that up—although he had been known to mess up boiled water, so I was ready for anything.

The funeral home and flower shop got tired of me calling, but at least I knew everything was okay. Reverend Bently was all set. He said it was easy for him because he knew my Mom so well. He asked if it was okay for him to add humor to her eulogy. I said sure I welcomed it. I remembered when he and Mom used to visit together and share a glass of wine, and they'd laugh often. If we had to have a religious service, he was the man. And even though I was a lapsed Christian, I sure appreciated a service honoring Mom. I didn't have to think about it, and I knew it would be great with him in charge.

Chapter 37

Brando

Brando woke up with a start. He regretted the two extra beers last night. In a few hours, they'd be at the wretched funeral home listening to an annoying religious ceremony in a hot room. He padded to the kitchen and got the jug of water out of the fridge, guzzling as much as he could in one go.

DeeDee walked into the kitchen and looked at him. "You okay, Dad?"

"Yup," he said.

"Do you want to talk about it?"

Brando paused. *Yes, I'd love to. But I can't bring myself to do it.* "It's okay, DeeDee." He didn't want his daughter worrying about him. He thought about all the things he wanted to say about the frustrations with Courtney, who nagged him constantly with questions and bullied him into decisions that he wasn't ready to make. She wouldn't stop. He wondered why she couldn't just keep it simple.

Weeks ago, when he was out golfing with Jeff and Conrad, Jeff surprised him at the twelfth hole when he brought out a jar and walked over to the boxwoods. He unscrewed the cap and dumped the contents of the jar under the bush.

"What was that, dude?" Brando asked, glancing at Conrad.

Jeff closed the lid and tossed the jar into his golf bag. "Ashes. My old man wanted some dumped at the golf course. This was his happy spot because he wasn't that at home."

"You can do that?" Brando asked.

"Do what?"

"Dump the ashes under a bush. I mean, don't you have to ask someone?"

"Too late. What are they going to do now? At least now I've got my brother off my back. He's been nagging me for a year."

"I hear you," said Brando, envying his friend for keeping it real.

"Dad, Dad, are you there?" said DeeDee, snapping her fingers near his face. "You seem far away."

Just then, Roxy entered the kitchen and wrapped her arms around him from behind. Brando would normally enjoy her moves, but not this time. Anxiety crept up through his body. He didn't want a session of touchy-feely hugs or conversations. What he really wanted was to be left alone to deal with this mess, this stupid day. Needing to get away without hurting her feelings, he patted Roxy's hands and moved away from the counter. She'd get the message.

"What time are we going to the funeral home?"

Brando checked his watch. Five hours to go. "I have to go for one o'clock, says Queen Bea, but there's no need of you two going that early. Quarter to two is fine."

"We don't mind going early, do we, DeeDee?" asked Roxy.

"I said, quarter to two is fine," Brando snapped. He needed to build in time to pick up Mona and the ashes and urn and smoke a little dope along the way, to cope with the service. If Roxy and DeeDee joined him, Roxy would comment that he was smoking too much dope and DeeDee would spout off all the toxic chemicals that were in a single joint.

He watched Roxy's lip curl up at the edge. "Sorry, babe. It's just that the air conditioning is broken, and there's no need for you two to sweat it out for an hour." He'd been told over and over that he needed to keep a lid on his temper in these situations. And he'd been doing better in the last year, but sometimes he got so fed up, having to argue about everything.

"I was only trying to help. Don't push me away," she pouted.

It was a conversation they recycled; every time they disagreed. Plus, Roxy always had to have the last word. Today, he was granting her wish because he couldn't deal with a confrontation. Summoning his best behavior, he put his arm around her and hugged her. "I know you were trying to help. I'm sorry, hon." He kissed her forehead and said, "We okay?"

She looked up at him and nodded. "Yup. Tell me, how can I best support you today?"

"Well, if I could know that you two were okay to go there together, and I could make my way there on my own, I'd be a happy camper."

"You got it, Brando," said Roxy. "DeeDee, you with me?"

"No problem, Dad. Roxy and I can handle that."

Crisis averted. That was one thing he didn't have to worry about and no arguing for hours on end. Now he could do what he wanted; organize his stuff for the service and get his stash of dope prepared with some for Darlene. A doobie sounded like a terrific way to take the edge off the morning. Knowing he could get a little sidetracked when he was stoned, he set his cell alarm in plenty of time to remind him it was time to go.

***

When Roxy and DeeDee announced they were going to brunch, he walked them out the door to the driveway. He said it was a great plan and he'd see them at the service. Relieved to have the place to himself, he went inside the house to his bedroom closet to look for something to wear. He was in no mood to iron, so he hoped he could pull something out of his work wardrobe. After flipping through his clothes three times, he realized he wasn't paying attention. He finally settled on a navy shirt and tie, and a pair of cotton pants that were new and still folded in a way that looked like they had just come off the shelf. He shoved everything into the washer and pressed go. If he kept an eye on it, they'd roll out of the dryer wrinkle-free and be ready to wear.

He set his timer for the length of the wash cycle and went outside to smoke a small joint. He looked at the truck. After driving on a side road last week, it looked like a hippo in a muddy pond. This wasn't how he wanted to present himself at his mother's service. He got out the hose and bucket and went at it. It was a bit hot, and he felt sluggish, so he guzzled his favorite energy drink which made him feel speedy. Then he wiped down the interior dashboard and seats with his favorite chamois cloth. *This is going well*, he thought. He grabbed the shop vac and did a quick turbo vacuum in the truck cabin. Judging by the clicking and clanging, he hoped he wasn't sucking up valuable items from the floor. By this point, he didn't care. But he was hungry. Very hungry.

When Courtney drove by at ten to one, she slowed down and lowered her window.

"What do you think?" Brando said, proudly showing off his gleaming truck that looked ready for a TV ad.

"What do I think? I think you've got ten minutes to get your sorry butt to the funeral home," she said, closing the window. Then she stopped long enough to yell, "Jerk!" With that, she screeched her tires and pulled away like a posse of crazy people was pursuing her.

Brando fumbled in his pocket for his phone, wondering why the alarm hadn't rung for his laundry or to remind him about leaving. "Oh shit," he said out loud when he realized he'd left his cell in the house. That meant the laundry was still in the washer. *There's going to be hell to pay.*

Texts pinged on the phone. He didn't have time to deal with whatever people wanted, so he ignored them until he could get organized. But first, he needed food.

Grabbing the peanut butter and jam on the counter, he slathered them on slices of bread that were still in the toaster from earlier and gulped a glass of milk. As he ate, he threw his clothes in the dryer, wiping away a smidge of peanut butter on his shirt. He set the dryer to high and pressed start. He gulped the rest of the sandwich, which made him feel like a snake that had just swallowed a small animal. With no time to lose, he stepped in the shower.

Minutes later, he stepped out of the shower and felt relieved that he was officially clean, especially after the mess he'd made with the truck. He opted for his electric shaver to avoid arriving with cuts all over his face. He shaved so fast he could have set a world record. Yet the eco dryer continued to tumble the clothes he needed; he couldn't believe it. Why wasn't it finished? Now he was pushing the deadline, and he could already feel the angst from everybody, especially Courtney.

He waited two more minutes, but the dryer somersaulted in slow motion as if it had all day. Finally, he stopped the cycle and pulled out his clothes. They were damp, hot and wrinkly. *Too bad, no time to iron.* He pulled them on his body, getting frustrated at every step. The shirts and pants were so hot, he felt steam rising from his body. Now he was sweating buckets. He was late, and sweaty, his face was red with razor burn, and his outfit was full of wrinkles. Why was it that one hour ago, cleaning the truck seemed so important? If he hadn't shooed Roxy out of the house, she would have pointed out the stupidity of him cleaning the truck, and she would have reminded him he was officially running late. *Why was all this so hard?*

He wondered if he should check in with the thread, *Am I an A**hole?* So far, from only reading the stories, he could tell they were straightforward people, who called things as they saw them. But then again, maybe asking them wasn't such a hot idea. He was quite sure how they'd respond.

Chapter 38

Mona

By noon, Mona hadn't heard from Rochella about when she was picking up Shiva. She was starting to get the feeling that her friend had forgotten, even though she had reminded her yesterday. Mona had done so many errands for her in the past year, she figured her karma bank was well in credit. As a backup, Mona texted other friends who had begged her to get in touch if she needed anything. Well, she needed something now, but not a single person responded. Raj was out of the country on business; she even tried to get him to find someone on her behalf. No luck.

She also hadn't heard back from Brando about when he was picking her up. She texted him and heard nothing. He usually had his cell in his pocket, so she wasn't sure what was going on. After the snide response he gave earlier, she was sure he hadn't forgotten. Ten texts to Rochella, and still no answer. Desperate, she decided to call her. That would catch her by surprise. She dialed and waited until she heard a mousy voice say, "Hello?" as if shocked that she had to answer a call.

"Hey, Rochella, it's Mona. Just wondering if you got my texts." She took a deep breath, trying not to sound panicked, when in fact that's how she felt. "When are you picking up Shiva?" There was one of those long pauses that worried Mona. She sensed Rochella was trying to dream up a lame excuse. Then Mona heard their other friends laughing and joking in the background.

"Oh gee, Mona. I'm so sorry. I had a chance to go to Martinique Beach today with the girls. You know I don't have a car, so I couldn't resist."

Mona reeled. "Does that mean you are neither looking after Shiva nor coming to the service?" She heard Rochella shush the others who were all giggling.

"I'm so sorry, sweetie. Didn't we tell you? We're going to hold our own sister ceremony for you later. We didn't like the idea of a church-y, patriarchal service," she said with a little too much enthusiasm. "I hope that's okay—we're discussing our plans today. Right now, as we speak."

"I guess," said Mona. She was so upset she didn't know what to say. She wanted to argue that a memorial service was about the loved one who had passed away, not her group's standards of what was cool for a service. "Listen, I have to go."

"LOVE YOU, SWEETIE!" they shouted together.

"Whatever." Mona hung up, in tears. Like her Mom said, the true character of a person was what they did when nobody was watching. Rochella had chosen to go to the beach, which she could do any time, instead of supporting Mona.

She took a deep breath, held it and counted to five, several times. That helped calm her anger and slow her breathing. Checking the clock, she realized it was time to go, or she'd get an earful from Courtney. Fortunately, she had set out her clothes earlier and had showered, so she was ready to roll. The lightweight, flowing purple dress was one of her favorites. It would be great in the hot sun, especially if she had to ride her bike. Whenever she wore it, her mother told her she looked so beautiful. She slipped it on and twirled in the mirror. "This one's for you, Mom," she said, feeling teary and alone. Fetching her macrame purse, she filled it with her phone, a comb and her wallet.

She texted and called Brando again; no reply. Great. Now she had no dog sitter, she had to get the ashes to the funeral home, and she was running late. As she placed the big box and other items into the carrying basket on her bike, she sensed she was missing something. Then she remembered her sunglasses and was relieved that she had addressed her nagging concern. Now with her helmet and sunglasses on, she pushed off on her bike.

Halfway down the road, she heard Shiva barking like a maniac. She hadn't left her alone in ages and knew the dog would have a nervous breakdown if left to her own devices. Worse, she could chew up everything in their mother's house. Sighing, she turned around. It no longer mattered if Courtney was angry; Mona had no choice. She opened the door and Shiva was ready with her leash in her mouth, dancing and whining with happiness to see Mona. She wasn't sure what to do with the dog, but then she thought, of all the sentient beings in her life, Shiva was the only one who hadn't let her down. "Okay, you win, girl," said Mona kissing the dog's head. "You can come to the service if you promise to behave."

She tossed the leash into the basket and Shiva trotted alongside, happy as a lark, while Mona rode her bike.

The lightweight dress fabric fluttered as she peddled, then settled like a purple mist when she came to a stop sign. As she started to peddle again, she felt a pull and noticed her dress was caught in the bicycle chain. She stopped and yanked it out, which tore the delicate fabric. *That dickhead Brando was supposed to pick me up.*

She knew if she kept peddling, the tear would continue, so she bundled it all up and sat on the fabric, which gave her the appearance of wearing a mini skirt. That triggered some catcalls from young guys as they drove by her. She flipped them the bird and kept cycling. Maybe they didn't mean any harm, but frankly, she couldn't take much more today, and the day was just beginning.

Chapter 39

Brandi

Brandi shuffled around the house in slow motion. She had things she was supposed to do but couldn't quite get into gear. The air conditioning ran at full blast, which meant it was muggy outside—and she dreaded the thought of what it would be like in the funeral home with only the fan on.

"Where's my blue-collared shirt, babe?" hollered Milo from upstairs.

Just where you left it, she wanted to say, like her mother did when one of her kids was looking for something obvious. "Laundry room, on a hanger on the drying rack, hon," Brandi shouted up the stairs. It amazed her, the number of times a day that Olivia and Milo asked where something was located when they were the last ones using it.

"Okay," he said. "Does it need to be ironed?"

She knew that was code for Milo asking her to do it. For some reason, it was beneath him as an artist to iron. The few times he'd done it, he made sure he did a lousy job and once, he even scorched the shirt. She suspected he had let it happen to prove how bad he was at ironing. "Would you like me to iron it, Milo?" she hollered.

"Oh, would you mind?"

He always sounded pleasantly surprised when she offered, but she knew the drill. She knew that's exactly what he expected. Brandi didn't mind because he did things for her. Besides, she liked that he cared enough to wear a dress shirt and show respect to her Mom. However, she had observed that once he offloaded the ironing responsibility to her, he became meticulous about the job. He was not shy about returning it to her to point out a tiny crease that was not supposed to be there and asking her to spray it with water and redo it. She finished it, put it on a hanger and took it into the bedroom for Milo. Now she was ten minutes behind schedule.

She returned to the kitchen and saw Olivia stumbling around. Bastet, the Sphynx cat was weaving around her legs as a big hint that she needed to be fed, which Olivia ignored. Brandi noted the cat limping as she walked, and the limp had seemed more pronounced in the past few days. She wondered if she should call Tim, the vet. She entered the pantry and grabbed a tin of cat food, which caused Bastet to limp over to the one feeding her. Now it was clear that she was favoring her front paw. Brandi bent down and petted her, her soft leathery hide rising and falling. It had taken her a long time to get used to a hairless cat. Funny, it was Milo and Olivia who insisted on this type of cat, but neither of them ever fed or played with her. She was more like a prop, or a conversation piece. "We have a Sphynx cat named after an Egyptian goddess, Bastet," they would announce to friends. When Brando visited, he always showed his dislike of pretentiousness in cats, calling it "Baldy," or "Baldy Pach" especially if Milo was around, since Pach was his last name. Milo would scowl at him and walk away. Brandi never laughed if Milo were nearby, but she'd giggle with Brando.

She looked at Olivia's outfit and cringed when she saw her current goth uniform of a black T-shirt dress, lengthy black tights, a bit wrinkled at the ankles and leather burgundy stomping boots. When she wore this outfit (which was most of the time), Brando nicknamed her "Olive Oyl", and asked where Popeye was. Olivia was tall and skinny, with stylish glasses; she fit in well in Milo's international art world, but not so much in Danbyville (which she called "Danby*vile*"). Brandi hoped and prayed that Olivia would be changing into something more appropriate for the service. But she had to watch what she said to her stepdaughter because Olivia would immediately run to Milo to complain if she didn't like the comment. Brandi worked hard to simply get along. "Want something to eat, hon?" she asked.

"Yes.... No. I don't know," Olivia snapped.

"How about some yogurt, granola and nuts?" Brandi didn't like the idea of Olivia with low blood sugar at the funeral. She could get quite ugly. "Or I can make you a nice omelet with peppers, mushrooms and cheese."

"How about a Western sandwich?"

"Fine," Brandi said. The items were the same, except one was served with the egg in between two slices of toast, and the other was with toast on the side. *Whatever, at least she's eating something.*

Milo trundled down the stairs but stopped on the landing to button one cuff, then the other one. "What time are we going to the funeral home?" he asked, kissing her lightly.

"The service starts at two. I need to be there earlier to go over things, so I'll leave in ten minutes," she said, biting into a piece of cheese while she stirred the eggs. "I figure you and Olivia could go together. Does that work for you?"

Olivia shrugged. Milo pressed his chin on her shoulder and hugged her. "I know how hard this is for you to lose your mother. And then you have to deal with your crazy family."

Brandi stiffened. "That's a bit harsh," she said, sliding a plate of toast toward him, a little more forceful than usual. It was one thing for her to complain about her family, but she didn't like him commenting. "We all have our jobs today at the funeral home and we know what to do."

"Mark my words," he said, reaching for a mug and filling his coffee. "At least one, and likely all your siblings will act up today. Except you, of course. Why do you think Courtney wants you there early?" he laughed as he stirred his coffee.

Brandi knew exactly why Courtney set an early start time for the family: Brando and Mona were perpetually late. Family estate meetings had turned into a ridiculous pattern. Courtney would set an early time because they were always late, and then they'd ignore her timing knowing she'd set it earlier. Then they'd arrive late, puffing, panting and disrupting everything. But she didn't want to explain this pattern to Milo because that would just confirm his theory about her family.

"Gotta run," she said, gathering her items for the funeral home and stuffing them into a carrying bag. "I'll see you two at McIsaac's." She kissed Milo on the cheek but pretended not to notice his arms out for a hug. So much for setting boundaries; she was behaving passive-aggressively right now but couldn't stop herself. Today wasn't a day for him to pick apart her family; it was a day for all of them to come together and support one another. At least, that's what she hoped and prayed for last night when she couldn't sleep.

Chapter 40

Courtney

When I walked into McIsaac's, a wall of muggy air walloped me. Mrs. McIsaac wore a long-sleeved dress, and her face looked damp with a pink flush. We chatted briefly and she toured me through the place, reminding me of all the key features like accessible washrooms, ramps and other assistance for the elderly or immobile. There was still an hour to go, but we could already see cars with elderly people arriving. They'd need ample time to move from the car to the inside.

Fortunately, Mrs. McIsaac was ready for the "earlies" as she called them. She had distributed little seat signs to establish social distancing and had boxes of masks at each entrance, along with a large container of hand sanitizer with a sign asking everyone to clean their hands. While I hated the idea of all the Covid precautions and how it sucked the life out of most events, these days, there wasn't much choice. Besides, with frail seniors or people with illnesses, I didn't want our event pinpointed as the source of an outbreak.

I was relieved that Brandi's caterers were in full swing. We agreed the sandwiches should be stowed in the fridge until after the service so that those with mayo wouldn't turn into a germ festival. And I asked them to cover sweets with plastic wrap to keep unwanted pests out (they assumed flies; I meant family). My goal was to prevent certain relatives and friends from hoovering up the sweets before the service. When it came to events with food and drink, Nova Scotians weren't just punctual, they arrived heart-stoppingly early—except my siblings, of course. Everybody knew that seniors, particularly those who lived on their own, brought a hearty appetite to events. Brandi had ordered lots of food and they'd be ready for them.

I saw Brandi's blue SUV pulling up in the parking lot and whipping into a space. It was one-twenty, and she was a little late, but there was still time. I was glad to finally have someone in the family to talk to.

"You look great, Brandi," I said, as we hugged, noting she had chosen a lightweight linen outfit with natural fibers that allowed the air to circulate. Smart move.

"Sorry, I'm a bit late. I had to iron Milo's shirt."

"You are likely forty-five minutes ahead of Brando and Mona, so you're good."

Brandi scanned the room and the placement of everything. "I see the Good Bites Catering van is here," she said, looking relieved. "Since it's so hot, they'll wait a bit to put the food out, right?"

"Exactly," I said.

"Let's look at the food trays; I just want to make sure everything is right."

"Sure." We walked into the kitchen area and stuck our heads in the fridge. "Wow, Brandi, look at these little sandwiches. The crusts are cut off... oooh, they are like the finger sandwiches we had at weddings, showers and funerals as kids."

Brandi beamed. "Exactly. When I talked to the caterers, I wanted to pay tribute to Mom and the food she prepared when she volunteered with the church. As soon as I said, 'I'm thinking something like Ladies' Auxiliary food you'd find at church events,' Donna got it right away. She suggested egg, and tuna salad on white, with crusts cut off and deviled eggs. And I added cream cheese sandwiches, with canned asparagus in the middle that were then rolled and cut. Not that they're good, just for old time's sake."

"This is awesome, Brandi." I laughed, moving to the sweets. "Check out these trays with squares: there are cherry-walnut, pineapple, lemon and date squares, plus pinwheel cookies, fudge and brownies."

"I love it." I could see Brandi was excited to talk about her catering choices.

"I ordered the larger napkins because I know a lot of the people will want to wrap up sandwiches and sweets to take them home for a nice easy dinner."

"Great idea," I added and let her talk. She was on a roll.

"And you know what? Donna liked the idea so much she's going to add 'The Ladies' Auxiliary Special' as a vintage package with her catering!"

"No wonder. This is a brilliant idea, Brandi. Mom would be so impressed."

"Really?" asked Brandi, looking genuinely moved.

"You bet," I said. At the same time, we both teared up and hugged each other, complete with heads on shoulders. It was the longest hug we'd had in years, maybe even since childhood.

"I miss Mom so much," Brandi cried softly.

"Me too, sweetie," which was all I could manage without falling apart. She hadn't said much before, but that was Brandi being the sibling who didn't make a big fuss. With all the demands the funeral had put on us, sometimes it was easy to forget we were all grieving. But Brandi was doing an amazing job with her catering task and was a model of grace under pressure until that moment when we both thought of Mom.

Just then a caterer arrived at our side and gently tapped my hand that had been resting on the fridge door. "Sorry, ladies, but I need to keep the fridge closed."

"Whoops, I'm sorry," I said, closing the door. "We best get out of the kitchen, eh, Brandi?"

She nodded and we linked arms, walking into the main salon. I pointed to the video screen, with a shot of the family on a beach with the Brandies and me. "I got Ava to create a photo presentation. Thanks for sending me photos."

I walked her past the speaking podium to a large table. "And on this side, we've got flowers and a beautiful picture of Mom. What do you think?"

"Looks great," she said, turning her head.

"Sorry, Brandi, I'll stop yakking. I just wanted everything to be perfect."

"I'm not even sure what to do," Brandi said, looking lost.

"Me either. But don't worry, Reverend Bently will guide us through today," I said. "We'll be in the family room at the back before the service and from there, he'll walk us to the two reserved rows at the front where we will each sit with our family."

A rattling, mint green Toyota with a duct-taped fender rumbled outdoors. Three people got out and stretched in every direction. "Look, it's Aunt Darlene and her sidekicks, Mickey and Minnie," said Brandi, walking toward the door. "That was so nice of them to come all the way from Cape Breton. Let's go say hi."

"Sure."

Brandi and I walked down the ramp, towards the car. "Aunt Darlene!" we shouted.

She turned sideways and her eyes lit up as she saw us. "Courtney and Brandi," she cried, scooping us both into her arms at the same time. "My God, loves, how are ya?" Then she spun us around. "You remember Mickey and Minnie, right?"

"Yes, of course. How are you two?" I said. "How was your trip?" I asked politely, not overly interested in full details.

"Don't get me started," said Mickey. "It took way longer to get here than I thought."

"Did you get a bite to eat along the way?" Brandi asked.

"Hell, no," said Minnie. "We were busy getting lost. It's such a trial coming to the mainland from Cape Breton. None of us could agree about the highway turnoffs—"

"She argued so much that I took a wrong turn at Antigonish, one in Truro and one in Halifax," said Mickey. "Minnie hasn't been across the causeway in a few years, so she was having conniptions every time she saw a highway sign."

"Anyhoo, we made it," said Darlene. "However, I do need to ask a favor here."

"Sure. What do you need?" I asked.

Darlene walked over between the couple and slung her arms around them. "We didn't get a chance to eat along the way. Mickey here is diabetic, and Minnie and I, well, we don't like more than an hour in between snacks," she said. "Do you have any food you can spare?"

"Of course," Brandi said. "Come with me, I'll sort you out in the kitchen. We've got all kinds of sandwiches and sweets. But don't tell anyone!"

"Perfect!" said Darlene perking up. "And then I want to see that crazy brother of yours. Oh, and Mona too." She linked arms with Brandi and started walking toward the kitchen.

By now, it was one forty-five, and people were taking their seats. I was getting nervous because there was no sign of Brando and Mona. As usual, they were cutting it close. Roxy and DeeDee were already there, and they were chatting with Jamie, Ava and Jacob, with Milo and Olivia standing at an angle nodding their heads, but not participating. Reverend Bently was doing a fantastic job talking to everybody. People were already turning their programs into fans for their faces.

I saw Brando swing into the parking lot, jam his truck into park and jump out all in one move. He burst through the door and marched over to where Brandi and I were standing. He looked hassled and weird.

"The *late* Mr. Brando Martin," I said, glancing at the clock, then peering at his face. "What's wrong with your face?" He looked crammed into his suit and underneath the jacket, it was clear he was sweating all over. His eyes were also glassy, which likely meant he was stoned. I hated the lack of respect he was showing our mother. "Steam is pouring off you."

"Just a little razor burn, and I'm finding it hot," he said, walking toward the old mercury thermometer nailed to the wall. "It says eighty-eight Fahrenheit. What's that in English?"

"Celsius," I said, unable to stop myself from correcting him. "That's about thirty-one, but with the humidex, more like thirty-nine." I shifted my weight. My pumps were already throttling my baby toes. "And why don't you answer texts?"

"Busy," he snapped.

I looked at his empty hands. "Where are the ashes?" I asked, my stomach preparing for unwelcome news. His face flashed an *oh-no-I-messed-up* look. "Um," he said looking around for somebody or something. "Out in the truck..."

"You know it's almost time for the service, right? Any chance you could move your butt and get them?" Just then, the screen door snapped, and Mona pushed the storm door open into the family room. Her hair looked damp, her arms were full of heavy items and Shiva was by her side.

"Jerk," Mona barked at Brando. "Why didn't you answer my texts? I've been waiting for you to pick me up for the past hour."

Brando ran his hand through his hair. "Mona, I completely forgot."

"Forgot what?" I said, sensing strange behavior. "And what are you carrying, Mona?"

"The ashes, because he forgot to pick me up. You had one job, Brando. And you messed up. I had to ride my bike here in this heat," she said gulping from her bottle of water.

The Reverend poked his head through the velvet curtain with a silly grin on his face, and said, "How are we doing, folks?" When nobody responded, he added, "Ready to go in about five minutes?"

"Sure," I squeaked. But something didn't feel right. "We're just sorting things out here, Reverend Bently."

"Arthur," he said with a warm smile.

"Thanks, Arthur," I said, on autopilot. I turned to Mona. "What are you doing with the ashes? Brando was going to bring them."

"Long story. Brando will explain later," she said, pulling out a large cardboard box bound tightly with clear packing tape.

"Okaaay," I said slowly, trying to understand what was going on. "So, the ashes weren't placed in the urn before the event. Where's the urn?"

Mona slapped her forehead. She and Brando exchanged dirty looks. "I knew I was forgetting something. This is your fault, Brando."

"What's going on, you two?" I snapped. "We have five minutes to the service which we can't delay because of the heat, with a taped-up cardboard box that looks like it was just delivered by the post office. That will look lovely on the podium."

A hand pushed its way through the dark curtains like an annoying magician trying to get everybody's attention. "Three minutes, folks," Arthur said, a little too cheerily.

"You should have done the ashes yourself, then it would have been perfect," sniped Brando. "How am I supposed to know what you want?"

"It's easy. I went over all the details with you, but you didn't bother to listen or ask questions."

"Big whoop," Brando said. "You love making a big deal about nothing."

"Nothing? Oh yeah? That's how you almost killed poor little Fluffy!" I spewed.

The room fell silent.

"What?" gasped Mona, glaring at Brando. "You almost killed Fluffy?"

"Brando?" asked Brandi.

"That's right," I continued. "Brando didn't understand the instructions in the will. Despite finding it odd and not asking any questions, he thought he was supposed to put Fluffy down and add her to Mom's gravesite, instead of waiting until the cat passed away in the future. He even went to Pet Vet and asked Tim to do it."

Arthur opened the curtains with a little snap. "Folks, it's getting a little testy in here, and super hot out there. How can I help?"

I realized I was sounding a bit too loud and scary. Through tears, I summarized what had almost happened to our mother's cat. He nodded through the story as if he were used to such insane scenarios.

"Deep breath, folks," said Arthur. "I know this is upsetting, but it didn't happen," he said with a hand on my shoulder. "If we park the Fluffy issue for the time being, and reduce this to its simplest issue, there is no urn for your Mom's ashes, right? We just won't put anything out at the service. And after the service, Brando can drive Mona to her place and get the urn. We'll do something special for your dear Mom at the gravesite."

"I guess we have no choice," I said. Then I turned to Mona. "Why is Shiva here? I thought your little friend was going to look after her all day."

"Rochelle couldn't make it," Mona said. "I couldn't get anyone else. She won't stay at home alone."

"You aren't bringing a panting dog to the service!" I had had enough from Brando and Mona. "Take her outside and put her under the big oak tree. Here's a bowl. Fill it with cold water," I said passing her a mixing bowl that the caterers had left on the table.

"But...but," said Mona, her face pained.

"She'll be fine for twenty minutes," I said, staring back. "It's probably cooler outside than in here."

Mona shot me a dirty look, followed by a worse one for Brando. Her dress was torn, and she looked weary. I knew we had to get the service started. We all walked into the service area and sat together—the last thing we all wanted to do. Everybody stared; they must have heard the shouting in the family room.

I looked around at the attendees: there were antique sellers, a group of Mom's friends who were auctioneers, and people from town. Our lawyer Megan was seated by herself, secretly scrolling through her texts and emails. I made a mental note to check the invoice when it came in—she'd better not bill us for attending the service. Heather the bank teller sat beside Megan, and I could see her looking over Megan's shoulder to see if she could glean any legal dirt from her emails. Cliff and his wife were there; Janice was fanning herself. I spotted a group that looked familiar, but I couldn't place them. Finally, I remembered it was the Santos family that was squatting on Mom's land. Nice touch. Then there was Doris, sitting arm in arm with Darlene, the two of them yakking up a storm. While it wasn't surprising to hear them gabbing—they had all gone to high school together—it was still galling. I wondered if Doris had updated Darlene about trying to defraud the family of a Maud Lewis painting. To round things off, Brando's ex-wife Twyla was there with her new boyfriend. Good thing it was a booze-free event.

Mona led Shiva outside under the big oak tree. It was near the window that was open into the room where the guests awaited the beginning of the service. Mona snuck back into the front row and settled in her seat.

I was impressed that Arthur looked so calm at the podium next to the window, especially after witnessing the heated exchange in the family room. While I imagined he had seen plenty of inappropriate behavior at funerals before, I figured we'd hit a new low for him. I could picture him at a post-retirement dinner party recounting the nutbars he'd encountered during his career, and we'd be right up there in his anthology of anecdotes.

A whiff of a breeze slipped through the window. Relief washed over the crowd. Arthur closed his eyes, took a deep breath and opened his mouth starting to say, "Welcome, everyone." At that precise moment, Shiva leaped vertically in front of the window and let out a whiny bark. It sounded for all the world like a ventriloquist had planted a bark at the back of Reverend Bently's mouth.

A nervous giggle rippled through the crowd as everybody tried to pretend it hadn't happened. I shot a look at Mona as if to say, "That better be the last bark." Not that Mona could control her annoying dog. The Reverend looked out the window, then turned to the crowd and smiled, "I couldn't have said it better myself!" Everybody laughed and resettled in their seats. Thank God for this man with a quick wit, who by the looks of things, specialized in curveballs. As he returned to his prepared notes, Shiva jumped up again and barked like a maniac. This time, there was no stopping her, and she was drowning out Reverend Bently. "Mona!" I hissed. "Do something!"

Mona froze like a deer caught in the headlights. Then she leaned to me and said, "The only thing I can do is bring her inside." Shiva continued with her eight-hundred-rounds-a-minute barking jag to join the indoor party.

No. No. No. This can't be happening, I thought, looking at Mona. "She'll disrupt the service."

"Less so than if she stays outside," Mona said, "Unless I sit with her outside." She paused, then said, "But I'd like to be at Mom's service. Can I bring her in?"

What choice did we have? "OK, but be quick."

With that, Mona stood up and bent over, creeping across the front chairs in front of the large screen that projected a big shadow of a woman hunched over, bobbing up and down like an Indonesian shadow puppet. Shiva carried on jumping and whining outside. On her way out, Mona whispered to Arthur that she'd be right back with Shiva, who sounded barking mad by this time. Reverend Bently stood smiling the whole time and made gentle comments while waiting for Mona. Those of us who could see out the window watched as she unhooked Shiva, picked up the bowl and brought her inside. Beaming, Shiva walked in with Mona and took her place at the bottom of the chair, panting and lapping up water in the bowl.

By then, my ability to be embarrassed had peaked. There was nothing left. I felt sad, tired and overheated. Jamie on one side and Ava on the other each took one of my hands and patted them to comfort me. And I cried like I hadn't cried in months. I wanted to scream, but I managed to keep it to a general sob at the service. I felt sad that we couldn't behave better as a family. I felt shortchanged in having such a dick of a brother. But worse, I felt ashamed that we couldn't do better for my beloved Mom who deserved so much more.

The Reverend spoke comforting words, but I could hardly focus. I wasn't known to cry, so I spent most of the service receiving tissues from kind people beside or behind me who felt sorry for me. The other siblings sniffled and cried too, but they had no idea that at that moment I was tired of being an executor. I wanted to walk away from the entire mess, but I couldn't because I desperately wanted to honor my mother. And we were nowhere near done.

Chapter 41

Mona

After the service, the guests were invited to have tea, sandwiches and sweets all laid out on the tables. Reverend Bently then invited the immediate family to go to the cemetery plot for the burying of the ashes. Brando took Mona and Shiva in the truck to pick up the urn at Mom's, and they joined everybody at the plot.

The immediate family arrived and stood in clumps by the gravesite. There was Jamie, Courtney, Jacob and Ava; to the side, Roxy and DeeDee; and on the opposite side, Brandi, Milo and Olivia. Everybody knew the heated exchanges with the siblings at the funeral home were still percolating. Darlene had joined them as well and stood near the center, her hands folded. Nobody said a word as Brando, Mona and Shiva pulled in and parked, then rejoined the group.

Mona carried the urn, while Brando carried the box of ashes to the site. Arthur smiled gently and nodded to them as they arrived. Mona was moved by his patience and kindness—not all clergy would be as helpful as he had been.

Reverend Bently turned to everyone. "Look, I know it's been a tough day for everyone, but that's normal. Maybe things didn't work out the way we planned back at the service, but we are all here together now. I knew your mother well, and that would have meant everything to her."

"Plus, she was a big forgiver of everybody," added Darlene. "So, let's not dig in our heels here." Her face flushed. "Whoops, sorry, Father. Bad choice of words at the burial grounds."

Mona watched as Brando exchanged glances with Darlene, then Brandi, then her. They all smiled lightly with their mouths closed. They sobered up quickly when Courtney met their eyes. Courtney then leaned over to tell Aunt Darlene that *Father* was the title for a Catholic priest and *Reverend* for a United Church minister. Darlene nodded a thanks to Courtney and stood at attention.

"Okay, Brando, did you place the ashes in the urn?" said Arthur.

Brando looked at Mona, with a *What now?* look on his face. "Uh, I was hurrying to get the urn, so Mona and I forgot to do that. Sorry. Give me five minutes."

"Not a problem," said Arthur, smiling at everyone. "Take your time."

Mona checked Courtney's expression, but she appeared defeated. Brando nodded to Mona and Brandi to help him. They stepped near him and held the box, while Brando fumbled for a pocketknife. Sweating, he flipped it open and started sawing at what looked like twenty layers of tape. A light breeze blew across the cemetery which helped everybody to relax while waiting in the blazing sun. Brando didn't look happy that his struggle to open a box was serving as graveside entertainment.

For the first time in her life, Mona felt sorry for Brando as he tried to cut his way through the box with a blunt pocketknife. He looked puzzled, like a surgeon in a bad dream, starting an operation only to discover the tools weren't ready. She also noticed he had sweated so much he'd likely ruined his suit.

Finally, he cut the tape and seams and opened the box. He looked dejected when he saw the next layer—a box lined with heavy sealed plastic. He stabbed desperately at the lining with the knife, only yielding a small puncture. Frustrated, he put his two fingers in the hole and applied brute strength, just as the wind gusted, sending ashes over his suit and into the air. People coughed and stepped away. He pretended it didn't happen and continued pouring the rest into his mother's urn, with ashes spilling over the side.

"There. Done!" he barked, holding up the urn in angry triumph.

Mona looked at Courtney and tried not to laugh because she was sure they shared the same thought: he sounded like a caveman. She wanted to respond "Ugh!" but with nervous laughter teetering on everybody's radar, she decided against it.

"Thanks. Great job, Brando," said Arthur. He pulled a bottle of water out of his kitbag and offered it to Brando, who nodded in appreciation. Mona watched him open and guzzle the bottle in one go. Then he turned his head away from the family, tapped his chest and let out a small gurgling belch, mumbling, "Sorry." DeeDee and Olivia snickered. The Reverend handed the urn to Courtney to hold. "Ready, everyone?" he said gently, trying to settle everyone, indicating it was time to get serious about the service.

"Yes, sir," Brando replied.

Reverend Bently drew a deep breath. "We are gathered here to say farewell to Barbara Ann Nichols—"

Mona felt a rush of emotion when she thought about the near-miss with Fluffy. She was still shaking and just couldn't take it.

"Wait a minute," Mona said. "I am sorry to interrupt, but I'm trying to process what nearly happened to Fluffy. It feels traumatic to think about it." She turned to Brando. "I forgive you, Brando, but I'm still terribly upset about Fluffy. She was everything to Mom."

Arthur looked at Mona. "Thank you for sharing, Mona. I know we all love Fluffy, and we're glad she's still with us. How can we support you right now?"

She paused. "I know it's been a stressful day, but we stumbled through it. I think I need something positive now. How about making this a celebration of life for Mom *and* a family commitment to hold a safe space for our beloved Fluffy."

Arthur smiled. "Great idea, Mona."

"Thanks. Here are a few details about Fluffy," she said handing him a large napkin with scribbles on it.

"Is that okay with everyone?" Arthur asked, scanning the crowd. The warm sun beat down on everyone. Looking dazed and confused, everybody nodded as if to say, "Whatever, let's just get through this."

"Okay," said Arthur quietly. "Let's begin." He opened his book and placed the napkin on the left side. "Good afternoon, everyone. We are gathered here today to celebrate the lives of—"

He coughed and bowed his head briefly.

Why did he do that? Mona wondered.

He raised his head. "Pardon me. We celebrate the lives of Barbara Ann Nicols and... Fluff...Fluffy—" He stopped again.

This time, Mona noticed his body language, as if he trying to hold back laughter. *It couldn't be. Ministers didn't laugh at times like this.*

"Sorry," he said, reaching into his bag and taking a swig of water. "Catch in my throat."

Relieved, Mona adjusted her dress that was sticky under the arms and patted Shiva lightly on the head while she waited. Shiva panted heavily.

Arthur smiled. "Once more with feeling. Barbara Ann Nichols and Fluffity-Fluff..." he halted, his lips quivering. Everybody leaned in toward the grave. "Fluffity-Fluff Muggins Nichols," he finally coaxed out of his mouth. He then suppressed a snort and lowered his head. He twitched as if trying to pull himself together, but kept his head bowed.

The family froze.

"*No shit*," mumbled Brando. "Fluffy's middle name is Muggins?"

At that moment, Arthur and the whole family laughed themselves silly. It was like a tension dam had burst and hysteria poured out everywhere. And every time the Reverend tried to reel them in and start over, he'd start laughing. Everybody joined in, even Courtney. Shiva chirped happily. Nobody could bring the collective laughing to a halt, so it ran rampant for several minutes while tension raced out of their bodies like a hot air balloon with a giant leak.

Just as it looked like they were cooling down with the out-of-control laugh track, one of Brando's friends drove by, looking puzzled by the spectacle of a dozen people laughing their butts off at a gravesite. Brando gave him the thumbs up, laughed, and it started up again.

Finally, Reverend Bently waved at everybody and held one hand in the air to get attention. "I am so sorry, folks. That has never happened to me before."

"It's okay, Arthur. It's been a weird day," Mona said. She couldn't imagine how difficult it must have been for him to witness such insanity.

"Thank you." He smiled at me. "And I have an idea. And this is also a first for me at a gravesite. Before we continue, I suggest we all take time to do what I call, 'shake the sillies' out."

"What's that?" beamed Darlene, looking ready for fun.

"I do this at Sunday School when the kids are too wound up. We stand up. We shake our heads and our bodies, make crazy noises, and laugh like maniacs for thirty seconds. Then we stop," he said rubbing his hands together. "Ready, Set, Go!" Everybody participated, although Mona noted that Milo and Olivia looked dubious. But she was relieved when it finally worked.

The rest of the service unfolded beautifully. Each person spoke lovingly about Babs, and Fluffy. At the end, everybody hugged.

"Well done, *Father*," said Darlene, forgetting what Courtney had told her to call him. "I don't know how you turned around such a sideshow. And you know what?"

"What's that, Darlene?"

"That was the best service I've ever been to. And I just know Babs is up there in heaven laughing so hard. Thank you," Darlene said, hugging him. "Time for a drink, everybody! Let's go back to the funeral home to wrap up, then over to Babs' place. I know where she kept her stash of rum."

Chapter 42

Courtney

After the graveside ceremony, we returned to the funeral home for the reception. Gradually the guests left, and we all stood around unsure of what to do with ourselves—should we stay or call it a day? There wasn't much left to do, but somehow leaving felt like it would end one era and remind us of the next, with a big void in our lives. Then we realized Aunt Darlene's idea was a good one, and we all descended on Mom's house, inviting the hangers-on at the funeral home. It seemed a fitting way to wrap things up. Aunt Darlene had to accompany Mickey and Minnie to the hotel to check in first but promised to make her way to Mom's place later.

The house soon filled with family and friends including people who couldn't get into the service due to lack of seating. We found the stash of rum and bottles of wine in the wine rack, and let people help themselves. Even Reverend Bently poured himself a tipple of wine—and who could blame him? He was likely battling PTSD after dealing with our family.

Although I had a headache, sharing memories calmed me down and gradually eased the pain. Everybody chatted and laughed as they recounted story after story. Someone opened the garage and people wandered around in the "retail" shop where Mom sold her stuff. Despite a successful estate sale, there were still items waiting to be sold. I could see Mona had done little to sell the goods. She was doing exactly as Brando had predicted: living rent-free, contributing nothing towards upkeep and expenses, selling nothing and showing no signs of moving on.

Gradually, our spouses and children departed, and Aunt Darlene went to get Mickey and Minnie from the hotel, leaving the four siblings together in the house where we continued to drink. We were still miffed at each other, for various infractions before, during and after the service. And we had future estate tensions to sort out, yet we found ways to poke fun at each other. Somehow, that was the rhythm of our family. When I kicked off my pumps and wore Mom's furry slippers with my fancy outfit, Brando snapped pictures and posted them online.

Minutes later, there was a knock on the door. I wandered to the front of the house, my mood lightened. "Hey, Olivia, come on in," I said.

"That's okay, I've had enough family for one day," she replied. Holding up the cat carrier with Bastet quivering inside, she handed it to me. "Dad will text Mom, but here's the headline: Bastet's limp got worse. And she needs to take her to the vet when she finishes here." With that, she turned and scuttled down the steps as if trying to escape before she got trapped in another family moment.

I looked at the cat and smiled. She gave me a sneer and edged toward the back of the carrier. I carried the cage into the living room, holding it up like a lantern. "Brandi, you have a visitor. Milo is going to text you with instructions." I handed the little live wire to her.

"Got it, thanks." Brandi took the cage and spoke sweetly to her cat, promising to take care of her. She set the carrier on the table. Everybody stared at the cat.

Glancing at the cage, Brando asked, "Brandi, why do you have a leather catcher's mitt in a cat cage?"

Brandi raised one eyebrow at her brother. "Ha ha, you dork. Bastet has a limp. Apparently, I am the only one who knows how to take her to the vet," she said, moving the carrier to the piano bench. Shiva immediately darted over to check out the cat, who didn't show appreciation for being investigated. The dog sat down and patiently watched Bastet as if she were settling in to watch a TV show.

"Hey, it's Baldy Pach," Brando said, placing his fat fingers near the carrier. In his best falsetto, he cooed, "Here kitty, kitty." The cat hissed and swatted at him. He laughed.

"Don't torment her, Bro," Brandi said, slurring her words slightly. "Whatever you do, don't open the kitty's door. And since you listen to no one, watch that latch, it needs to click. If not, she could escape, and you'll be recapturing her."

"Who me?" Brando joked. "Don't worry."

Mona walked over and took Shiva by the collar, gently leading her across the room "Shiva loves her, but Bastet doesn't like Shiva."

Brandi nodded. "Exactly, Mona. Bastet looks regal, but underneath, she's a freakin' scrapper and won't back down if she feels threatened."

"Baldy and I have a bond. I know how to handle her," said Brando.

"I'd be nervous if I was a cat, Brando," I said. "Your track record isn't exactly impressive." As soon as the words rolled out of my mouth, I realized I had stepped on a nerve.

Brando shot me a dirty look. "Let's not go there, Miss Perfect who isn't as perfect as she thinks."

"What do you mean?" I fumed. I shouldn't have taken the bait with Brando, but whenever he felt pushed into a corner, the guy came out swinging.

"You've had months to sort out the estate, and all you do is procrastinate. Followed by endless complaining."

"Are you kidding me?" I pulled out my phone and scrolled quickly, then turned the phone toward him. "This is my task list, now logging over two hundred items. If you want to speed things up, you could take on tasks."

"Nah. If there's one thing I know, I could never meet your standards. Even Mom said you were a perfectionist beyond hope."

"Easy, Brando," said Brandi, walking toward him. "This isn't the time—"

"Oh yeah?" said Brando. "I think it's the perfect time."

"Now you're acting like our father when he was drinking," I shot back, trying to hit him harder. "That's what Mom told me."

Mona jumped up and stood in the middle to block the exchange. "Okay, everyone, take it easy. This is a day for remembering Mom with love. Enough with the insults. That's how wars start."

"Oh, Mona's so deep and profound," said Brando. "How about singing us a round of 'Kumbaya'?"

My head throbbed and I knew Brando was preparing for a big brawl. I wouldn't be part of it.

"You make a good point, Mona. So, I'll leave," I said, walking toward the door. At the last minute, something snapped. I'd put up with enough crap today. I turned back and walked to the china cabinet, opening the door, and picking up the sugar bowl. "And I'm taking this, since I spoke for it first."

"NO!" thundered a chorus from the Brandies and Mona.

"You are *so NOT* taking the sugar bowl," growled Brandi, holding out her hand. "Give it to me."

I had never seen such a maniacal look in her eyes and worried she'd well and truly lost it.

"I'm the sole male heir," shouted Brando. "I'm having that sugar bowl."

Brandi, Mona and I laughed. "You're the sole heir duking it out over a sugar bowl?" I held the bowl in my hand and looked at the three of them, all of us pumped up on too much humidity, caffeine and sweets at the funeral home, and now booze. "What's with you? I asked you numerous times to pick something of Mom's and you all insisted you didn't care. Then I speak for it, and you all jump on the bandwagon. Brando and Brandi, admit it: you only wanted it once I claimed it. And Mona, you have no attachment to it other than you secretly think it's valuable," I said glaring at her. "Yes, Aunt Darlene told me you cornered her to help you identify it, in case it's from the Ming Dynasty or something." I grasped the small, covered bowl in my right hand and held it like it was a live grenade. "I'm leaving, and this is going with me."

Fuming, Brando turned and opened the carrier, which triggered Bastet to leap out like a flying squirrel. Excited, Shiva squealed like a banshee and prepped her muscles to tackle the cat who was jumping into the thick of things. Feline and canine forces smashed head-on, with my outstretched hand in the epicenter. Their collision knocked the sugar bowl out of my hand. I remember it flying upward and me trying to catch it. In shock, I watched the lid flipping over and over to the left, the bowl dropping to the right. My mind couldn't decide which to catch. I missed both. Time froze. It was like being in an accident that seemed to take forever yet was over in a split second.

Suddenly I remembered a valuable black and white photo Mom had sold in her shop years ago. It was taken in the forties by a Parisian photographer, Philippe Halsman. Mom called it "The Flying Cat" photo. As a kid, it fascinated me. The main subject, Salvador Dali, was captured on camera, frozen in mid-air along with three leaping cats, a flying chair and a bucket of water splashed in front of everything. Chaos ensued. Mom loved it but had to sell it to keep things rolling in our household.

By the time I registered what was going on, the inevitable happened: the ceramic bowl crashed to the floor, smashing into pieces. The lid fared better because it had landed on a folded blanket. Cold comfort. The sugar bowl was now rubble. The frenzied cat and dog raced down the hallway and back until Bastet dove under the sofa, then resurfaced and jumped on the piano bench, then the top of the piano. We stood like statues.

Brandi finally corralled Bastet back into the carrier and Shiva was banished to one of the rooms with the door shut behind her. I realized the one thing of Mom's that I treasured more than anything could never be mine again. Infuriatingly, the Brandies and Mona had each contributed to the breaking of the sugar bowl. While the rational side of me knew it wasn't planned, the emotional side of me felt like they had somehow secretly decided if they couldn't have it, nobody could.

Finally, Mona got up from the chair. "Oh dear," she said, bending over to examine the scene of the crime. "I'm so, so sorry," she whispered. Genuinely shaken, she walked into the kitchen and grabbed a whisk and dustpan, and a zipper seal bag. It looked like she was gathering evidence as she gently eased everything into the bag and pressed the two tracks of the bag together for a tight seal.

"What are you doing?" asked Brandi.

"I don't know," she said. "I'll think of something."

Yeah, right. I nearly laughed at Mona's efforts to gather pieces and shards—it seemed so futile.

Tears streamed down my face for the umpteenth time that day. Once again, Brando's ugly mug looked like he had just recognized that he'd done something impulsive and wished he hadn't. Brandi looked sheepish. It was as if she suddenly realized that the sugar bowl meant way more to me than to her.

"Sorry, squeaked Brandi.

"I'm done," I said quietly, gathering my things.

"What's that supposed to mean?" Brando asked.

I shrugged. Truth was, I didn't know exactly what I meant by that, but it felt serious. All I knew was that I was done with all of them.

"Courtney?" said Mona. "Can we talk about this?"

"Too late," I said with a tone of eerie calmness.

"How can we make things right, Courtney?"

I stopped to think about it because Mona sounded sincere.

"One, you all owe me an apology. Not one of your fake 'sorry, not sorry' apologies you'd say to get through the moment. I want a real one."

"Not gonna happen, sister," said Brando. "You owe me an apology for the way you've treated me since Mom passed away."

That didn't surprise me in the least, but it wasn't going to stop my rant. "I also want you to think about how you conspired early on. I know your motivations were devious—you two were trying to hurt me by fighting for the bowl. And Mona was motivated by money. "If you'd just let me take it home when I first mentioned it, it wouldn't have been broken today."

"Shoulda, coulda, woulda," snapped Brando. "What now?"

"If you all think I'm doing such a bad job, one of you can do it," I said, surprising myself. "You three can discuss it and let me know."

"Well, I'm not doing a thing until you apologize to me and Brandi," said Brando, looking around the room. Spotting Mona, he added as an afterthought, "Oh, and Mona too."

"Thanks for having my back," sniffed Mona, obviously aware Brando had forgotten her.

"To hell with all of you." With that, I walked out and slammed the door.

Chapter 43

Mona

Courtney wasn't gone five minutes when a car pulled in and Aunt Darlene jumped out with her entourage. Mona watched as they joked and laughed their way up the front steps to the house. "Don't look now, but here comes Aunt Darlene, Mickey and Minnie, and Doris."

"Batten down the hatches if Doris is wandering around the house," said Brando, which broke the tension in the room. Brandi and Mona laughed.

Without knocking, Darlene opened the door and yelled in a friendly tone, "Anybody home?" Mona knew they were thrown off because it was so quiet in the house. They'd be expecting a Cape Breton-style wake that would include chatting and visiting with family and friends, followed by food and booze, and live music. And it might even end up with what Darlene called "B and B," bawling and brawling. Darlene and Minnie had told Mona the last funeral they went to back home, one family got a little belligerent which resulted in three brothers in fisticuffs in front of their Dad's casket. After hearing that, Mona didn't feel quite so bad about her family's behavior earlier that day at the funeral home.

"In here, Aunt Darlene," Mona shouted back. She saw their joviality cease when they entered the living room. They looked at the Brandies and her, a triple bill of morosity.

"Well, aren't you just havin' a time," said Darlene looking at the three of them. "What gives?"

"We just had a situation," said Brando, not saying anything else.

"Where's Courtney?"

"She left," said Brandi. "She was the focus of the situation."

"Tell me more," said Darlene.

Mona picked up the bag and walked over to Darlene, placing it in her palm on display. "Remember this sugar bowl?"

Darlene eyed it and looked disappointed. "Yeah. Your Mom loved it. What happened?"

Mona looked over at Brando. There was no point in stirring everything up again. "Long story, but the headline is the bowl broke, two pets are in custody and Courtney's totally pissed. She left."

"I gathered that," said Darlene. "Too bad."

Mona figured it was time to get to the bottom of the mystery, even though they might be discovering they had accidentally smashed something worth thousands. "Aunt Darlene, I'm worried this was valuable. Before she died, Mom was telling me about numerous items that were rare or could fetch a big price, so that we wouldn't sell them for a buck or two at a yard sale." Mona felt ashamed because she had been hardly listening. "She even mentioned the Ming Dynasty at one point. But she covered so many items at once, my mind got overwhelmed."

"That's understandable, love," said Darlene.

"Do you know anything about it?" asked Mona. "We never got to finish our conversation the other day." She saw Darlene slowly nod her head. Mona prepared for the worst.

"Sure do, like it was yesterday. She bought it at the church fair when she was eight years old. She was fascinated because it was six-sided, and she loved the flowers on the side and the lid. I don't know why; it just tickled her fancy." Darlene pulled out the lid and turned it over, smiling. "They were asking three dollars. She marched over and asked the deacon why it was so expensive. He told her it was from the 'Ding Dynasty.'"

"You mean Ming?" Mona asked.

"No. It had several nicks and dings, so that's how he came up with the Ding Dynasty. He was pulling her leg," she laughed.

"So, it wasn't worth much?" asked Brando.

"Nope, but that didn't matter to Babs. It was priceless to her. She insisted we use the sugar bowl at home. And when she moved away from home, that was the first thing she packed. I know it sounds silly now, but money was tight, so we had to spend wisely."

"That's not silly at all," said Mona. She felt relief wash over her to learn the broken heirloom wasn't worth a fortune, though it had significant sentimental value. She thought of Courtney and the terrible anguish heaped on her today of all days. Because Courtney was the oldest, their mother had likely told her the story and that's why she was so enamored with it. Mona now felt foolish. She should have talked to Courtney when she had an inkling it was worth something; instead, she joined in the antics that the Brandies had started. She got sucked into all the stupidity and wasn't even coming close to living her values. Shame swept through her body, and she wondered if Courtney would ever speak to her again. She vowed to somehow make it up to her.

Chapter 44

Courtney

Months passed. Nobody got in touch to apologize or offer to be the executor. I wasn't surprised. For my sanity, I had taken a break after the funeral. Even though I threatened to walk away if nobody else would step up to work on the estate, I couldn't follow through on my threat. Megan pointed out that I could hire a professional to do the work, but I felt a strong commitment to honor my mother's wishes.

It was a small town, so I had bumped into the Brandies and Mona at various places: the grocery store, café and post office. At first, we each looked away, but gradually Brandi nodded at me, and I nodded back. Then one day as I left the café, we bumped into each other, making eye contact.

"How are you doing, Brandi?" I asked. That was the best I could do.

"Good, thanks," she said pausing and looking off in the distance. "I just wanted to say..."

"Say what?" I encouraged her to talk. *Could she be ready to apologize?*

"Well, it's not fair that I got lumped in with your anger about the funeral. I didn't do anything wrong. Bastet contributed to the breaking of the sugar bowl, but it wasn't on purpose."

I was all prepared to launch into a big rant because I had pent-up anger that needed to be released. How many times had I mentally rehearsed what I would say? (well, yell was more like it.) But as I thought about the day of the funeral, she was right. She had shown up on time, she had booked the caterers who did a great job, and she wasn't part of the near-miss Fluffy debacle, she would have stopped Brando if she'd known.

I took a deep breath and said, "You know what, Brandi? You're right. It's just that I assumed you took Brando's side on this—"

"You shouldn't always assume," she cut in. "I agree with Brando often, but not all the time. But you and I both know, when he's in that frame of mind, there's no arguing with him or pointing out his faults. It drives him crazy."

"I guess."

Brandi looked at me, her eyes full of sadness. "And you know something you've never learned with Brando?"

I shook my head.

"You always make him wrong about things. Yes, he does mess up; we all do. But for some reason, with Brando, you not only have to be right about everything, but you also feel compelled to point it out and lord it over him. It makes him nuts," said Brandi.

"I know—"

"I'm not finished," she said. "Then, on the toughest day of his life, you humiliated him in front of the family. As if he didn't feel bad enough about his mistakes, you made it ten times worse." She sighed and said, "And then you tarred me with the same brush."

I shifted on my feet. "You're right." I realized Brandi was lumped in with Brando's activities because she was a nice person and didn't complain much. She didn't like confrontation; she just wanted the family to get along. "I am sorry, Brandi," I said, in as heartfelt a way as I could.

She kicked at the dirt a bit. "Thanks. Now can we just move on?"

I nodded. "Sounds good, Brandi." However, I wasn't about to let Brando off the hook. He needed to apologize. She gave me a quick hug and ran off.

Days later, I spotted Mona at the hardware store and said hello. The approach worked with Brandi, so I wondered if I could do the same thing with my other sister. Also, I needed to pry her out of the house to sell it. One thing at a time. "Hi, Mona."

"Hey, Courtney," she said, her face lighting up.

I was surprised; it was as if she'd never been angry or upset with me or anybody. While I felt a little angrier with her than with Brandi, I realized we needed to let go of this angst if we were to move on. "How are things?" I added.

"Good, thanks..." She drifted off in mid-sentence, then picked up again, as if now ready to tackle the topic. "I was going to get in touch with you."

"What's up?"

"You remember Maria Santos?"

You mean the squatters on Mom's land? I wanted to let loose with a little sarcasm, but Mona had that deeply sincere look on her face for all those facing problems and trauma in their lives. "Sure, I remember Maria and Juan."

"They asked for a meeting with you and me."

"What's it about?"

Mona shrugged. "I assume it's about the land."

I wondered why they had invited the two of us. "I would have expected just me as the executor or all four of us. Any ideas, Mona?"

"Maybe it's because I got to know them a bit at the hospital. They know I would always offer a safe space for talking, so maybe they feel more comfortable with me there."

"Okay, I will reach out to them and let you know a day and time. Any days when you aren't available in the next couple of weeks?"

"Nope, wide open."

I decided it wasn't the time to make a snide comment about Mona's lifestyle. Since there were no reports from her, I figured Mona was making little to no progress on selling things.

***

I pulled into Mom's driveway for our meeting at the house. Mona had suggested it because she knew Maria and Juan would be intimidated to come to my home. I told her I couldn't understand why. I'd offer a layer cake and lemonade and would do everything to make them comfortable. Mona explained that a giant, expensive house in the town's most expensive subdivision and being served a fancy layer cake that looked like it was in a magazine could put a person off. She also pointed out that the long and winding road to my house forced poor people to look at all the overpriced, grandiose homes that they could never afford.

When they knocked on the door, Mona asked me to stay at the table while she greeted them. They hugged each other like old friends; judging by their conversation, they were socializing at common events. Mona led them into the kitchen, and they shook my hand warmly and set homemade sweets on the counter. I left the over-decorated cake on a glass pedestal on the counter. It looked entirely out of place. Thank heavens there was an opaque cover on it.

After endless chit-chat, Maria and Juan looked at each other. "First, thank you so much for your generosity in letting us stay on your Mom's land," Maria said. "We wouldn't have been able to get our start in Danbyville," added Juan.

"Well, Mom was only too happy to help," said Mona, taking Maria's hand. "It's not like we even remembered we had it."

I shot Mona a look for allowing that detail to slip out, but I relaxed a little because I could see they were good, honest people.

Maria sat straight up. She looked nervous as if she had practiced the speech a million times. "As we told you that day on the land, we are saving money for a down payment to buy our own home, or land to build on."

I nodded. I couldn't imagine there would be much progress given the salaries they must be making. "And how's that going?" I tried to sound polite, but Mona didn't seem pleased with my question.

"Good, thanks," said Maria, "Even though we have two jobs, and the boys contribute through their part-time jobs, it's taking time." She looked at Juan, then across the table. "However, we now have twenty-five thousand."

"Oh," I muttered involuntarily. I was impressed with their progress, especially at the thought of their kids contributing.

"We wondered...."

She paused for so long, I had to help. "Yes, Maria...?"

"We'd like to buy your mother's land. It's extremely hard for immigrants to get a loan or mortgage in Canada because we have no credit rating," said Juan, blurting it out. "If we could do it without a bank or a real estate agent, both parties could save a lot of money."

I pulled out my notebook. "Okay, so back up a bit. Tell me what you are proposing."

Suddenly the two of them talked excitedly, and I could hardly follow the thread of the conversation. But I soon got the gist—they would give us the twenty-five grand for a down payment and then make monthly payments to us until the whole thing was paid off. Like a ping-pong dialogue, Maria would point out how consistently they'd saved their money. Then Juan would talk about all the work they'd done to improve the land. She continued to explain how they'd also helped other family and friends when they arrived in Danbyville.

"And think about the contribution you are making to our town," gasped Mona, in tears.

I glanced at Mona to remind her that she wasn't supposed to be part of their team to sell the idea, but she was having none of it. Finally, I'd heard all the selling points. "Okay, thanks Maria and Juan, you've given us lots to think about." As I thought about it, I loved that this plan would allow us to pay the back taxes on the land, with a little left over. After months of little progress on the estate, there was suddenly hope.

"So will you do it?" they asked together.

"I can't promise anything. We still have to talk to our other siblings and discuss it as a group."

"Of course, we understand," Maria said. Yet it was as if I'd hosed everybody down and extinguished a fire. Maria and Juan looked at each other, their faces disappointed. Mona looked dejected as if she'd personally lost the round. I shook hands and thanked them, promising to get back to them as soon as I spoke to the others. They smiled sweetly and left.

"Wow, you were a downer," said Mona.

"You were forgetting whose side you were on."

"It wasn't about sides," said Mona. "I want them to succeed. Do you see how hard they work?"

Yeah, and you could learn from them. I figured it would only antagonize her to point this out. However, I did see an opportunity in this proposal. "Mona, you refused to sign the papers earlier about selling the land. If the Brandies agree to this, would you sign?"

"In a heartbeat," she said. "They even offered me the chance to stay in the tiny house on the land if necessary. Can you believe that?"

I could see how motivated Mona was, and even possibilities for putting Mom's house up for sale. But I knew I had to get her involved if I wanted things to happen. "Tell you what, Mona. I'll get an appraisal on the land. Let's first see if Maria and Juan agree on the price. Since Brando won't talk to me or answer emails, you need to set up a meeting with the Brandies and make your case. If they say yes, and the Santoses accept our price, I will vote yes too. Deal?"

Mona jumped up and high-fived me. "Deal!" she shouted.

"And that means we'll put up Mom's house for sale too."

"I'd need some notice," Mona replied.

"Look, it could take a long time. Let's put it up for sale now and we can ask for a long closing date," I said. In my mind, Mona posed a greater risk as a squatter than the Santos family. At least they were motivated to make a deal.

"Sure," said Mona, gathering the teacups and placing them in the dishwasher. She then popped a sweet into her mouth. "But I reserve the right to turn down the offer if they want a short closing date."

I smiled lightly as if to show I heard what she said. But I didn't care. There was no way I was going to let Mona dictate the terms of the sale. I figured the best course of action was to nod agreeably and let the situation unfold as it should. I was also tired of worrying. "We'll jump off that bridge when we come to it," I joked.

Chapter 45

Brando

Brando, Brandi, Mona and Courtney sat staring at each other in the lawyer's office. This was the first time Brando had encountered Courtney up close in months. He'd seen her at the arena in the winter, the pub and the car wash, but they'd carefully sidestepped each other. Brando had no idea if Brandi and Mona had seen her, and he didn't care.

Months ago, against his better judgment, he'd agreed to meet Mona in the pub, where she attempted a debrief after the funeral to reboot their relationship. She was all sweetness and polka dots, but Brando saw right through her, although he wasn't sure what her hidden agenda was. When she finally took a breath, he told her he was done with family and there was no need to keep covering the same arguments.

She asked how he felt about his behavior on the day of the funeral. Mostly it was a blur for him because he was in a serious funk and smoking too much weed. She recounted the highlights of the day, (or lowlights, as she called them), until he finally said, "Enough, Mona."

After his conversation with Mona, he needed a more neutral opinion. The next night he'd gone on the forum *Am I an A**hole?* and had described to the group what had happened at the funeral. He presented himself as a good guy who was misunderstood. However, the group embraced "tough love" and voted overwhelmingly that he was indeed in this instance. No hard feelings, they said. He shot back, "Well, excuse me if I don't cut the mustard," which prompted a bunch of grammar fans to argue about whether it was "pass muster" or "mustard." He couldn't win for trying. While some on the thread were sympathetic, many pointed out the entire mess could have been avoided if he had 1) taken the time to listen to the assignments he was given 2) asked questions about anything he didn't understand, or thought was odd (like putting down the cat) and 3) reduced the amount of dope he'd been smoking. He disputed these points, but the court of public opinion wouldn't budge.

Today in the law office he sat across from Courtney. She looked busy writing in her notebook to avoid making eye contact, while Megan was out of the room. He felt irked that Courtney had never offered an apology and therefore felt he had to follow through on his threat of not socializing with the family anymore or he'd look like a jerk. His involvement with her was now on a strictly as-needed basis—like today—signing papers to sell the land. When they finished signing, Brando whispered to Brandi to ask Courtney when they would receive the money. As usual, Courtney blathered on about this factor and that, outstanding debts and taxes, and waiting for blah-de-blah. It was the same answer every time and he figured they'd never see any money.

One day, he asked to meet with Megan but wouldn't explain why until he got there. He then said he wanted to get Courtney expelled from being the executor. Instead of agreeing with him and making recommendations, she took half an hour to explain all the things Courtney was doing and why the estate moved at the speed of honey oozing down a hill. She shocked him by telling him many estates took two to ten years to settle. He had no idea. Finally, she berated him for giving his sister a tough time and made him read her to-do list that now topped one hundred and fifty items. Then she sent him a bill for four hundred dollars.

He was annoyed with the outcome, and when he saw Mona at the café, he explained his annoyance over an overpriced coffee that she'd managed to have him pay for. When he finished, Mona said she thought he was angry about other things and was deep in grief. She added it wasn't helpful to direct his wrath at his sister. Deep inside, he knew she was right, but he couldn't stop himself. He was pissed off about losing his mother so young and not spending time with her at the end. There were things he wished he'd asked her, and he would have loved to listen to her wonderful stories again. Also, she had made him promise to be good to his sisters and family, and he wasn't doing that either. Even though he wanted to, he couldn't reverse the negative roll he was on.

Because of him, they hadn't gotten together as a family last Christmas for the first time. Courtney had hosted everybody for years, but she didn't invite anybody last time. Everybody else called each other and discussed it—except nobody called Courtney to see if she'd reverse her stand. That made him sad, but he couldn't bring himself to end the stalemate. He figured she'd never get over Fluffy or breaking the sugar bowl—which he didn't do on purpose. Well, maybe he shouldn't have let Bastet loose, but why couldn't everybody move on? Yet he struggled with lingering sadness.

Chapter 46

Courtney

After three months of rigamarole, we finally sold the land. The transaction plunged me right back into the estate game that felt like the world's longest and most tedious game of snakes and ladders. When we presented the paperwork to the Santos family, I watched the family whoop, cheer and hug each other with tears of joy. I envied their closeness. They thanked Mona repeatedly for her assistance, and she insisted it was the universe delivering what she had envisioned for them. As airy-fairy as it sounded, I had to give Mona credit: curiously, she made a lot happen. She was especially good at bringing others in the community together. If only she could mend our broken family.

Soon after we paid back taxes, we put Mom's house up for sale and it sold quickly. Fortunately, it had a long closing date so that Mona could find a new place. She eventually found a room in her girlfriend's apartment. I felt sad that settling the estate had torn our family apart. I missed our Christmas get-togethers even though I always hosted them, and everybody drove me crazy. I felt the void, especially without Brando. He was like a giant barnacle on the side of a boat that you stare at all the time and plan to scrape off, then never get around to it. But when it's gone, you kind of miss it. Full of seasonal spirit, he happily wore ugly sweaters with obnoxious blinking lights and ornaments hanging from his sleeves which broke as soon as the rum flowed. But the kids got a kick out of him, even when he played Santa badly.

I had no idea if everybody was happier at their own homes last year, but we weren't in our household. Yes, everything was calm and on time, but I missed the chaos that the family brought to the dinner table. It felt too quiet at home. We were a month away from another Christmas and no closer to patching up family differences. I worried it might be irreversible.

Aunt Darlene called me and said she had a ride to Danbyville this Christmas and wondered if everybody was getting together. I told her I didn't know and felt terrible when I hung up.

A brisk knock on the door shook me out of my stupor. I peeked around the drapes and saw Mona standing outside with a gift box in her hand. I couldn't imagine why. I swung open the door and she beamed, with a bright glow surrounding her. I smiled but was on my guard. "Hey, Mona, how are you?"

"Great," she smiled. "I have something for you."

Surprised, I stood there, looking at the box in her hands. Why was she giving me a gift? All family interactions had ceased, so this seemed like a curveball. I wondered if I was being pranked.

"Can I come in?" She asked, walking across the threshold, not waiting for an answer.

"Sorry. Of course," I said, wondering what happened to my manners.

She kicked off her cowboy boots, sending snow, slush and salt all over the boot mat. She handed the box to me and said, "This is for you."

"Should I open it now?" I asked.

She nodded.

"Let's go into the living room," I said, extending my arm. I offered her a glass of wine along with crackers and cheese, which she inhaled as if she hadn't eaten for days.

I sat on the sofa and picked up the gift. I started removing ribbons and bows, which led to another layer of paper and then another box. The item was wrapped in recycled tissue paper. Mona appeared delighted with my puzzled expression and how long it was taking me to open it. Finally, I pulled out the treasure. Gasping, I glanced at her. "Oh my," I said, my eyes tearing up. "The sugar bowl, but different... it's put back together with beautiful gold seams."

She gulped. "The lid is in there too. Miraculously, it landed on a blanket, so it didn't break," she said. "You may recall seeing me on my hands and knees, gathering pieces into a zip bag."

I winced. "I wondered what you were doing but was too distraught to ask."

"To be honest, I wasn't sure what my plans were either," she laughed. "All I knew is that it felt wrong to throw the pieces out."

I unwrapped the lid and placed it on top. "Mona, this is stunning. How did you do this?"

"It's a fifteenth-century Japanese tradition called *Kintsugi*, which translates to 'the art of broken pieces.' When an item breaks, it is honored and given a new life by being repaired with a gold adhesive filling, rather than discarded."

"It's got a special feel to it," I said, turning it gently.

"That's right. You aren't meant to fit in every single piece. Filling the cracks with gold means that the flaws are seen as a unique part of the object's history. Which adds to its overall beauty and character," said Mona.

I held it up to the shimmering rays of the afternoon sun. "And look how the light catches the gold. Mona, this is gorgeous. Where did you get the idea?"

"I belong to an international group called the Artisan Ideas Collective. Any artisan can ask for help, whether it's for feedback, business advice, or to present a new craft idea. We meet by video, so I showed them a photo of the original sugar bowl, then held up the bag of pieces and asked, 'How can I repurpose this?' There were many great ideas, but near the end, this quiet woman, Himari, suggested Kintsugi and explained how it worked. Her Mom holds workshops, so she sent me a Kintsugi repair kit from Japan. Then I got a few friends to help me hold pieces while I applied the gold glue. It took us ages, but we had a wonderful time."

"Amazing story and look at the outcome."

"So, you like it?" Mona beamed, her smile like a bouquet of summer daisies.

"*No*, I love it!" I felt my throat constricting. "All I ever wanted was this lovely memory of Mom. I was so sad when it broke."

"I know," Mona blushed. "And I'm sorry for causing so much pain. I don't know why I behaved like I did that day. You were so right; the bowl didn't mean anything to me."

"Call it a big learning moment." The hard pain I felt about that day started to melt. "It was an accident. Besides, it doesn't all fall on your shoulders."

"Well, I'm relieved I could make it up to you in some small way."

I looked at Mona, surprised by her thoughtfulness. While her behavior and characteristics sometimes irritated the hell out of me, I realized she was just being true to herself. And this gift was a kind gesture on her part. I held it out to look it over. "You know this broken sugar bowl is a bit of a family metaphor."

She stood up and stretched. "Yeah," she said softly. "But it doesn't have to be that way. I know we're the weirdest family ever, but we're family. I miss seeing everybody together."

"Me too," I whispered. "What are your plans for Christmas?"

She shrugged. "Not sure."

"What did you do last year?"

"The Santos family invited me to join the Filipino community at someone's house decorated with crazy flashing lights, tinsel, and Jose Mari Chan singing at full volume. It was packed to the rafters. They had a big feast and music. They were so welcoming."

"Are you going back this year?" I asked.

"No. The Santos family is heading back to the Philippines for the holidays. I'll figure something out."

I felt ashamed that she spent the holiday without family around her, the first year after our Mom had passed away. *How could I have let that happen?* "Well, I'd love it if you'd join our family this year."

"Really?" Her eyes widened.

"Yes, I insist, Mona," I said, putting my arm around her.

"Thanks, although I have one caveat."

There goes Mona, I thought. With Mona, there were always strings attached. "What?"

"I want all the family to be together. So, if everybody comes, then I come. If they say no, then I say, 'Thanks but no thanks.'"

I released her from my hug. "Well, I'd be happy to host everybody, including Brando, but I doubt he'd come."

"Funny, when I asked him, he doubted you'd invite him," she stated matter-of-factly.

I sighed. Yes, of course, there had to be a stand-off—and I'd have to extend the olive branch. That was just Brando's way. "You've already discussed it?"

"Sort of... I'm just trying to get us back to where we were: one big, crappy family. Are some of us plain nutty?" she asked, not waiting for an answer. "Yes, but it's our family."

"I appreciate your idea, Mona, but Brando behaved like a jerk. He didn't apologize and I feel like he didn't learn a thing. I don't know how to process that."

"How would you feel if you knew he'd had a heart attack?"

"What? Why didn't anyone tell me?" My heart pounded. I pulled out my cell to call him.

"Relax, he didn't. It was a theoretical 'how would you feel' question," she said. "But you see your reaction just now? That tells me you still care. A lot."

"You got me."

"You know, Mom said something one day when I was complaining about family. She said, 'Keep in mind, everybody is doing their best. Of course, they aren't perfect, but in their heart, they're doing their best.'"

"Good point, Mona," I said, watching her stand up.

"And, while I'm on the topic, what's so hard about saying sorry?" She looked me directly in the eye. "Life's short. Why insist on an apology from Brando? Five months, or five years from now, you two won't even remember what you were angry about."

She had a point, but I had standards. "Did he apologize to you for the ashes debacle?"

Mona shook her head. "We exchanged heated words at the funeral home. Then we met for coffee with no resolution, but it didn't matter. I have no interest in holding a grudge."

Who was this wise, young wonder who often behaved like a child but was now acting like the most mature adult in the family? She was a full-blown walking contradiction—one minute so entitled and self-centered, the next, so forgiving and full of love for others. And when I thought about her, I wondered: why had I always focused on her faults? I had given up on the sugar bowl, but thanks to her, I now had a special memory of my Mom that I'd treasure forever.

"I believe love is the cure for everything," Mona said, pausing at the door. "So, will you consider sending the Christmas invitation?"

"I promise to think about it," I said, hugging her. "Thank you, again. And what a gorgeous item. I could see you creating new pieces for families with broken heirlooms."

"Funny you should say that," she laughed. "I posted a photo on social media and forty people asked me to re-purpose their family's teacups, plates and vases—some of which weren't even broken. They liked the vibe of it."

"I'll bet we're the only family that's had a family heir-loom break over a sibling brawl and two frenzied animals colliding mid-air."

Mona laughed. "We all have our life lessons to learn."

"So true. Anyway, I'm not surprised that people reached out—you seem to have your finger on the pulse of what people want. I have no doubt you could launch a very successful business."

She opened the door and paused, carefully consider-ing my suggestion. "Maybe... maybe not. It could take all the fun out of it," she said with a devious smile, easing the door closed.

That was classic Mona. So brilliant with a bottomless well of creative ideas where she could make a fortune, yet she was utterly ambivalent about it all.

Chapter 47

Courtney

Mona's visit made me reflect on everything. The more I thought about what she said, the more I agreed with her suggestion, "Let's move on." Why was that so hard for me?

Like a good family that lived in denial, I wondered if we could skip the blamestorming session about who did what and why and forget demands for an apology. I figured enough time had passed with our bickering about the estate and the cone of silence. I didn't want this family feud to be permanent—somebody had to make the first move. Why not me? Was I crazy? Could I learn to see everybody differently and accept them for who they were?

Looking back, I realized it took incredible persistence on Mom's part to make our family work. Whenever we got together, we were like two separate families: there was me and the Brandies, and then Mona and George tacked on years later. It was like we were puzzle pieces all tossed into one box, never quite adding up to the beautiful scene on the cover.

As siblings, we all had individual quirks. First, our sense of money was totally warped. The Brandies and I acted like fearful paupers clinging to every cent because the financial rug had been yanked out from under us as children. Even when we all earned good money as adults, fear ruled us, and we were always searching for more. It was never enough. Plus, the three of us all had abandonment issues about our father. As children, we desperately wanted a real father, but not our birth father. George Nichols tried to help, and he was a good man, but he never felt like *our* father.

There was Brandi who never caused a fuss, so why did I always lump her with Brando's deeds? She was a good person. It must have been hard to be part of the Brandies; it was as if things were automatically decided as a unit, except Brando was the puppet master. She never got the chance to decide anything on her own. Maybe it was time to stop calling them the Brandies and show some respect for each of them as individuals.

I recalled that Milo and Olivia tolerated the family at Christmas, except they drew the line at the Martin tradition of wearing ugly sweaters. Brando loved to wind up Olivia when she'd arrive at our home. He'd compliment her "ugly Christmas sweater." She'd retort that it was a high-fashion sweater from Europe. "Could have fooled me!" Brando would joke. "It's a fine line between a four-hundred-dollar designer sweater and a four-dollar one from the second-hand shop." Olivia and DeeDee would roll their eyes, which made Brando chuckle.

Mona had the opposite attitude toward money. Thanks to the secure life that Mom and George had given her, Mona believed that money gushed out of a mythical fountain of wealth, forever and ever, amen. She couldn't help that she had no money worries anymore than the rest of us couldn't help that we had constant money woes.

That left Brando and me as the outliers. We were probably too much alike—competitive, highly driven and very insecure. We battled constantly growing up, yet the minute a boyfriend would hurt me or Brandi, he'd come to our defense. Given our challenging childhood, he had turned out surprisingly well. He could have behaved like our father; instead, he was a caring and super attentive father to his daughter DeeDee. Yes, he fell apart when Mom was ill; but acting out was always his fallback when he couldn't handle a situation.

Would we ever return to our regular family before Mom's passing? Not likely; our grieving exposed cracks in our family's foundation. Minor issues flared into running feuds. We behaved like a family of charged electrons that were sometimes attracted to, and other times repulsed by each other.

Nobody can tell you how hard grief is, how to respond to it, or how long it will last. Sometimes it feels like a lingering houseguest who won't reveal their departure date. For me, it often felt like an invisible veil of sadness draped over me.

There were books about grief, but I didn't buy into the "five stages" concept because grief doesn't unfold neatly like a well-behaved set of dominoes. To me, the stages and emotions looked more like a laptop circuit board, where the connected parts have a journey and an end goal but bounce all over the map to get there.

Sometimes I felt one emotion: shock, pain, numbness, denial, anger, fear, guilt, frustration, isolation or loneliness. Other times, it felt like all of them were hurtling towards me at warp speed.

Added to that was being an executor on top of life, work and family commitments. Back when Mom asked me to be the executor, I nodded enthusiastically and felt a smidge of superiority to my siblings. I had no idea the estate work would idle in the background for years.

But the biggest hurt was my siblings not trusting me. Trust is everything for an executor; without it, all decisions are disputed. Added to that was miscommunication which led to near-disastrous results (sorry Fluffy!).

Despite the domestic mess, I'd hate for our family to stay divided. After all we'd weathered, Mom would have cried her eyes out at the thought of this. I hoped we could mend our collective broken hearts, but it could go either way.

I talked to Jamie and the kids, who encouraged me to resurrect the family Christmas tradition at our home. That surprised me, but then again, I had never asked them how they felt about it. Jamie's parents had passed away, and his only sister lived out west, so he said the Martin family at Christmas was his family. Plus, I wanted to add in Aunt Darlene, who had friends near her, but no family.

Somebody had to make the first move and I knew it wouldn't be Brando. I spent an hour trying to compose an email to invite everybody to our home for the holidays. When I read it, it sounded long and tortuous. I had wasted endless words setting the context and rationalizing my thoughts. It was a rambling mess. I knew even if Brando opened it, he'd get fed up or bored and stop reading. I took pride in writing to cover every detail, but if nobody liked it or read it, it was useless. A long time ago, Mom told me I took the pride thing too far. She reminded me there was no need to be perfect—and at times, I should let go, or it would be my downfall. How right she was.

I deleted the email and started over, wondering how to tackle the message. Then I thought about it and realized, we were an on/off, yes/no, black/white kind of family. Shorter was better. This time I wrote an invitation in two simple sentences which was truly out of my comfort zone, but it felt right. I could almost hear my Mom urging me to do it. I hovered my right index finger in the air for an agonizing two minutes, wondering if I should send the message, and if so, would we be able to patch things up as a family? Finally, I pressed send.

I was about to find out.

Acknowledgments

Writing a book is hard work, yet it's also incredibly rewarding. And the journey from page one to a published book poses endless distractions and obstacles. That's where my network of family, friends and loved ones were invaluable—they supported me until I stumbled across the finish line. Some people offered practical help, inspiration, moral support, marketing ideas, cheerleading, and even laughter. It all helps.

Elizabeth Peirce—you are a fine editor with astonishing attention to detail. In addition to your vast knowledge of grammar, structure, voice and more, you have a way of highlighting changes without crushing a person! Any errors that were missed are mine. Thank you, Elizabeth.

Thanks to Peggy Issenman, with Peggy & Co. Design, for a compelling book cover. And to Bob Young, with Robert George Young Photography, for capturing the beauty of the sugar bowl on the cover.

Thank you to the Brown family: Dale Brown, Reisa Muir, Al Muir, Connor Muir, Tanya Brown and Ric Hamilton. It's impossible to express the many ways you have supported me over the past few years. I'm especially grateful to Reisa for your guidance through the messy world of estates. And in loving memory of my Dad, Floyd "Brownie" Brown and my Mom, Christina (Stronach) Brown. Miss you both.

To the Stronach family and relatives on my Mom's side, thanks for being such a connected and fun group of people—love those family potlucks! On my Dad's side, thanks to Lorraine and Richard Lalonde and the others in the Brown family, as well as my newfound Tuttle cousins, Ann Liebenberg and Shelagh Greenaway. I hope to meet more family someday!

To the Crockett Clan, and in memory of Robert Crockett, my loving partner of ten years. It's wonderful to have his family in my life: Rigel Crockett, Ariel Janzen and Zella Crockett; Laurel Crockett, Drew Rector and Luke Rector; Joe Zsebenyi, Aidan Zsebenyi and Ryan Zsebenyi, and Tami Lee Malin; and Bobby Crockett's siblings: Carol, Jeanie and Mary. Thanks to Sue Crockett for your wonderful children, Rigel and Laurel. And to Michael Fuller, Buzz would have loved the Japanese word "Nakama" to describe you: one who is loved like family, even if not related by blood.

For Kelly Hennessy and Cathy Jacob, co-founders of the writing group, "Word Salad." For 11 years, we have written and grown together, read each other's work, and organized retreats ("And we aren't drinking wine this year!"). We have laughed and supported each other through happy, as well as tough times. And most importantly, we celebrate each other's wins and writing achievements.

To the Beta Readers' Circle: Tanya Brown, Dana Dean, Kelly Hennessey, Cathy Jacob, Reisa Muir and Susan Smith, who provided helpful and hilarious feedback on the first draft of my novel. You spent hours reading the manuscript and did so enthusiastically, even with busy lives. My heartfelt thanks to you all.

Local business supporters: Bookmark in Halifax—your commitment to local writers is incredible. To Room 152 in Dartmouth, with special thanks to Trina

Matheson and Morgan Currie for carrying my first novel and your continued enthusiasm. Emma Bent with Read Between the Vines. And Halifax Public Libraries for carrying my book.

Thanks to many health and wellbeing stalwarts who keep me immersed in fitness activities. The Saturday Morning Group: Susan Smith, Steve Smith, Shawna O'Hearn, Malcolm Boyle, Dave van de Wetering, Lisa Tilley, Mike Tilley, Peter Harrison and Gisella Alecce Harrison, Kim Thompson, Glynis Woodman; and the early members, JK Keeping, Vicki Balcolm, Andrea Power, Jim Power and founder, Gerry Walsh.

My Regatta Point friends and neighbors, including "Mayor" Donald D'Entremont and "Deputy Mayor" John Webb (and Rozanne Webb), Pedal Peter (Meagher) and his band of merry cyclists, too many to mention. TY to the wonderful team and yogis of Halifax Yoga.

Thanks to Gayle Lunn for the conversations about our favorite Japanese words, including the word "Kintsugi," the art of broken pieces. And thanks to Ariel Janzen and Zella Crockett in Tokyo, who shed more light on Kintsugi while I was visiting them.

Appreciation to Renée Hartleib, Shelley Murphy, Nancy Laberge, Monica MacDonald, Maureen Medved, Michael Roberts, Derek Sarty, Alan Stanbridge, Corinne Boudreau, Matt Higgins, Erika Williams, Andy Willies, plus Tanya Butler, Jamie Angus and team with Touchstone Legal Inc.

Thanks to Damhnait Doyle on CBC radio, for coincidentally playing Blue Rodeo's "We are Lost Together" at the precise moment I was gazing off into space and wracking my brain trying to think of a classic Canadian song that would unite the family in my book. And to Blue Rodeo, for creating such an emotionally moving song that sounds like it's always existed!

A portion of my book sales will be donated to selected charities with a humanitarian focus.

About the author

Gina N. Brown

Born and raised in Nova Scotia, Gina Brown has written two novels, *Lucy McGee's Moment of Truth* in 2021 and *The Sugar Bowl Feud* in 2024, both set in Nova Scotia. Her freelance travel, memoir and lifestyle articles have been published in newspapers, magazines and online.

Following a lengthy career where she worked as a marketing and communications specialist in music, film, museums, special events, advertising and education, she founded NovaHeart Media, an independent publishing platform.

After living away for many years in Montreal, Birmingham (England), Ottawa and Toronto, she returned to her beloved home port of Halifax, Nova Scotia in 2004. For more information, visit novaheartmedia.com.

Book Club Questions

1. Author Gina Brown cites her own experience as a starting point for *The Sugar Bowl Feud*: "While my loved ones settled several estates with no issues, during the same time, friends, neighbors and strangers told me stories about settling their families' estates. Some stories were very sad, a few were outrageous, and a number were hilarious. It made me realize how tough it is to deal with estates, memorial services, and bureaucracy while trying to cope with the demands of work and family in a fog of grief." Have you (or any of your friends) experienced a similar strain in family relationships as the result of settling an estate? What happened as a result?

2. In this book, family dynamics played a huge role in how everybody interacted. What do you think was the main source of tension within the family?

3. Courtney, Brando and Brandi grew up in extreme poverty with nothing, while Mona never had to worry about money—she got whatever she wanted. How do you think this affected the siblings' relationship? Do you think the three older siblings were fair to Mona, or did they judge her and/or stereotype her as a millennial?

4. The siblings treat Mona as the family outsider throughout the book. Yet by the end, Mona is the

one who takes steps to reunite the family. Why do you think she did that?

5. Even if they don't acknowledge it, each sibling plays a certain role which sometimes triggers sibling rivalry. Have you noticed sibling rivalry or birth order expectations in your own family or other people's families?

6. Each sibling changes during the story—some more than others. Which character changed the most? Did your opinion of any of them change by the end of the novel? In what way?

7. Which sibling did you feel the most sympathy for and why?

8. Grief affects people in many ways, and it can take a long time for some people to process it. Some try to ignore it. Early on, when Mona is talking about her grief groups and supportive girlfriends, Brando says, "There's no time to grieve Mona." What do you think he meant by that?

9. Doris was Babs' best friend since childhood, yet she tried to defraud the estate of a painting by Maud Lewis. Do you think she would have followed through with it, or were her actions born out of frustration about the treatment she received from the siblings?

10. During the settling of an estate, beneficiaries sometimes clash over who gets certain items. Usually, it's an emotional or sentimental con-

nection, not the resale value. Have you seen instances in your own or your friends' situations where that happened? How did it get resolved (if, in fact, it got resolved)?

11. In the last chapter, Courtney realizes that Brando will probably never apologize, and she acknowledges that sometimes they clash because they're too much alike. Should Courtney hold out for an apology, or just accept that Brando is who he is?

12. Do you think the family will reunite? Why or why not?

Your Reviews help!

Whether you bought this book from an online retailer or borrowed it from a library, many platforms offer the opportunity to review the book. I would encourage you to do so—whether it's taking the time to write a sentence or two, or simply clicking on one of the five stars. Both help the author tremendously!

Why? Because readers read reviews before they buy. Also, reviews help search engines to move books upward in the listings where they will be noticed. Thanks for supporting an independent author!

Stay in Touch

Thank you for reading this book. If you enjoyed it and want to learn more about the author, sign up for updates or check out other books published by NovaHeart Media, please visit novaheartmedia.com.